ASIAN POLITICAL, ECONOMIC AND SECURITY ISSUES

NORTH KOREA: NUCLEAR WEAPONS AND THE DIPLOMACY DEBATE

ASIAN POLITICAL, ECONOMIC AND SECURITY ISSUES

Additional books in this series can be found on Nova's website under the Series tab.

Additional E-books in this series can be found on Nova's website under the E-book tab.

ASIAN POLITICAL, ECONOMIC AND SECURITY ISSUES

NORTH KOREA: NUCLEAR WEAPONS AND THE DIPLOMACY DEBATE

BRIAN N. THOMPSON
EDITOR

Nova Science Publishers, Inc.
New York

Copyright © 2012 by Nova Science Publishers, Inc.

All rights reserved. No part of this book may be reproduced, stored in a retrieval system or transmitted in any form or by any means: electronic, electrostatic, magnetic, tape, mechanical photocopying, recording or otherwise without the written permission of the Publisher.

For permission to use material from this book please contact us:
Telephone 631-231-7269; Fax 631-231-8175
Web Site: http://www.novapublishers.com

NOTICE TO THE READER

The Publisher has taken reasonable care in the preparation of this book, but makes no expressed or implied warranty of any kind and assumes no responsibility for any errors or omissions. No liability is assumed for incidental or consequential damages in connection with or arising out of information contained in this book. The Publisher shall not be liable for any special, consequential, or exemplary damages resulting, in whole or in part, from the readers' use of, or reliance upon, this material. Any parts of this book based on government reports are so indicated and copyright is claimed for those parts to the extent applicable to compilations of such works.

Independent verification should be sought for any data, advice or recommendations contained in this book. In addition, no responsibility is assumed by the publisher for any injury and/or damage to persons or property arising from any methods, products, instructions, ideas or otherwise contained in this publication.

This publication is designed to provide accurate and authoritative information with regard to the subject matter covered herein. It is sold with the clear understanding that the Publisher is not engaged in rendering legal or any other professional services. If legal or any other expert assistance is required, the services of a competent person should be sought. FROM A DECLARATION OF PARTICIPANTS JOINTLY ADOPTED BY A COMMITTEE OF THE AMERICAN BAR ASSOCIATION AND A COMMITTEE OF PUBLISHERS.

Additional color graphics may be available in the e-book version of this book.

Library of Congress Cataloging-in-Publication Data

North Korea : nuclear weapons and the diplomacy debate / editor, Brian N. Thompson.
   p. cm.
 Includes bibliographical references and index.
 ISBN 978-1-62100-450-9 (hardcover)
 1. Nuclear weapons--Korea (North) 2. Korea (North)--Military policy. 3. Korea (North)--Foreign relations. I. Thompson, Brian N.
 U264.5.K7N66 2011
 355.8'25119095193--dc23
                        2011034214

Published by Nova Science Publishers, Inc. † New York

CONTENTS

Preface		**vii**
Chapter 1	North Korea: U.S. Relations, Nuclear Diplomacy and Internal Situation *Emma Chanlett-Avery*	**1**
Chapter 2	North Korea's Nuclear Question: Sense of Vulnerability, Defensive Motivation and Peaceful Solution *Kwang Ho Chun*	**21**
Chapter 3	North Korea's Nuclear Weapons: Technical Issues *Mary Beth Nikitin*	**45**
Chapter 4	North Korea's 2009 Nuclear Test: Containment, Monitoring, Implications *Jonathan Medalia*	**75**
Chapter 5	North Korea's Second Nuclear Test: Implications of U.N. Security Council Resolution 1874 *Mary Beth Nikitin, Mark E. Manyin, Emma Chanlett-Avery and Dick K. Nanto*	**113**
Index		**137**

PREFACE

North Korea has been among the most vexing and persistent problems in U.S. foreign policy in the post-Cold War period. The United States has never had formal diplomatic relations with North Korea. Negotiations over North Korea's nuclear weapons program have consumed the past three U.S. administrations, even as some analysts anticipated a collapse of the isolated authoritarian regime. This book provides background information on the negotiations over North Korea's nuclear weapons program that began in the early 1990s under the Clinton Administration. Although negotiations have reached some key agreements that lay out deals for aid and recognition to North Korea in exchange for denuclearization, major problems with implementation have persisted. With talks suspended since 2009, concern about proliferation to other actors has grown.

Chapter 1- North Korea has been among the most vexing and persistent problems in U.S. foreign policy in the post-Cold War period. The United States has never had formal diplomatic relations with the Democratic People's Republic of Korea (the official name for North Korea). Negotiations over North Korea's nuclear weapons program have consumed the past three U.S. administrations, even as some analysts anticipated a collapse of the isolated authoritarian regime. North Korea has been the recipient of well over $1 billion in U.S. aid and the target of dozens of U.S. sanctions.

Chapter 2- With little faith in reaching a peaceful and sustainable solution to the nuclear question through engagement and negotiations with the regime in Pyongyang, some scholars argue that nuclear nonproliferation can be forced on North Korea only through the use of coercive tools within a general framework of containment. Other scholars, alarmed by the catastrophe that might result from a vigorous attempt to confront and/ or topple the regime in Pyongyang, suggest bypassing it and engaging the North Korean people, hoping that they will gain enough power to transform North Korea into a democratic nuclear-free country. Indeed, to a great extent, current American policy toward North Korea reflects both stances.

Chapter 3- This report summarizes what is known from open sources about the North Korean nuclear weapons program—including weapons-usable fissile material and warhead estimates—and assesses current developments in achieving denuclearization. Little detailed open-source information is available about the DPRK's nuclear weapons production capabilities, warhead sophistication, the scope and success of its uranium enrichment program, or extent of its proliferation activities. In total, it is estimated that North Korea has between 30 and 50 kilograms of separated plutonium, enough for at least half a dozen nuclear weapons. While North Korea's weapons program has been plutonium-based from the start, in the last decade, intelligence emerged pointing to a second route to a bomb using highly enriched uranium. North Korea openly acknowledged a uranium enrichment program in 2009, but has said its purpose is the production of fuel for nuclear power. In November 2010, North Korea showed visiting American experts early construction of a 100 MWT light-water reactor and a newly built gas centrifuge uranium enrichment plant, both at the Yongbyon site. The North Koreans claimed the enrichment plant was operational, but this has not been independently confirmed. U.S. officials have said that it is likely other, clandestine enrichment facilities exist.Beginning in late 2002, North Korea ended an eight-year freeze on its plutonium production program, expelled international inspectors, and restarted facilities. In September 2005, members of the Six-Party Talks (United States, South Korea, Japan, China, Russia, and North Korea) issued a Joint Statement on the verifiable denuclearization of the Korean Peninsula. On October 9, 2006, North Korea conducted a nuclear test, with a yield of less than 1 kiloton. In February 2007, North Korea and the other members of the Six-Party Talks agreed on steps for phased implementation of the 2005 denuclearization agreement. Phase 1 included the shut-down of plutonium production at the Yongbyon nuclear complex in exchange for an initial heavy fuel oil shipment to North Korea. Phase 2 steps included disablement of plutonium production facilities at Yongbyon and a "complete and correct" declaration of DPRK nuclear activities, in exchange for delivery of energy assistance and removal of certain U.S. sanctions. The declaration was submitted in June 2008. Thereafter, President Bush removed North Korea from the Trading with the Enemy Act (TWEA) list and notified Congress of his intent to lift the State Sponsor of Terrorism (SST) designation after North Korea agreed to verification provisions. North Korea did not accept initial U.S. verification proposals, and in September 2008, threatened to restart reprocessing plutonium. U.S. officials announced a verbal bilateral agreement on verification in October 2008, and the Bush administration removed North Korea from the SST List. North Korea soon after said that it had not agreed to sampling at nuclear sites, a key element for verification of plutonium production. The Six-Party Talks have not convened since December 2008.

Chapter 4- On May 25, 2009, North Korea announced that it had conducted its second underground nuclear test. Unlike its first test, in 2006, there is no public record that the second one released radioactive materials indicative of a nuclear explosion. How could North Korea have contained these materials from the May 2009 event and what are the implications?

As background, the Comprehensive Nuclear-Test-Ban Treaty (CTBT) would ban all nuclear explosions. It was opened for signature in 1996. Entry into force requires ratification by 44 states specified in the treaty, including the United States and North Korea. As of November 2010, 153 states, including 35 of the 44, had ratified. North Korea has not signed the CTBT. President Clinton signed it in 1996; in 1999, the Senate voted not to consent to its ratification. In 2009, President Obama pledged to press for its ratification.

Chapter 5- The United Nations Security Council unanimously passed Res. 1874 on June 12, 2009, in response to North Korea's second nuclear test. The resolution puts in place a series of sanctions on North Korea's arms sales, luxury goods, and financial transactions related to its weapons programs, and calls upon states to inspect North Korean vessels suspected of carrying such shipments. The resolution does allow for shipments of food and nonmilitary goods. As was the case with an earlier U.N. resolution, 1718, that was passed in October 2006 after North Korea's first nuclear test, Resolution 1874 seeks to curb financial benefits that go to North Korea's regime and its weapons program. This report summarizes and analyzes Resolution 1874. In summary, the economic effect of Resolution 1874 is not likely to be great unless China cooperates extensively and goes beyond the requirements of the resolution and/or the specific financial sanctions cause a ripple effect that causes financial institutions to avoid being "tainted" by handling any DPRK transaction.

In: North Korea: Nuclear Weapons and the Diplomacy Debate
Editor: Brian N. Thompson
ISBN: 978-1-62100-450-9
© 2012 Nova Science Publishers, Inc.

Chapter 1

NORTH KOREA: U.S. RELATIONS, NUCLEAR DIPLOMACY AND INTERNAL SITUATION[*]

Emma Chanlett-Avery

SUMMARY

North Korea has been among the most vexing and persistent problems in U.S. foreign policy in the post-Cold War period. The United States has never had formal diplomatic relations with the Democratic People's Republic of Korea (the official name for North Korea). Negotiations over North Korea's nuclear weapons program have consumed the past three U.S. administrations, even as some analysts anticipated a collapse of the isolated authoritarian regime. North Korea has been the recipient of well over $1 billion in U.S. aid and the target of dozens of U.S. sanctions.

This report provides background information on the negotiations over North Korea's nuclear weapons program that began in the early 1990s under the Clinton Administration. As U.S. policy toward Pyongyang evolved through the George W. Bush presidency and into the Obama Administration, the negotiations moved from mostly bilateral to the multilateral Six-Party Talks (made up of China, Japan, Russia, North Korea, South Korea, and the United States). Although the negotiations have reached some key agreements that lay out deals for aid and recognition to North Korea in exchange for denuclearization, major problems with implementation have persisted. With talks suspended since 2009, concern about proliferation to other actors has grown.

Meanwhile, North Korea's reclusive regime has shown signs of strain under its ailing leader Kim Jong-il. Pyongyang may be struggling as a result of the impact of international sanctions, anxiety surrounding an anticipated leadership succession, and reports of rare social unrest in reaction to a botched attempt at currency reform in November 2009. North Korea has initiated a string of provocative acts, including an alleged apparent torpedo attack on a South Korean warship that killed 46 South Korean servicemen in March 2010 and an artillery attack on Yeonpyeong Island that killed two South Korean Marines and two civilians.

---

[*] This is an edited, reformatted and augmented version of a Congressional Research Service publication, CRS Report for Congress R41259, from www.crs.gov, dated June 17, 2011.

The Obama Administration, like its predecessors, faces fundamental decisions on how to approach North Korea. To what degree should the United States attempt to isolate the regime diplomatically and financially? Should those efforts be balanced with engagement initiatives that continue to push for steps toward denuclearization, or for better human rights behavior? Is China a reliable partner in efforts to pressure Pyongyang? Have the North's nuclear tests and alleged torpedo attack demonstrated that regime change is the only way to peaceful resolution? How should the United States consider its alliance relationships with Japan and South Korea as it formulates its North Korea policy? Should the United States continue to offer humanitarian aid?

Although the primary focus of U.S. policy toward North Korea is the nuclear weapons program, there are a host of other issues, including Pyongyang's missile program, illicit activities, and poor human rights record. Modest attempts at engaging North Korea, including joint operations to recover U.S. servicemen's remains from the Korean War and some discussion about opening a U.S. liaison office in Pyongyang, remain suspended along with the nuclear negotiations.

This report will be updated periodically.

This report covers the overall U.S.-North Korea relationship, with an emphasis on the diplomacy of the Six-Party Talks.

LATEST DEVELOPMENTS

Food Aid Debate Continues

Beginning in early 2011, North Korea issued an appeal for international food aid. A subsequent World Food Program (WFP) assessment reported in March that a quarter of the North Korean population nation is facing severe food shortages due to an unusually cold winter, fertilizer shortages, and rising international food prices. A U.S. delegation, led by Special Envoy for Human Rights in North Korea Robert King, visited the nation in May to carry out its own assessment. The United States maintains that its food aid policy follows three criteria: demonstrated need, severity of need compared to other countries, and satisfactory monitoring systems to ensure food is reaching the most vulnerable. Obama Administration officials are reportedly divided on whether to authorize new humanitarian assistance for North Korea. Among critics, strong concerns about diversion of such aid to the elite exist, although assistance provided in 2008-2009 had operated under an improved system of monitoring and access negotiated by the Bush Administration. Another complicating factor involves taking a different stance than South Korea, which explicitly links food aid with diplomatic concerns. Several Members of Congress have spoken out against the provision of any assistance to Pyongyang because of concerns about supporting the regime.

More Instability in North-South Relations

Relations between Pyongyang and Seoul under the Lee Myung-bak Administration have steadily deteriorated. After the sinking of the South Korean warship *Cheonan* in March 2010 and the artillery shelling of Yeonpyeong Island in the Yellow Sea in November 2010, North-South relations fell to their worst point in decades. Although relations warmed briefly, tension between the two capitals resumed and intensified through the spring and summer of 2011. In May, President Lee publicly invited North Korea to attend next year's Nuclear Security

Summit in Seoul and revelations of secret contacts between the two governments emerged. In response, North Korea's National Defense Commission issued a statement vowing never to deal with the Lee government and pledging to defend itself against its "gang of traitors." Many analysts have concluded that Pyongyang has given up on any form of negotiation with the Lee government and instead hopes to influence South Korean politics before his successor is elected in December 2012.

Six-Party Talks Impasse

Multilateral negotiations on North Korea's nuclear program have not been held since December 2008. Pyongyang's refusal to take responsibility for the *Cheonan* sinking has left the international nuclear negotiations frozen. Seoul has insisted that North Korea must apologize for the incident, as well as show "sincerity" in implementing major denuclearization commitments made in the 2005 landmark accord among the six nations. (See "Six-Party Talks" section below.) China has worked aggressively behind the scenes to restart the negotiations, but the United States has remained steadfast that an improvement in North-South relations is a pre-requisite for forward movement on the talks. Hopes for a resumption of the negotiations have risen periodically, including when former U.S. President Jimmy Carter visited North Korea in April 2011 along with three other former leaders from the group "The Elders." North Korea claims to be willing to return to the talks "without preconditions," but U.S. and other officials point to Pyongyang's failure to implement previous agreements.

INTRODUCTION

An impoverished nation of about 23 million people, North Korea has been among the most vexing and persistent problems in U.S. foreign policy in the post-Cold War period. The United States has never had formal diplomatic relations with the Democratic People's Republic of Korea (DPRK, the official name for North Korea). Negotiations over North Korea's nuclear weapons program have consumed the past three administrations, even as some analysts anticipated a collapse of the isolated authoritarian regime in Pyongyang. North Korea has been both the recipient of billions of dollars of U.S. aid and the target of dozens of U.S. sanctions. Once considered a relic of the Cold War, the divided Korean peninsula has become an arena of more subtle strategic and economic competition among the region's powers.

U.S. interests in North Korea encompass crucial security, economic, and political concerns. Bilateral military alliances with South Korea and Japan obligate the United States to defend these allies from any attack from the North. Tens of thousands of U.S. troops occupying the largest U.S. military bases in the Pacific are stationed within proven striking range of North Korean missiles. An outbreak of conflict on the Korean peninsula or the collapse of the government in Pyongyang would have severe implications for the regional—if not global—economy. Negotiations and diplomacy surrounding North Korea's nuclear weapons program influence U.S. relations with all the major powers in the region and have become a particularly complicating factor for Sino-U.S. ties.

At the center of this complicated intersection of geostrategic interests is the task of dealing with an isolated authoritarian regime. Unfettered by many of the norms that govern international diplomacy, the leadership in Pyongyang, headed by its dynastic "Dear Leader" Kim Jong-il, is unpredictable and opaque. U.S. policymakers face a daunting challenge in navigating a course toward a peaceful resolution of the nuclear issue with a rogue actor.

In the long run, the ideal outcome remains, presumably, reunification of the Korean peninsula under stable democratic rule. At this point, however, the road to that result appears fraught with risks. If the Pyongyang regime falls due to internal or external forces, the potential for major strategic consequences (including competition for control of the North's nuclear arsenal) and a massive humanitarian crisis, not to mention long-term economic and social repercussions, loom large. In the interim, policymakers face deep challenges in even defining achievable objectives, let alone reaching them.

Overview of Past U.S. Policy on North Korea

Over the past decade, U.S. policy toward North Korea has ranged from direct bilateral engagement to labeling Pyongyang as part of an "axis of evil." Despite repeated provocations from the North, since 1994 there is no publicly available evidence that any U.S. administration has seriously considered a direct military strike or an explicit policy of regime change due to the threat of a devastating war on the peninsula. Although there have been periodic efforts to negotiate a "grand bargain" that addresses the full range of concerns with Pyongyang's behavior and activities, North Korea's nuclear program has usually been prioritized above North Korea's human rights record, its missile program, and its illicit and criminal dealings.

Even as the strategic and economic landscape of East Asia has undergone dramatic changes, North Korea has endured as a major U.S. foreign policy challenge. As Washington has shifted from a primarily bilateral (during the Clinton Administration) to a mostly multilateral framework (during the Bush and Obama Administrations) for addressing North Korea, the centrality of China's role in dealing with Pyongyang has become increasingly pronounced. North Korea is dependent on China's economic aid and diplomatic support for its survival. (See "China's Role" section below.) Cooperation on North Korea has competed with other U.S. policy priorities with Beijing such as Iran, currency adjustment, climate change, and human rights.

Relations with other countries, particularly Japan and South Korea, also influence U.S. policy toward North Korea; power transitions in other capitals can bring about shifts in the overall cooperation to deal with Pyongyang. In recent years, Japan's approach to North Korea has been harder-line than that of other Six-Party participants. South Korean President Lee Myung-bak is seen as more hawkish on Pyongyang than his recent predecessors, particularly since the sinking of the *Cheonan* in March 2010.

Identifying patterns in North Korean behavior is challenging, as Pyongyang often weaves together different approaches to the outside world. North Korean behavior has vacillated between limited cooperation and overt provocations, including testing two nuclear devices and several missiles between 2006 and 2009. Pyongyang's willingness to negotiate has often appeared to be driven by its internal conditions: food shortages or economic desperation can push North Korea to re-engage in talks, usually to extract more aid from China or, in the past, from South Korea. North Korea has proven skillful at exploiting divisions among the other five parties or taking advantage of political transitions in Washington to stall the Six-Party Talks negotiating process.

At the core of the North Korean issue is the question of what Pyongyang's leadership ultimately seeks. As the negotiations have endured dozens of twists and turns, analysts have remained divided on whether the regime truly seeks acceptance into (or is capable of entering) the international community, or remains resolutely committed to its existence as a closed society with nuclear weapons as a guarantor. If the latter, debate rages on the proper strategic response, with options ranging from trying to squeeze the dictatorship to the point of collapse to buying time and trying to prevent proliferation or other severely destabilizing events.

OBAMA ADMINISTRATION NORTH KOREA POLICY

Beginning with his presidential campaign, Obama indicated a willingness to engage with "rogue" governments. Although not mentioning North Korea by name, he pledged in his inaugural address to reach out to isolated regimes. With a commitment to retaining the six-nation forum, U.S. officials have stated that they seek a comprehensive package deal for North Korea's complete denuclearization, which would include normalization of relations and significant aid. On the personnel side, Ambassador Stephen Bosworth has assumed the position as Special Representative for North Korea Policy, Sung Kim serves as the Special Envoy for the Six-Party Talks, and Robert King has assumed the post of Special Envoy for North Korean Human Rights Issues.

However, a series of provocations from Pyongyang after Obama took office halted progress on furthering negotiations. In 2009, the North tested a second nuclear device, expelled U.S. and international nuclear inspectors, and declared it would "never" return to the talks. In response to the test, the United Nations Security Council unanimously passed Resolution 1874, which outlines a series of sanctions to deny financial benefits to the regime in Pyongyang.[1] After passage of the resolution, the Obama Administration named Philip Goldberg as the coordinator of the U.S. sanctions efforts, the fourth ambassadorial-level position devoted to North Korean efforts. Goldberg has since been replaced by Robert Einhorn, who also oversees sanctions efforts against Iran.

As these events played out, the Obama Administration adopted what Secretary of State Hillary Clinton dubbed a "strategic patience" policy that essentially waits for North Korea to come back to the table while maintaining pressure through economic sanctions and arms interdictions. Critics claim that this approach has allowed Pyongyang to control the situation, while fears of further nuclear advances and possible proliferation build. While the talks are frozen, Washington has maintained a strong united approach with Seoul and Tokyo. Despite reports of China's harsh reaction to North Korea's provocations, and Beijing support for adoption of U.N. Security Council Resolution 1874, Beijing has remained unwilling to impose more stringent economic measures that might risk the Pyongyang regime's survival.

The *Cheonan* sinking and Yeonpyeong Island shelling (see "North Korean Behavior During Obama Administration" section below) drew the United States even closer to Seoul and, since then, U.S. officials have stated explicitly that they will wait for South Korea's cue to resume negotiations. American and South Korean policies appear in complete alignment, with both governments insisting that North Korea demonstrate a serious commitment to implementing the denuclearization aspects of the 2005 Six-Party Talks agreement. U.S.-South Korean cooperation has been underscored by a series of military exercises in the waters surrounding the peninsula, as well as symbolic gestures such as the joint visit of Secretary of State Hillary Clinton and Secretary of Defense Robert Gates to the Demilitarized Zone (DMZ) in June 2010. During the visit, a new set of unilateral U.S. sanctions targeting North Korea was announced.[2]

The Administration has formulated its approach to North Korea against the backdrop of its global nonproliferation agenda. After pledging to work toward a world free of nuclear weapons in an April 2009 speech in Prague, President Obama has taken steps to further that goal, including signing a new nuclear arms reduction treaty with Russia, convening a global leaders' summit to secure stockpiles of nuclear materials, and releasing a new Nuclear Posture Review that outlines new U.S. guidelines on the use of nuclear weapons. The document narrows the circumstances under which nuclear weapons would be used, pledging not to attack nor threaten an attack with nuclear weapons on non-nuclear weapon states that are in compliance with the Nuclear Non-Proliferation Treaty (NPT). When announcing the strategy, officials singled out North Korea and Iran as outliers that are not subject to the security guarantees. The announcement that South Korea plans to host the second Nuclear Security Summit in 2012 further drew attention to Pyongyang's nuclear status.

While the denuclearization talks drag on, the concern about proliferation has intensified. Because of North Korea's dire economic situation, there is a strong fear that it will sell its nuclear technology to another rogue regime or a non-state actor. Evidence of some cooperation with Syria, Iran, and potentially Burma has alarmed national security experts. The Israeli bombing of a nuclear facility in Syria in 2007 raised concern about North Korean collaboration on a nuclear reactor with the Syrians. Reports surface periodically that established commercial relationships in conventional arms sales between Pyongyang and several Middle Eastern countries may have expanded into the nuclear realm as well.[3] The Obama Administration is faced with the question of whether it should pursue limited measures to prevent proliferation in the absence of a "grand bargain" approach to disarm the North.

North Korean Behavior During Obama Administration

Since Obama took office, North Korea has emphasized two main demands: that it be recognized as a nuclear weapons state and that a peace treaty with the United States must be a prerequisite to denuclearization. The former demand presents a diplomatic and semantic dilemma: despite repeatedly acknowledging that North Korea has produced nuclear weapons, U.S. officials have insisted that this situation is "unacceptable." According to statements from Pyongyang, the latter demand is an issue of building trust between the United States and North Korea. After years of observing North Korea's negotiating behavior, many analysts believe that such demands are simply tactical moves by Pyongyang and that North Korea has no intention of giving up its nuclear weapons in exchange for aid and recognition. In April 2010, North Korea reiterated its demand to be recognized as an official nuclear weapons state and said it would increase and modernize its nuclear deterrent.

Pattern of Conciliation and Provocations

North Korea's behavior has been erratic since the Obama Administration took office. After its initial string of provocations in 2009, most prominently its May 2009 nuclear test, North Korea appeared to adjust its approach and launched what some dubbed a "charm offensive" strategy. In August 2009, Kim Jong-il received former U.S. President Bill Clinton, after which North Korea released two American journalists who had been held for five months after allegedly crossing the border into North Korea. The same month, Kim met with Hyundai Chairperson Hyun Jung-eun. The following month, meetings with Chinese officials yielded encouraging statements about Pyongyang's willingness to rejoin multilateral talks. A North Korean delegation traveled to Seoul for the funeral of former South Korean President Kim Dae-jung and met with President Lee Myung-bak. In early 2010, Pyongyang called for an end to hostilities with the United States and South Korea.

Some observers saw this approach as a product of deteriorating conditions within North Korea. The impact of international sanctions, anxiety surrounding an anticipated leadership succession, and reports of rare social unrest in reaction to a botched attempt at currency reform appeared to be driving Pyongyang's conciliatory gestures. (See "North Korea's Internal Situation" section below.) Many analysts anticipated that North Korea would return to the Six-Party Talks.

String of Provocations in 2010

Expectations of a return to negotiations were altered by the dramatic sinking of the South Korean navy corvette *Cheonan* on March 26, taking the lives of 46 sailors on board. A multinational investigation team led by South Korea determined that the ship was sunk by a torpedo from a North Korean submarine. The Obama Administration expressed staunch support for Seoul and embarked on a series of military exercises to demonstrate its commitment. The attack may have been an effort to shore up support for the succession of Kim Jong-un. According to some analysts, the provocation may have been designed to bolster Kim Jong-il's credibility as a strong leader confronting the South, and therefore his authority to select his son as his replacement.[4]

After the *Cheonan* incident, Pyongyang initiated further provocations. In November, North Korea invited a group of U.S. nuclear experts to the Yongbyon nuclear complex to reveal early construction of an experimental light-water reactor and a small gas centrifuge uranium enrichment facility. The revelations of possible progress toward another path to a nuclear weapon prompted speculation that North Korea was attempting to strengthen its bargaining position if the talks resumed, or perhaps trying to advertise its goods to potential customers. Further, the sophistication of the uranium enrichment plant took many observers by surprise and renewed concerns about Pyongyang's capabilities and deftness in avoiding sanctions to develop its nuclear programs.

On November 23, shortly after announcing its new nuclear facilities, North Korea fired over 170 artillery rounds toward Yeonpyeong Island in the Yellow Sea, killing two ROK Marines and two civilians, injuring many more and damaging multiple structures. The attack, which the North said was a response to South Korean military exercises, was the first since the Korean War to strike South Korean territory directly and inflict civilian casualties. Again, the U.S. military joined the ROK for military exercises, this time deploying the USS *George Washington* aircraft carrier to the Yellow Sea. Despite Pyongyang's threats of retaliation, South Korea staged its previously scheduled live fire exercises near Yeonpyeong Island, prompting an emergency meeting of the United Nations Security Council amid fear of the outbreak of war. Perhaps due to Chinese pressure, the North refrained from responding.

Reaching out Again in 2011?

In early 2011, Pyongyang appeared to be re-launching a diplomatic offensive, presumably to secure new economic assistance and food aid. As of June, no new provocations had been undertaken in 2011. During this Pyongyang has welcomed foreign delegations, including the Elders group led by former U.S. President Jimmy Carter and a U.S. team led by Special Envoy for Human Rights in North Korea Ambassador Robert King. Leader Kim Jong-il has visited China three times since May 2010 with his itineraries heavy on stops that showcase Chinese economic development. China has urged Kim to embrace economic reform for years; some analysts see the repeated trips as an indication that he is seeking further aid and support from Beijing. Although rhetoric toward the South remains harsh, Pyongyang appears to be in an outreach mode to the international community.

SIX-PARTY TALKS

Background: History of Negotiations

North Korea's nuclear weapons programs have concerned the United States for nearly three decades. In the 1980s, U.S. intelligence detected new construction of a nuclear reactor at Yongbyon. In the early 1990s, after agreeing to and then obstructing IAEA inspections, North Korea announced its intention to withdraw from the Nuclear Non-Proliferation Treaty (NPT).[5] According to statements by former Clinton Administration officials, a pre-emptive military strike on the North's nuclear facilities was seriously considered as the crisis developed.[6] Discussion of sanctions at the United Nations Security Council and a diplomatic mission from former President Jimmy Carter diffused the tension and eventually led to the 1994 Agreed Framework, an agreement between the United States and North Korea that essentially would have provided two light water reactors (LWRs) and heavy fuel oil to North Korea in exchange for a freeze of its plutonium program. The document also outlined a path toward normalization of diplomatic relations.

Beset by problems from the start, the agreement faced multiple delays in funding from the U.S. side and a lack of compliance by the North Koreans. Still, the fundamentals of the agreement were implemented: North Korea froze its plutonium program, heavy fuel oil was delivered to the North Koreans, and LWR construction commenced. In 2002, U.S. officials confronted North Korea about a suspected uranium enrichment program, dealing a further blow to the agreement. After minimal progress in construction of the LWRs, the project was suspended in 2003. After North Korea expelled inspectors from the Yongbyon site and announced its withdrawal from the NPT, the project was officially terminated in January 2006.

Under the George W. Bush Administration, the negotiations to resolve the North Korean nuclear issue expanded to include China, South Korea, Japan, and Russia. With China playing host, six rounds of the "Six-Party Talks" from 2003-2007 yielded occasional incremental progress, but ultimately failed to resolve the fundamental issue of North Korean nuclear arms.

The most promising breakthrough occurred in 2005, with the issuance of a Joint Statement in which North Korea agreed to abandon its nuclear weapons programs in exchange for aid, a U.S. security guarantee, and normalization of relations with the United States. Some observers described the agreement as "Agreed Framework Plus." Despite the promise of the statement, the process eventually broke down due to complications over the release of North Korean assets from a bank in Macau and then degenerated further with North Korea's test of a nuclear device in October 2006.[7]

In February 2007, Six-Party Talks negotiators announced an agreement that would provide economic and diplomatic benefits to North Korea in exchange for a freeze and disablement of Pyongyang's nuclear facilities. This was followed by an October 2007 agreement that more specifically laid out the implementation plans, including the disablement of the Yongbyon facility, a North Korean declaration of its nuclear programs, and a U.S. promise to lift economic sanctions on North Korea and remove North Korea from the U.S. list of state sponsors of terrorism. Under the leadership of Assistant Secretary of State for East Asia and Pacific Affairs Christopher Hill, the Bush Administration pushed ahead for a deal, including removing North Korea from the terrorism list in October 2008.[8] Disagreements over the verification protocol between Washington and Pyongyang stalled the process until the U.S. presidential election in November 2008.

China's Role

As host of the Six-Party Talks and as North Korea's chief benefactor, China plays a crucial role in the negotiations. Beijing's decision to host the talks marked China's most significant foray onto the international diplomatic stage and was counted as a significant achievement by the Bush Administration. Formation of the six-nation format, initiated by the Bush Administration in 2002 and continued under the Obama Administration, confirms the critical importance of China's role in U.S. policy toward North Korea. The United States depends on Beijing's leverage to relay messages to the North Koreans, push Pyongyang for concessions and attendance at the negotiations, and, on some occasions, punish the North for its actions. In addition, China's permanent seat on the United Nations Security Council ensures its influence on any U.N. action directed at North Korea.

In addition to being North Korea's largest trading partner by far, China also provides considerable concessional assistance. The large amount of food and energy aid that China supplies is an essential lifeline for the regime in Pyongyang, particularly since the cessation of most aid from South Korea under the Lee Administration. It is clear that Beijing cannot control Pyongyang's behavior—particularly in the cases of provocative nuclear tests and missile launches—but even temporary cessation of economic and energy aid is significant for North Korea. In September 2006, Chinese trade statistics reflected a temporary cut-off in oil exports to North Korea, in a period which followed several provocative missile tests by Pyongyang. Although Beijing did not label the reduction as a punishment, some analysts saw the move as a reflection of China's displeasure with the North's actions.[9] In instances when the international community wishes to condemn Pyongyang's behavior, such as the sanctions imposed in U.N. Security Council Resolution 1874, Beijing's willingness to punish the regime largely determines how acutely North Korea is affected.

China's overriding priority of preventing North Korea's collapse remains firm.[10] Beijing fears the destabilizing effects of a humanitarian crisis, significant refugee flows over its borders, and the uncertainty of how other nations, particularly the United States, would assert themselves on the peninsula in the event of a power vacuum. While focusing on its own economic development, China favors the maintenance of regional stability over all other concerns. To try to stabilize North Korea's economy, China is expanding economic ties and supporting joint industrial projects between China's northeastern provinces and North Korea's northern border region. Many Chinese leaders also see strategic value in having North Korea as a "buffer" between it and the democratic, U.S.-allied South Korea.

North Korea's Internal Situation

The remarkable durability of the North Korean regime despite its intense isolation and economic dysfunction may be undergoing its biggest test. The combination of a botched currency reform campaign, Kim Jong-il's failing health, and continued food shortages has heightened uncertainty about the regime's future. In addition, the impact of international sanctions and the virtual cessation of aid from Seoul under the Lee Administration leaves the government with limited options for providing for the elite and holding on to power.

In November 2009, the government abruptly announced a revaluation of the North Korean won, forcing citizens to exchange their old notes for new currency, and putting caps on the total amount that could be converted, thereby instantly wiping out many families' savings. Prices of goods skyrocketed and distribution channels were disrupted, worsening an already dire situation of food shortages. Reports of isolated unrest emerged, rare in a society where public expression of anger toward the government is harshly punished. Authorities were forced to ratchet back the initial reform and issued an apology. The government official in charge of the reform was reportedly executed, although those reports could not be confirmed.[11] Analysts have described the move as a misguided attempt to stamp out any free-market enterprise and consolidate the state's control over commercial activity.

The North Korean regime remains extraordinarily opaque, but a trickle of news works its way out through North Korean exiles and other channels. These forms of grass-roots information gathering have democratized the business of intelligence on North Korea. Previously, South Korean intelligence services had generally provided the bulk of information known about the North. Surveys of North Korean defectors reveal that some within North Korea are growing increasingly wary of government propaganda and turning to outside sources of news.[12]

Succession Process Moves Ahead

Since Kim Jong-il suffered a stroke in August 2008, international observers have speculated about an anticipated succession process in Pyongyang. In September 2010, a rare session of the Supreme People's Assembly confirmed that the regime is preparing to transfer leadership. Many analysts believe that the regime is aiming for a formal appointment in 2012. 2012 will mark North Korean founder Kim Il-sung's 100th birthday, and is the year designated by Kim Jong-il for North Korea to become "militarily strong and economically prosperous." Kim's youngest son, Kim Jong-un, believed to be about 27 years old, appears to be the chosen successor. The younger Kim was appointed as a four-star general as well as a vice-chairman of the Central Military Commission, a powerful organ of the Korean Workers Party (KPA). He also became a member of the Central Committee of the KPA. He later appeared by his father's side during military exercises and, following the death of a prominent military figure, was named to the state funeral committee, again indicating his elevated status.

The haste surrounding these succession steps is in marked contrast to the transfer of power to Kim Jong-il after his father Kim Il-sung's sudden death in 1994: the younger Kim had been publicly groomed as the inheritor of his father's position for several years. The risks of pulling off a dynastic succession are high, particularly if Kim Jong-il passes quickly. Though looking frail and requiring support to walk at recent public appearances, many observers noted that his condition did not seem as dire as some had suggested. Kim Jong-un has barely been introduced to the public, making many analysts question whether the North Korean people will embrace his leadership.

Perhaps more importantly, Kim Jong-un's legitimacy among the established power constituencies may be questionable. Other senior figures also were elevated recently, leading to speculation that the young Kim will be buffeted by a group of close advisors. Most prominently, Kim Jong-il's brother-in-law, Jang Song-taek, earlier was appointed as vice-chairman of the National Defense Commission, making him second in command under Kim. Analysts speculate that Jang may serve as a regent with Kim Jong-un as the bloodline figurehead. Kim Kyong-hui, Jang's wife and Kim Jong-il's sister, also received promotions in the military and political elite. Despite his major postings, Kim Jong-un did not receive an appointment to the Politburo, the highest party body; Kim Kyong-hui is a member and Jang is an alternate. Because of Kim's youth and inexperience, it appears that a group of senior advisors may serve as a collective leadership unit if he has not established authority at the time of his father's death.

Kim Jong-un's and others' appointments to high-level party positions have led some analysts to posit that the Korean Workers' Party may be gaining in stature over the military establishment. The emphasis on the Central Military Commission, the tool through which the Party controls the military, may indicate that the regime is moving away from the concentrated power in the National Defense Commission exploited by Kim Jong-il and instead returning to a Party-centric order, as was the case under Kim Il-sung. The *Songun*, or "Military First," policy is likely to remain in place, but Kim Jong-un may seek to establish his authority over the military by developing authority within the Party.[13] The September conclave highlighted the restoration of several formal Party organs as the mechanism through which a new generation would rise.[14]

The implications for the United States of how succession planning proceeds are significant. In the event of Kim Jong-il's death, the United States and its allies could face potentially explosive dangers. Many analysts point to the danger of a power vacuum in a state with a nuclear arsenal, with competing elements possibly locked in a struggle against one another. However destructive Kim Jong-il has proven to be, his leadership has provided a degree of stability. The future scenarios of collective leadership, dynastic succession, or foreign intervention all present tremendous risks that would almost certainly disrupt any existing channels of negotiation with North Korea. Though some may hold out hope that the young, European-educated Kim could emerge as a reformer, most analysts conclude that the

North's outdated ideology and closed political system will not allow for divergence on the part of a new leader.[15]

Solidifying Ties with China

As North Korea faces the end of the Kim Jong-il era, the regime appears to be drawing closer to China. This process has taken form in both internal party-to-party interactions as well as on the international scene. In early May 2010, as South Korean President Lee Myung-bak's administration weighed how to respond to the *Cheonan* sinking without risking an escalation into general war, Kim Jong-il visited China for the first time in four years, a move that infuriated Seoul. Beijing has resisted U.S. and others' appeals to condemn the attack, including fighting for language in a United Nations Security Council statement that avoided directly blaming North Korea. Kim returned to China in August 2010 and again in May 2011. Observers speculate that Kim was seeking China's support for his son's succession, as well as perhaps more food aid.

The possible increase in the Korean Workers' Party power in Pyongyang's decision-making process has implications for China's influence. Analysts have noted deepening links between the Korean Worker's Party and the Communist Party in China. Some analysts have identified Beijing's pursuit of economic cooperation with North Korea—including the provision of capital and development of natural resources within North Korea—as channeled through the Communist Party of China (CPC) International Liaison Department, that is, through party-to-party engagement.[16] If indeed the KWP's power becomes paramount in Pyongyang, Beijing could stand to increase its clout.

Both sides have some reservations about becoming too interlinked: Beijing faces condemnation from the international community, and deterioration of relations with an important trade partner in South Korea, for defending North Korea, and Pyongyang seeks to avoid complete dependence on China to preserve some degree of autonomy. However, both capitals appear to have calculated that their strategic interests—or, in the case of Pyongyang, survival—depend on the other.

OTHER U.S. CONCERNS WITH NORTH KOREA

North Korea's Human Rights Record

Although the nuclear issue has dominated relations with Pyongyang, U.S. officials periodically voice concerns about North Korea's very poor human rights record. The plight of most North Koreans is dire. The State Department's annual human rights reports and reports from private organizations have portrayed a little-changing pattern of extreme human rights abuses by the North Korea regime over many years.[17] The reports stress a total denial of political, civil, and religious liberties and say that no dissent or criticism of leader Kim Jong-il is allowed. Freedoms of speech, the press, and assembly do not exist. There is no independent judiciary, and citizens do not have the right to choose their own government. Reports also document the extensive ideological indoctrination of North Korean citizens.

Severe physical abuse is meted out to citizens who violate laws and restrictions. Multiple reports have described a system of prison camps that house 150,000 to 200,000 inmates, including many political prisoners.[18] Reports from survivors and escapees from the camps indicate that conditions in the camps for political prisoners are extremely harsh and that many political prisoners do not survive. Reports cite executions and torture of prisoners as a frequent practice.

A 2011 study of DPRK defectors indicates that in recent years many North Koreans have been arrested for what would earlier have been deemed ordinary economic activities. North Korea criminalizes market activities, seeing them as a set of challenges to the state. Its penal system targets low-level or misdemeanor crimes, such as unsanctioned trading or violations of travel permits. Violators face detention in local-level "collection centers" and "labor training centers." Defectors have reported starvation, suffered beatings and torture, and witnessed executions in these centers.[19]

In addition to the extreme curtailment of rights, many North Koreans face significant food shortages. In a recent survey, the World Food Program identified urgent hunger needs for 3.5 million citizens in North Korea, out of a total population of 24 million. UNICEF has reported that each year some 40,000 North Korean children under five became "acutely malnourished," with 25,000 needing hospital treatment. About one-third of the population reportedly suffers from stunting.[20]

North Korean Refugees

For over a decade, food shortages, persecution, and human rights abuses have prompted perhaps hundreds of thousands of North Koreans to go to neighboring China, where they are forced to evade Chinese security forces and often become victims of further abuse, neglect, and lack of protection. There is little reliable information on the size and composition of the North Korean population located in China. Estimates range up to 300,000 or more. The United Nations High Commissioner for Refugees (UNHCR) has not been given access to conduct a systematic survey. Reports indicate that many women and children are the victims of human trafficking, particularly women lured to China seeking a better life but forced into marriage or prostitution.[21] Some of the refugees who escape to China make their way to Southeast Asia or Mongolia, where they may seek passage to a third country, usually South Korea. If repatriated, they risk harsh punishment or execution.

The North Korean Human Rights Act

In 2004, the 108th Congress passed, and President George W. Bush signed, the North Korean Human Rights Act (H.R. 4011; P.L. 108-333). Among its chief goals are the promotion and protection of human rights in North Korea and the creation of a "durable humanitarian" option for its refugees. The North Korean Human Rights Act (NKHRA) authorized new funds to support human rights efforts and improve the flow of information, and required the President to appoint a Special Envoy on human rights in North Korea. Under the NKHRA, North Koreans may apply for asylum in the United States, and the State Department is required to facilitate the submission of their applications. The bill required that all non-humanitarian assistance must be linked to improvements in human rights, but provided a waiver if the President deems the aid to be in the interest of national security.

In 2008, Congress reauthorized NKHRA under P.L. 110-346 at the original levels of $2 million annually to support human rights and democracy programs, $2 million annually to promote freedom of information programs for North Koreans, and $20 million annually to assist North Korean refugees. Appropriations for the reauthorization were extended to 2012. The legislation also requires additional reporting on U.S. efforts to resettle North Korean refugees in the United States.

Implementation

Relatively few North Korean refugees have resettled in the United States. According to the State Department, as of May 2011, 120 North Korean refugees now reside in the United States.[22] The Government Accountability Office (GAO) reports that in spite of the U.S. government's efforts to expand resettlements, rates did not improve from 2006-2008.[23] Several U.S. agencies were involved in working with other countries to resettle such refuges, but North Korean applicants face hurdles. Some host countries delay the granting of exit permissions or limit contacts with U.S. officials. Other host governments are reluctant to antagonize Pyongyang by admitting North Korean refugees and prefer to avoid making their countries known as a reliable transit points. Another challenge is educating the North Korean refugee population about the potential to resettle in the United States, many of whom may not be aware of the program.

Under the NKHRA, Congress authorized $2 million annually to promote freedom of information programs for North Koreans. It called on the Broadcasting Board of Governors (BBG) to "facilitate the unhindered dissemination of information in North Korea" by increasing Korean-language broadcasts by Radio Free Asia (RFA) and Voice of America (VOA).[24] A modest amount has been appropriated to support independent radio broadcasters. The BBG currently broadcasts to North Korea ten hours per day. In FY2010, the BBG spent $8.49 million to cover the cost of transmission as well as of a news center for VOA Seoul and the RFA Seoul Bureau. For FY2011, it requested $8.46 million which includes funding for the VOA and RFA Bureaus.[25] Although official North Korean radios are altered by the government to prevent outside broadcasts, defectors report that many citizens have illegal radios that receive the programs. There have also been efforts in the past by the U.S. and South Korean governments to smuggle in radios in order to allow information to penetrate the closed country.

In 2009, Robert R. King, a long-time aide to the late Representative Tom Lantos, became the Obama Administration's Special Envoy on North Korean Human Rights Issues. Before joining the Administration, he was involved in the planning of Representative Lantos' human rights agenda, visited North Korea and played a role in the passage of the NKHRA. King is currently leading a mission to North Korea to assess the need for humanitarian food aid, as well as raise broader human rights issues with North Korean officials. His trip is the first by a Special Envoy on North Korea Human Rights to the country since the creation of the post under the 2004 law. According to the State Department, King's office is closely integrated with the Office of the Special Envoy on North Korea, Stephen W. Bosworth. As a result, he consults regularly with his counterparts in the Department and he works on a full-time basis. The office of the former Special Envoy, Jay Lefkowitz, fell under the Bureau of Democracy, Human Rights, and Labor. Lefkowitz worked on a part-time basis, which drew criticism from some Members of Congress.

North Korea's Illicit Activities

Strong indications exist that the North Korean regime has been involved in the production and trafficking of illicit drugs, as well as of counterfeit currency, cigarettes, and pharmaceuticals. DPRK crime-for-profit activities have reportedly brought in important foreign currency resources and come under the direction of a special office under the direction of the ruling Korean Worker's Party.[26] Although U.S. policy during the first term of the Bush Administration highlighted these activities, they have generally been relegated since to a lower level of priority compared to the nuclear issue.

In September 2005, the U.S. Treasury Department identified Banco Delta Asia, located in Macau, as a bank that distributed North Korean counterfeit currency and allowed for money laundering for North Korean criminal enterprises. It ordered the freezing of $24 million in North Korean accounts with the bank. This action prompted many other banks to freeze North Korean accounts and derailed potential progress on the September 2005 Six-Party Talks agreement. After lengthy negotiations and complicated arrangements, in June 2007 the Bush Administration agreed to allow the release of the $24 million from Banco Delta Asia accounts and ceased its campaign to pressure foreign governments and banks to avoid doing business with North Korea. Since the second nuclear test and the passage of U.N. Security Resolution 1874, there have been renewed efforts to pressure Pyongyang through the restriction of illicit activities, particularly arms sales.

North Korea's Missile Program

North Korea has a well-developed missile program, as evidenced by its repeated tests over the past several years.[27] The missiles have not been a high priority for U.S. North Korea policy since the late Clinton Administration and have not been on the agenda in the Six-Party Talks. In 1999, North Korea agreed to a moratorium on long-range missile tests in exchange for the Clinton Administration's pledge to lift certain economic sanctions. The deal was later abandoned during the Bush Administration. In 2006, U.N. Security Council Resolution 1718 barred North Korea from conducting missile-related activities. North Korea flouted this resolution with its April 2009 test of the long-range Taepodong II.

According to South Korean defense officials, Pyongyang's arsenal includes intermediate-range missiles that have a range of about 1,860 miles, which includes all of Japan and the U.S. military bases located there.[28] Some military analysts believe that North Korea is close to deploying ballistic missiles that could eventually threaten the west coast of the continental United States. Pyongyang has sold missile parts and technology to several states, including Egypt, Iran, Libya, Pakistan, Syria, United Arab Emirates, and Yemen.[29] Of key concern to the United States is the North Koreans' ability to successfully miniaturize nuclear warheads and mount them on ballistic missiles. Military experts have cited progress in North Korea's missile development as evidenced by its tests. They note that the April 2009 test of the Taepodong II, which Pyongyang claimed was a satellite launch, failed but still indicated advancements in long-range missile technology.[30]

During a visit to China in January 2011, U.S. Secretary of Defense Robert Gates called for missile and nuclear testing moratoria by North Korea and said that while the North Korean missile threat to the United States will be "very limited" in five years, it is still cause for concern. Press reports in mid-February 2011 showed a completed launch pad and launch tower at a second missile launch facility in North Korea's northwest, close to the border with China, near Tongchang-dong. The DPRK has been constructing the site, a more sophisticated set-up than the current launch facility at Musudan-ri, for the past decade, and analysts say it could be used to test inter-continental ballistic missiles.

U.S. ENGAGEMENT ACTIVITIES WITH NORTH KOREA

U.S. Assistance to North Korea[31]

Since 1995, the United States has provided North Korea with over $1.2 billion in assistance, of which about 60% has paid for food aid and about 40% for energy assistance. Except for a small ongoing medical assistance program, the United States has not provided any aid to North Korea since early 2009; the United States provided all of its share of pledged heavy fuel oil by December 2008. Energy assistance was tied to progress in the Six-Party Talks, which broke down in 2009. U.S. food aid, which officially is not linked to diplomatic developments, ended in early 2009 due to disagreements with Pyongyang over monitoring and access. (The North Korean government restricts the ability of donors to operate in the country.) In 2011, North Korea issued appeals to the international community for additional food aid (see "Latest Developments" section above).

From 2007 to April 2009, the United States also provided technical assistance to North Korea to help in the nuclear disablement process. In 2008, Congress took legislative steps to legally enable the President to give expanded assistance for this purpose. However, following North Korea's actions in the spring of 2009 when it test-fired a missile, tested a nuclear device, halted denuclearization activities, and expelled nuclear inspectors, Congress explicitly rejected the Obama Administration's requests for funds to supplement existing resources in the event of a breakthrough in the Six-Party Talks. Prior to the spring of 2010, the Obama Administration and the Lee Myung-bak government in South Korea had said that they would be willing to provide large-scale aid if North Korea took steps to irreversibly dismantle its nuclear program.

POW-MIA Recovery Operations in North Korea

In 1994, North Korea invited the U.S. government to conduct joint investigations to recover the remains of thousands of U.S. servicemen unaccounted for during the Korean War. The United Nations Military Command (U.N. Command) and the Korean People's Army conducted 33 joint investigations from 1996-2005 for these prisoners of war-missing in action (POW-MIAs). In operations known as "joint field activities" (JFAs), U.S. specialists recovered 229 sets of remains and successfully identified 78 of those. On May 25, 2005, the Department of Defense announced that it would suspend all JFAs, citing the "uncertain environment created by North Korea's unwillingness to participate in the six-party talks" concerning North Korea's nuclear program, its recent declarations regarding its intentions to develop nuclear weapons, and its withdrawal from the nuclear nonproliferation treaty, and the payments of millions of dollars in cash to the Korean People's Army (KPA) for its help in recovering the remains.[32]

The United States has not undertaken any JFAs with the KPA since May 2005. On January 27, 2010, the KPA proposed that the United States and North Korea resume talks on the joint recovery program. On April 5, the KPA issued a public statement criticizing the Department of Defense for failing to accept its proposal. It said the DPRK would not assume responsibility for the loss of remains because of delays in the Six-Party Talks, specifically: "If thousands of U.S. remains buried in our country are washed off and lost due to the U.S. side's disregard, the U.S. side should be wholly responsible for the consequences as it has developed the humanitarian issue into a political problem."[33] The Department of Defense has said that the recovery of the remains of missing U.S. soldiers is an enduring priority goal of the United States and that it is committed to achieving the fullest possible accounting for POW-MIAs from the Korean War.

Potential for Establishing a Liaison Office in North Korea

One prospective step for engagement would be the establishment of a liaison office in Pyongyang. This issue has waxed and waned over the past 16 years. The Clinton Administration, as part of the 1994 U.S.-North Korea Agreed Framework, outlined the possibility of full normalization of political and economic relations. Under the Agreed Framework, the United States and North Korea would open a liaison office in each other's capital "following resolution of consular and other technical issues through expert level discussions."[34] Eventually, the relationship would have been upgraded to "bilateral relations [at] the Ambassadorial level." Under the Bush Administration, Ambassador Christopher Hill reportedly discussed an exchange of liaison offices. This did not lead to an offer of full diplomatic relations pursuant to negotiations in the Six-Party Talks. In December 2009, following Ambassador Stephen Bosworth's first visit as Special Envoy to Pyongyang, press speculation ran high that the United States would offer relations at the level of liaison offices. The Obama Administration quickly dispelled these expectations, flatly rejecting claims that Bosworth had carried a message offering liaison offices.[35]

Non-Governmental Organizations' Activities

Since the reported famines in North Korea of the mid-1990s, the largest proportion of aid has come from government contributions to emergency relief programs administered by international relief organizations. Some non-governmental organizations (NGOs) are playing smaller roles in capacity building and people-to-people exchanges, in areas such as health, informal diplomacy, information science, and education.

The aims of such NGOs are as diverse as the institutions themselves. Some illustrative cases include NGO "joint ventures" between scientific and academic NGOs and those engaged in informal diplomacy. Three consortia highlight this cooperation: the Tuberculosis (TB) diagnostics project, run by Nuclear Threat Initiative (NTI), Stanford Medical School, and Christian Friends of Korea; the Syracuse University-Kim Chaek University of Technology digital library program; and the U.S.-DPRK Scientific Engagement Consortium, composed of the Civilian Research and Development Foundation Global (CRDF Global), the American Association for the Advancement of Science (AAAS), Syracuse University, and the Korea Society. The following is a sample of such efforts.

- In 2008, NTI, Stanford Medical School, and Christian Friends identified multiple drug resistant TB as a serious security threat. By providing North Korean scientists with the scientific equipment, generators, and other supplies to furnish a national tuberculosis reference laboratory, they hope to enable North Korean researchers and physicians to take on this health threat.[36] Over the course of 2010, the partners completed the TB reference laboratory, and installed a high voltage cable for more regular energy supply.[37] In September 2010, North Korea health representatives signed a grant agreement for a two-year period with the Global Fund to Fight AIDS, Tuberculosis, and Malaria. The $19 million dollar grant will support procurement of laboratory supplies as well as vaccines through July 2012.
- In 2001, Syracuse University and Kim Chaek University (Pyongyang) began a modest program of modifying open-source software for use as library support and identifying the international standards necessary to catalog information for the library at Kim Chaek. Over time this expanded to include twin integrated information technology labs at Kim Chaek and Syracuse and a memorandum to exchange junior faculty. North Korean junior faculty members are expected to attend Syracuse University in spring 2011.[38]
- In 2007, the U.S.-DPRK Scientific Engagement Consortium formed to explore collaborative science activities between the United States and North Korea in subjects such as agriculture and information technology. In December 2009, at the invitation of the North Korean State Academy of Sciences, Consortium members toured facilities and received briefings from researchers in biology, alternative energy, information sciences, hydrology, and health. Potential areas for collaboration include identification of shared research priorities, academic exchanges, joint workshops on English language, mathematics, biomedical research methods, renewable energy and digital science libraries, and joint science publications.

End Notes

[1] For more information, see CRS Report R40684, *North Korea's Second Nuclear Test: Implications of U.N. Security Council Resolution 1874*, coordinated by Mary Beth Nikitin and Mark E. Manyin.

[2] For more information, see CRS Report R41438, *North Korea: Legislative Basis for U.S. Economic Sanctions*, by Dianne E. Rennack.

[3] For more information, see CRS Report RL33590, *North Korea's Nuclear Weapons Development and Diplomacy*, by Larry A. Niksch.

[4] "U.S. Implicates North Korean Leader in Attack," *New York Times*. May 22, 2010.

[5] Walter Pincus, "Nuclear Conflict Has Deep Roots: 50 Years of Threats and Broken Pacts Culminate in Apparent Nuclear Test," *Washington Post*. October 15, 2006.

[6] "Washington was on Brink of War with North Korea 5 Years Ago," *CNN.com*. October 4, 1999 and North Korea Nuclear Crisis, February 1993 - June 1994," *GlobalSecurity.org*.

[7] For more details on problems with implementation and verification, see CRS Report RL33590, *North Korea's Nuclear Weapons Development and Diplomacy*, by Larry A. Niksch.

[8] For more information on the terrorism list removal, see CRS Report RL30613, *North Korea: Back on the Terrorism List?* by Mark E. Manyin.

[9] "China Cut Off Exports of Oil to North Korea," *New York Times*. October 30, 2006.

[10] For more information, please see CRS Report R41043, *China-North Korea Relations*, by Dick K. Nanto and Mark E. Manyin.

[11] "North Korea Official Reported Executed," *New York Times*. March 19, 2010.

[12] Marcus Noland, "Pyongyang Tipping Point," *Wall Street Journal* op-ed. April 12, 2010.

[13] "Amid Leadership Reshuffle, Role of Central Military Commission Strengthens in N. Korea," *Hankyoreh*, September 30, 2010.

[14] Ruediger Frank, "Hu Jintao, Deng Xiapoing or Another Mao Zedong? Power Restructuring in North Korea," *38 North*. November 2010. (http://38north.org/2010/10/1451/)

[15] Victor Cha, "Without a Loosened Grip, Reform will Elude North Korea," *CSIS Korea Platform*. October 15, 2010.

[16] John Park, "On the Issues: North Korea's Leadership Succession: The China Factor." *United States Institute of Peace* (http://www.usip.org). September 28, 2010.

[17] See U.S. Department of State, 2010 Country Report on Human Rights Practices: Democratic People's Republic of Korea, April 2011, available at http://www.state.gov/g/drl/rls/hrrpt/2010/eap/154388.htm, and Amnesty International Annual Report 2011 - North Korea, available at http://www.unhcr.org/refworld/country,COI,,,PRK,4562d8cf2,4dce154c3c,0.html.

[18] Radio Free Asia, North Korea: "Political Prison Camps Expand," May 4, 2011, available at http://www.unhcr.org/ refworld/docid/4dd288f128.html.

[19] Stephan Haggard and Marcus Noland, *Witness to Transformation, Refugee Insights into North Korea* (Peterson Institute for International Economics, 2011), p. 51.

[20] Amnesty International, Amnesty International Annual Report 2011 - North Korea, May 13, 2011, available at http://www.unhcr.org/refworld/docid/4dce154c3c.html.

[21] United States Department of State, Trafficking in Persons Report 2010 - Korea, Democratic People's Republic of, June 14, 2010, available at http://www.unhcr.org/refworld/docid/4c1883e6c.html.

[22] CRS email correspondence with U.S. Department of State, May 26, 2011.

[23] U.S. Government Accountability Office, *Humanitarian Assistance: Status of North Korean Refugee Resettlement and Asylum in the United States*, GAO-10-691, June 24, 2010, available at http://www.gao.gov.

[24] Broadcast content includes news briefs, particularly news about the Korean Peninsula; interviews with North Korean defectors; and international commentary on events occurring in North Korea. The BBG cites a Peterson Institute for International Economics survey in which North Korean defectors interviewed in China and South Korea indicated that they had listened to foreign media including RFA. RFA broadcasts five hours a day. VOA broadcasts five hours a day with three of those hours in prime-time from a medium-wave transmitter in South Korea aimed at North Korea. VOA also broadcasts from stations in Thailand; the Philippines; and from leased stations in Russia and eastern Mongolia. In January 2009, the BBG began broadcasting to North Korea from a leased medium-wave facility in South Korea. The BBG added leased transmission capability to bolster medium-wave service into North Korea in January 2010. RFA broadcasts from stations in Tinian (Northern Marianas) and Saipan, and leased stations in Russia and Mongolia.

[25] Data on funding supplied by the Broadcasting Board of Governors, November 8, 2010.

[26] For more information, see CRS Report RL33885, *North Korean Crime-for-Profit Activities*, by Liana Sun Wyler and Dick K. Nanto.

[27] For more information, see CRS Report RS21473, *North Korean Ballistic Missile Threat to the United States*, by Steven A. Hildreth.

[28] "North Korea Has 1,000 Missiles, South Says," *Reuters*, March 16, 2010.

[29] *Jane's Sentinel Security Assessment - China And Northeast Asia*, January 22, 2010.

[30] David Wright and Theordore A. Postol, "A Post-launch Examination of the Unha-2," *Bulletin of the Atomic Scientists*. June 29, 2009.

[31] For more, see CRS Report R40095, *Foreign Assistance to North Korea*, by Mark E. Manyin and Mary Beth Nikitin.

[32] "U.S. Halts Search for Its War Dead in North Korea," *New York Times*. May 26, 2005.

[33] "KPA Holds US Side Responsible for Leaving Remains of GIs," *Korean Central News Agency* (KCNA), April 5, 2010.

[34] 1994 US-DPRK Agreed Framework at http://www.kedo.org/pdfs/AgreedFramework.pdf.

[35] "U.S. has not proposed setting up liaison office in Pyongyang next year: White House." *Yonhap*, December 19, 2009 (Lexis-Nexis).
[36] "New Tuberculosis Lab Hailed as Breakthrough in Health Diplomacy." *Science*. March 12, 2010. p. 1312-1313.
[37] Christian Friends of Newsletter, November 2010.
[38] Hyunjin Seo and Stuart Thorson. "Academic Science Engagement with North Korea." *On Korea*. Washington, DC: Korea Economic Institute of America, 2010. p. 105-121.

In: North Korea: Nuclear Weapons and the Diplomacy Debate   ISBN: 978-1-62100-450-9
Editor: Brian N. Thompson   © 2012 Nova Science Publishers, Inc.

Chapter 2

NORTH KOREA'S NUCLEAR QUESTION: SENSE OF VULNERABILITY, DEFENSIVE MOTIVATION AND PEACEFUL SOLUTION[*]

Kwang Ho Chun

The Strategic Studies Institute (SSI) is part of the U.S. Army War College and is the strategic-level study agent for issues related to national security and military strategy with emphasis on geostrategic analysis.

The mission of SSI is to use independent analysis to conduct strategic studies that develop policy recommendations on:

- Strategy, planning, and policy for joint and combined employment of military forces;
- Regional strategic appraisals;
- The nature of land warfare;
- Matters affecting the Army's future;
- The concepts, philosophy, and theory of strategy; and
- Other issues of importance to the leadership of the Army.

Studies produced by civilian and military analysts concern topics having strategic implications for the Army, the Department of Defense, and the larger national security community.

In addition to its studies, SSI publishes special reports on topics of special or immediate interest. These include edited proceedings of conferences and topically-oriented roundtables, expanded trip reports, and quick-reaction responses to senior Army leaders.

The Institute provides a valuable analytical capability within the Army to address strategic and other issues in support of Army participation in national security policy formulation.

---

[*] This is an edited, reformatted and augmented version of a Strategic Studies Institute publication, from http://www.StrategicStudiesInstitute.army.mil/, dated December 2010.

SSI Monograph

The views expressed in this report are those of the author and do not necessarily reflect the official policy or position of the Department of the Army, the Department of Defense, or the U.S. Government. Authors of Strategic Studies Institute (SSI) publications enjoy full academic freedom, provided they do not disclose classified information, jeopardize operations security, or misrepresent official U.S. policy. Such academic freedom empowers them to offer new and sometimes controversial perspectives in the interest of furthering debate on key issues. This report is cleared for public release; distribution is unlimited.

*****

This publication is subject to Title 17, United States Code, Sections 101 and 105. It is in the public domain and may not be copyrighted.

Foreword

Why have efforts to dismantle the North Korean nuclear program failed so far? What can be done in order to achieve a peaceful and long-lasting resolution to this conundrum? To answer these questions, this monograph scrutinizes and refutes two prevailing academic-cum-policy approaches to the North Korean nuclear questions: the use of coercive tools within a general framework of containment and bypassing the regime in Pyongyang, and engaging the Korean people with the hope that they will gain enough power to transform North Korea into a democratic nuclear-free country. Dr. Kwang Ho Chun argues that neither of these can provide any meaningful solution to the North Korean nuclear questions. Instead, he suggests that engaging the regime in Pyongyang and forgoing endeavors to forcefully push democracy in North Korea are inseparable prerequisites to a peaceful and lasting solution to this problem.

DOUGLAS C. LOVELACE, JR. Director
Strategic Studies Institute

About the Author

KWANG HO CHUN is an International Scholar at the Department of Political Science at Kyung Hee University. Since September 2007, he has taught at the Defence Studies Department as a lecturer. He was previously a lecturer at Unite de science politique et des relations internationales, Universite Catholique de Louvain, Belgium. Dr. Kwang holds a B.A. and M.A. from Kyung Hee University, Seoul, Korea, an M.A. in European studies and a Ph.D. in international relations from Katholieke Universiteit Leuven, Belgium.

SUMMARY

With little faith in reaching a peaceful and sustainable solution to the nuclear question through engagement and negotiations with the regime in Pyongyang, some scholars argue that nuclear nonproliferation can be forced on North Korea only through the use of coercive tools within a general framework of containment. Other scholars, alarmed by the catastrophe that might result from a vigorous attempt to confront and/ or topple the regime in Pyongyang, suggest bypassing it and engaging the North Korean people, hoping that they will gain enough power to transform North Korea into a democratic nuclear-free country. Indeed, to a great extent, current American policy toward North Korea reflects both stances.

North Korea's history indicates that Pyongyang's sense of vulnerability is directly related to the developmental status of its nuclear program. This deviates from Nicholas Eberstadt's claim that the regime's rationale behind the program has been predominantly and persistently offensive since its initiation. On the other hand, this supports Joachim Krause and Andreas Wenger's claim that the predominant rationale behind Pyongyang's nuclear program is deterring what it perceives as a threat to the survivability of its regime--namely, to a large extent, American power. On the basis of this finding, it can be argued that if North Korea's perceived vulnerability can be significantly reduced, it is more likely to give up its nuclear arms program.

How, then, can Pyongyang's sense of vulnerability be significantly reduced? The observation herein suggests that Pyongyang's sense of vulnerability has been more influenced by its perception of its adversaries' hostility than its perception of its allies' guarantee for its security. During the 1960s, Pyongyang perceived that its allies had strong interests in guaranteeing North Korean security, but its perception of the continuous hostility from its adversaries increased its sense of vulnerability, which resulted in its continuous pursuit of developing a nuclear program. Despite the decreasing guarantee by Moscow and Beijing for Pyongyang's security since the late 1960s, Washington's progressive approach toward Pyongyang had so significantly reduced its sense of vulnerability from the late 1980s to the mid-1990s as to persuade North Korea to sign the Agreed Framework in 1994. This indicates that the key to reducing North Korea's sense of vulnerability and to bringing it back into compliance with international nonproliferation regimes is in the hands of its adversaries rather than those of its traditional allies. In this sense, it can be assumed that China is not bluffing when it claims that it lacks the necessary leverage to push North Korea into an internationally agreed solution to the nuclear problem. America's calling for China to put more pressure on North Korea may thus not yield a significant breakthrough in efforts to resolve the North Korean nuclear issue. The key factors determining Pyongyang's sense of vulnerability, and hence the future of its nuclear program, are U.S. projects and, more importantly, the manner in which its messages are perceived by North Korea.

In this sense, the two previous U.S. administrations' policies toward the North Korean nuclear question can provide invaluable lessons to the contemporary U.S. Government. The 1994 Framework Agreement manifested, among other attributes, tolerance towards diversity, a theme borrowed from President Richard Nixon and Henry Kissinger's foreign policy during the 1970s. President Bill Clinton, who included in the agreement the normalization of relations between Washington and Pyongyang, signaled the *de facto* acceptance of the totalitarian regime in Pyongyang, a clear divergence from his goal of spreading liberalism and democracy, which he had pursued since coming to office. Hence, the reasoning of the 1994 agreement was not to first wrest from North Korea its strategic deterrent and then proceed with toppling its regime. On the contrary, the purpose was to incorporate North Korea, as it is, into the international community, with the hope that time would yield a change in the nature of the regime as it mingles with the other members of the international community, particularly the United States. In other words, the purpose was not to convey the sense that the United States was planning to topple or coerce the regime in Pyongyang into a change of nature, but to patiently lure it, by its own consent, into such a change.

The Bush administration, seemingly, took an important step toward reducing Pyongyang's sense of vulnerability by expressing its willingness to give assurances to the security of North Korea, to respect its sovereignty, and to take steps toward the normalization of relations—all in return for North Korea's total nuclear disarmament. Nevertheless, overshadowing and contradicting those promises and guarantees are the North Korean Human Rights Act, which strives to promote democracy in North Korea at the expense of the totalitarian regime, and the ensuing appointment of a special envoy on human rights in North Korea. Without resolving these contradictions, Washington will continue to project through its foreign policy ambiguous intentions, hindering a significant change in North Korea's sense of vulnerability.

From these experiences, the contemporary U.S. Government must learn that engagement with the current regime in Pyongyang and forgoing endeavors to promptly and forcefully push democracy in North Korea are inseparable prerequisites to a peaceful and long-lasting solution to the North Korean nuclear question.

INTRODUCTION

North Korea's nuclear development has been one of the gravest threats to the security of not only the Korean peninsula, but also the Asian region and the world as a whole. The international community and the United States have thus made continuous efforts to end North Korea's nuclear program. The United States, in particular, has tried to address the proliferation challenges posed by North Korea through various policies, including military cooperation with its allies in the region and a wide range of sanctions. However, these efforts have not yet succeeded. Why have these efforts failed so far? How can a long-lasting and peaceful solution to the North Korean nuclear question be achieved?

These questions are highly relevant to understanding why North Korea has pursued a nuclear program. The more we understand about the motivation behind North Korea's drive for a nuclear program, the greater chance we have to find a peaceful and perfect solution to the North Korean nuclear question. This monograph therefore seeks to elucidate the motivation for North Korea's nuclear program, and to consider whether it is possible to achieve a peaceful and long-lasting solution to the North Korean nuclear question, and, if it is, how to accomplish this goal. This monograph does so by providing a historical review of North Korea's nuclear program.

The main finding revealed herein is that North Korea's nuclear program has been driven by the country's intention to use the possession of nuclear weapons as a deterrent against a perceived risk of attack. The historical narrative of North Korea's nuclear development since the 1950s has proved this defensive motivation for North Korea's nuclear weapon build up, indicating that Pyongyang's sense of vulnerability has been positively related to the developmental status of North Korea's nuclear program. Based on this finding, the author opines that some hard-line policies, built upon the assumption of North Korea's offensive motivation, cannot provide any meaningful solution to the North Korean nuclear question. Instead, he suggests that engagement with the current regime in Pyongyang and forgoing any endeavors to push promptly and forcefully for democracy in North Korea can offer a peaceful and long-lasting solution.

The monograph begins by considering the relationship among developing nuclear weapons, Pyongyang's motivations, and its sense of vulnerability. It then provides the history of the relationship between North Korea's sense of vulnerability and its development of a nuclear program. It concludes by considering the possibility of a peaceful solution to the North Korean nuclear question.

Nuclear Weapons, Motivation, and Sense of Vulnerability

Let us start with a fundamental but thus far unanswered question: Why has North Korea pursued a nuclear program since the mid-1950s? The technical school of proliferation holds that, "[T]he availability of nuclear weapons in itself constitutes sufficient motive for pursuing them. If states can acquire the bomb, this line of thinking goes, they will."[1] However, an examination of past efforts to prevent nations with nuclear aspirations from pursuing nuclear armament provides many cases of success. South Korea, Taiwan, Brazil, Argentina, and South Africa are all examples of states that abandoned their nuclear armament efforts.[2] This indicates that availability of technology and resources alone does not necessarily lead a nation to pursue vigorously a nuclear armament course.

An alternative explanation is provided by the motivational school of proliferation. According to Michael J. Mazarr, the motivational school holds that:

> [D]espite the pressures of a near-anarchic world system, states do not pursue the development of nuclear weapons without a reason. The associated costs, both financial and political, establish a presumption against acquiring nuclear arsenals. It is only when a state's perceived vulnerability or desire for attention or prestige overcomes that presumption that proliferation will take place.[3]

There have been two contradicting perspectives on the motivation for North Korea's developing nuclear weapons. The first ascribes a continuous and predominantly offensive rationale to North Korea's nuclear program, whereas the second argument sheds light on North Korea's perceived need to deter its adversaries from seeking to violate its sovereignty and topple its regime.

Nicholas Eberstadt puts emphasis on North Korea's desire to retrieve its lost pride. From his perspective, the North Korean nuclear program is not merely a deterrent, designed to warn the United States against any attempt to forcefully change the regime in Pyongyang, or an instrument used to blackmail the international community to get food and fuel; it is primarily a tool designed to "fulfill a grand ideological vision: the reunification of the now-divided Korean peninsula."[4] He argues:

> [The purpose of this nuclear program] is to settle a historical grievance, namely the failure of the famous June 1950 surprise attack against South Korea [due to American intervention]. . . . The total mobilization war states that Pyongyang has painfully erected over the decades (at the cost of, *inter alia*, the North Korean famine of the 1990s) is a response to this grievance and an instrument for fulfilling this vision . . . [of] unconditional annexation of present-day South Korea.[5]

Eberstadt contends that the North Korean statecraft has built on the very vision of "an ongoing war"[6] to reunify the peninsula under the regime in Pyongyang and that the regime has seen the nuclear program as a vital tool to realize such a vision—a tool never to be given away, at least until this goal is accomplished. This line of analysis thus presents us with pessimistic prospects for resolving peacefully the political tension surrounding the issue.

In contrast to Eberstadt's argument, Joachim Krause and Andreas Wenger present us with a different analysis regarding North Korea's motivation to acquire a nuclear-weapons capability, taking their cue from Scott Sagan's three models to explain why countries strive to acquire nuclear armaments. These consist of:

> the "security model," according to which states build nuclear weapons to increase national security against foreign threats, especially nuclear threats; the "domestic politics models," which envisions nuclear weapons as political tools used to advance parochial domestic and bureaucratic interests; and the "norms model," under which nuclear weapons decisions are made because weapons acquisition . . . provides an important normative symbol of state's modernity and identity.[7]

Based on the security model, Krause and Wenger ascribe a predominantly defensive rationale to North Korea's nuclear program. They point to the importance of Pyongyang's sense of vulnerability in driving North Korea's nuclear weapons program:

> North Korea perceives itself as threatened by other countries, such as the U.S., which have an important military presence in the region. It is believed that the possession of nuclear weapons can be used as a deterrent against a perceived risk of attack.[8]

The process by which a country evaluates its vulnerability has received much attention in literature dealing with armament, disarmament, and the causes of war. It is presented as an outcome of a calculated process in which a national leadership's perception of its adversaries' intentions toward it and its perception of its adversaries' capability to carry out offensive intentions are measured against its self-perceived capability to thwart such danger.[9] George Kennan, and later Secretary of State Henry Kissinger relying on Kennan, provide a similar definition of what creates and precipitates perceived vulnerability: "[T]he combination of hostility with the ability to do something about it."[10] Hence, the concept of a state's sense of vulnerability consists of two dimensions: its perception of the hostility of its adversaries and its perception of its capability to deter its adversaries from fulfilling their aggressive intentions.

It is also essential to consider alliances when measuring a state's sense of vulnerability. Allying with other nations is the most prevalent method used in *realpolitik* to deter an adversary from attacking.[11] Nevertheless, the existence of alliances with powerful nations, such as the Soviet Union and China in North Korea's case, is not a sufficient cause for reducing a state's sense of vulnerability. The key thing to affect a state's sense of vulnerability is its perception of its allies' interest in reacting against an attack of its adversaries. When a state detects a thaw between its allies and its adversaries, it tends to perceive its allies' interest in reacting against an adversary's attack as decreasing and this, in turn, is likely to increase the country's sense of vulnerability.

On the basis of these insights, indicators to measure Pyongyang's sense of vulnerability in each era mentioned above are: 1) the number of its adversaries' perceived proclamations and/or acts of conciliation toward North Korea; 2) the number of its adversaries' proclamations and/or actions perceived by North Korea as a challenge to its sovereignty; and 3) the number of its allies' perceived proclamations and/or acts of conciliation toward its adversaries. The first indicator listed is expected to have a negative relationship with North Korea's sense of vulnerability, whereas the second and third indicators are expected to have a positive relationship with it.

A Historical Review of North Korea's Perceived Vulnerability and Its Nuclear Program

The Height of the Cold War (1950-68)

This time frame can be divided into two consecutive periods. During the 1950s there was an increase in North Korea's sense of vulnerability. This reflected American attempts during the Korean War to overthrow the newly inaugurated communist regime and the introduction of U.S. nuclear weaponry into the peninsula in 1957. North Korea's increasing sense of vulnerability throughout this period led to the initiation of its nuclear program. Between the late 1950s and the late 1960s, North Korea's sense of vulnerability decreased slightly. Though the American threat remained in the background, there were no substantial proclamations or actions from either Washington or Seoul to be perceived as a challenge to North Korean sovereignty. Moreover, with the Cold War at its height, Pyongyang's allies were perceived as more committed than ever to guaranteeing its security.

The Korean War was the first opportunity for North Korea to evaluate Washington's intentions regarding its regime. The war, initiated by the North, which was as eager as the Syngman Rhee regime in the South to take control of the whole Korean peninsula, taught Pyongyang some valuable lessons. Although U.S. Secretary of State Dean Acheson excluded the peninsula from his January 1950 announcement of the defense perimeter that marked Washington's vital strategic outposts in the Pacific,[12] the North soon came to realize that it had underestimated the political-psychological importance of the peninsula to the decisionmakers in Washington. Not only was the United States willing to commit a huge military force into the peninsula in order to block the Northern attack and to protect Rhee's regime, but it was actually planning to seize the opportunity to proceed with a rollback of North Korean forces so as to reunify the whole peninsula under the regime in Seoul.[13] This was perceived as a grave threat to North Korea. Following the Inchon landing on September

15, 1950, the North could not balance and repel the combined American-South Korean forces by itself. It needed help.

Pyongyang's allies provided it with another valuable lesson. Allies, even brotherly ones like China, were first and foremost driven by their own interests. Joseph Stalin, then leader of the Soviet Union, who was the liberator of the Northern half of the peninsula and gave his consent to the June 25, 1950, invasion, offered no substantial support to the North following the outbreak of the conflict. Based on American intelligence sources, Bruce Cumings points out that, "[T]here is no evidence of an upturn in Soviet military shipments to North Korea after June 25; if anything, a decrease was registered."[14] Moreover, Stalin explicitly ordered Soviet ambassador to the United Nations (UN) Jacob Malik not to attend the Security Council meeting that dealt with the issue of Korea, which meant there would be no veto against U.S. plans for dealing with the situation on the peninsula under UN auspices. For Cumings, this Soviet behavior suggests that the shrewd Stalin may have hoped to pit American Soldiers against Chinese forces and thus to weaken MaoTse Tung and make him more submissive, even at the cost of abandoning the regime in Pyongyang to the threat of American military power.[15]

While China, unlike the Soviet Union, did commit its forces in an effort to halt the U.S./UN advance to the Yalu River, this was also driven by China's own interests. Cumings claims, based on retrieved North Korean and Chinese documents, that China entered the Korean War not out of fear of the American march toward the Yalu River, but rather as a response to the American rollback strategy that endangered the existence of an ally regime. As a bonus, Beijing was also toying with the notion of taking over the Soviets' position as the major patron of the infant state.[16] Other scholars who examined the rationale behind Mao's intervention in the war give more credit to his fear that North Korea would become a northern gate to China for American imperialism and to his perception of the Korean battleground as a test case for Communism in its fight against intruding Capitalism along the southern gate of China (i.e., Vietnam).[17]

In any case, both the Soviet Union and China were unwilling to risk an outbreak of a global conflict. As panic caused by the successful counterattack and the southward movement of the North Korean-Chinese forces spread throughout Washington, President Harry Truman warned that "the United States may use [in Korea] any weapon in its arsenal,"[18] thus hinting at the possibility of the use of nuclear weapons. This put Stalin on alert. Cumings wrote:

> According to a high official in the KGB at the time, Stalin expected global war as a result of American defeat in northern Korea; fearing that consequence, he favored allowing the United States to occupy all of Korea: "so what? Let the United States of America be our neighbors in the Far East . . . we are not ready to fight." Unlike Stalin, the Chinese were ready to fight, but only down to the middle of the peninsula, rather than to start World War III.[19]

The war ended with the July 1953 armistice that put the struggling forces along the opposite sides of approximately the same line that separated them in June 1950. Notwithstanding this, North Korea's sense of vulnerability was increased by American aggressive policies toward the peninsula in the aftermath of the Korean War. Just 4 years after the armistice, the United States introduced nuclear artillery shells, mines, and missiles in Korea, and kept increasing their number periodically.

The lessons Pyongyang drew from its allies' behavior during the Korean War, and from the continuous perceived American challenge to its sovereignty in its aftermath, became clearly expressed in the emerging post-war Juche ideology that emphasized self-reliance in defense, as in other fields. Kim Jung-il, current leader of North Korea, illustrates this point in his book *On the Juche Idea of Our Party*: "Of course, one may receive aid in national defence from fraternal countries and friends. But it is impossible to depend on others for the defence of one's own country."[20] From the late 1950s, North Korea started to send scientists to Soviet institutions to study nuclear technology. After receiving Soviet and Chinese assistance, the North established a research complex at Yongbyon and assembled a two-four megawatt Soviet IRT-2M research reactor next to it in 1965.[21] Nevertheless, no significant breakthrough was made during the 1960s with regard to obtaining nuclear weapons-production capability. There was no need to rush, as international and regional developments during the 1960s slightly decreased Pyongyang's sense of vulnerability.

The 1960s saw the Cold War at its height. The Soviet Union was catching up with American nuclear and missile capabilities, and China successfully achieved a nuclear capability of its own.[22] The unquestionable supremacy of American technology and weapons, which characterized the 1950s, was giving way to a more balanced power equation between East and West, contributing to North Korea's confidence in its allies' capability to balance the United States. Tension rose from time to time between Pyongyang and its patrons, who tried to meddle in internal North Korean politics and stall the solidification of former North Korean leader Kim Il-sung's regime at the expense of their proxies. Despite this, however, and despite being caught from time to time in the middle of the SinoSoviet quarrel, there were no major surface cracks in the hostile attitude of both Beijing and Moscow toward Washington.[23] On the contrary, tension reached new heights between the United States and the Soviet Union, a result of the Cuban Missile Crisis in 1962 and the entry of U.S. forces to Vietnam in 1965.

Moreover, during the 1960s there were no substantial proclamations or actions, either by the United States or the Republic of Korea (ROK), which could have been perceived as a challenge to North Korean sovereignty. Perhaps it was a result of the U.S. fear of entanglement in a second front, in addition to Vietnam, while having to cope simultaneously, in budgetary terms, with Soviet endeavors for strategic military parity. In South Korea, the toppling of the belligerent Syngman Rhee Regime was followed by the coming to power, after a short interim parliamentary republic, of Park Chung-hee, whose main goal, at least during the 1960s, was to reform and build the ill-treated South Korean economy. However, the picture of global politics soon began to change, which corresponded to changes in North Korea's sense of vulnerability.

Détente and Rapprochement (1969-89)

During this time frame, the designated indicators reflect a sharp increase in North Korea's sense of vulnerability. North Korea's strategic allies were approaching its traditional adversaries through arms control negotiations, treaties, and mutual visits, replacing political considerations with economic ones. On top of that, Park Chung-hee began to pursue more aggressive military goals that might change the strategic balance of power between the Koreas in favor of the South. A sharp increase in North Korea's sense of vulnerability drove it to achieve a major breakthrough in its nuclear program that enabled it to produce nuclear weapons.

The increasingly thawing atmosphere between Washington, Moscow, and Beijing also increased Pyongyang's sense of vulnerability. The rudiments of change in the nature of Washington and Moscow's relations from hostility to coexistence and cooperation started to appear during John Kennedy's presidency and came to maturity during Richard Nixon's tenure. The détente initiated in 1969 created an environment in which, according to Charles Kegley and Eugene Wittkopf, "visits, cultural exchanges, trade agreements, and joint technological ventures replaced threats, warnings, and confrontations."[24] The détente continued to characterize U.S.-Soviet relations throughout the 1970s and 1980s, with a brief interlude during the Soviet involvement in Afghanistan (1979-85). The détente manifested itself during that period in major confidence-building measures between the two: the Strategic Arms Limitation Talks Treaty (SALT I, 1972), the Anti Ballistic Missile Treaty (ABM, 1972), SALT II (1979), and the Intermediate-range Nuclear Forces Treaty (INF, 1987).[25]

In addition to the thawing relations with Moscow, the United States pursued a rapprochement with China. It was Nixon's national security advisor and later Secretary of State Henry Kissinger who brought a rapprochement between the United States and China. Kissinger, as a realist, held that China, though communist, did not pose a challenge to the United States since it lacked economic as well as military capabilities to challenge Washington. On the contrary, he believed on the basis of his multidimensional concept of power that China played an important role in balancing the Soviet Union on the ideological level. Unlike former Secretary of State John Foster Dulles, Kissinger did not see all communist states as part of one big octopus threatening the West. Having an eye to the bad blood running between Moscow and Beijing, especially along their Manchurian border, he determined to end China's isolation for the sake of global order.[26] Mao responded to the American initiative with a similarly realistic understanding. "'The leaders of China were beyond ideology in their dealings with us,' Kissinger recalled. 'Their peril had established the absolute primacy of geopolitics.'"[27] The new era of improved relationship between the two states was soon reflected in reciprocal state visits of their leaders (Nixon and Ford to China, 1972 and 1975, respectively, and Deng Xiaoping to the United States in 1979 and 1982), in exchanging ambassadors (March 1979), and in a booming trade exchange that, as early as 1987, was fourfold in comparison with the Sino-Russian trade exchange.[28] The trade volume between the two countries continued to increase from $9,790 million in 1987 to $20,043 million in 1990.[29]

With Pyongyang watching the thaw between Washington and its allies, Moscow and Beijing, with suspicion and fear, its sense of vulnerability was reinforced by the policies taken by its adversaries, particularly Seoul, which began to pursue an aggressive military enhancement. Although the United States remained as the largest threat to North Korea, the U.S. administration was transforming its security policy toward the peninsula so as to avoid any direct clash with North Korea. Behind this was Nixon and Kissinger's conviction that the United States should avoid a second Vietnam, their fear that American forces might get entrapped in a similar situation on the Korean peninsula, and Kissinger's multipolar concept of the balance of power. The U.S. administration thought that the stability of the peninsula could be maintained through a regional, as well as global, balance of power, which could be constructed through an American-Chinese rapprochement. Falling into the trap of North Korean provocations would have only jeopardized this rapprochement. Moreover, that would have been self-defeating and contrary to the retrenchment policy of an administration that believed in a strong economy as the key to all other ingredients in the calculus of power.

From this perspective, the Nixon administration carried out a policy of restraint in its dealings with North Korea in order to reduce the possibility of any clash with Pyongyang, disregarding South Korean protests.

It is not certain that this change in U.S. security policy toward the peninsula reduced Pyongyang's sense of vulnerability, but it is certain that this change increased that of Seoul. Nixon's administration continued Johnson's policy of projecting weakness toward Pyongyang, dealing too gently with incidents such as the seizure of the USS *Pueblo* on April 23, 1968, and forcing Seoul not to respond to the North's attack on the Blue House on April 21, 1968. What was worst of all, the U.S. administration committed a greater sin— reducing the number of U.S. troops on the peninsula.[30] The withdrawal of the 7th U.S. Infantry Division from South Korea and the pull back of the 2d Infantry Division from the front line in 1971 were carried out despite fierce South Korean protests against the American disregard of previous assurances the United States had given to the Park Chung-hee regime. Park claimed that Nixon had assured him that the retrenchment policy would not be applied in the Korean Peninsula, and, on the contrary, that Nixon had vowed to strengthen the U.S. forces in the South. Fearing that such a withdrawal would invite North Korean miscalculations, Seoul tried but failed to reach a compromise with Washington that would prevent the pull out of an entire division. Perhaps the utmost disregard of South Korean fears of the potential danger embodied in the planned withdrawal was manifested in Washington's answer to Park's plea to take note of the anxiety in the South, a feeling of déjà vu reminiscent of the pull out of U.S. troops that preceded the Korean War. Washington bluntly responded, as if explaining the facts of life to an infant, that there were no grounds for South Korea's concern, since the bipolar system of the 1950s had since turned into a multipolar one.[31]

From Park's point of view, Seoul could no longer rely solely on its bilateral alliance with the United States in order to guarantee its national security. One of the initiatives that Park took in order to cover for what Seoul perceived as conventional inferiority, in comparison to the North Korean Army, was the buildup of a nuclear capability. A South Korean general, reflecting on the period, remembered that President Park, "decided upon a secret 'Master Plan' for producing nuclear weapons in 1970 following President Nixon's announcement of possible U.S. force withdrawals from Korea under the 'Guam Doctrine'."[32] Park's June 1975 statement that "South Korea would and could develop its own nuclear weapons if the U.S. nuclear umbrella is withdrawn," was heard in Pyongyang as well.[33] While, in the face of American pressure, the South Korean nuclear adventure ended with Park's January 1977 announcement that South Korea would not develop nuclear arms,[34] it contributed to raising the sense of vulnerability north of the 38th parallel. It faced Pyongyang with a future scenario, although not imminent, that required preparation.

The aforementioned increase in Pyongyang's sense of vulnerability was followed by upgrades in its nuclear program that would enable the production of nuclear weapons. Pyongyang modernized its Soviet research reactor in 1974, bringing it to a capacity of eight megawatts, and began to build a second reactor with a capacity of five megawatts. Moreover, Pyongyang succeeded in persuading Moscow to supply it with a 50-megawatt and a 200-megawatt graphite reactor, "which would be installed at Yongbyon in the early 1980s and would become the focus of the world's concern."[35] In 1987, after its completion, the 5-megawatt reactor began operating with a capability of producing seven kilograms of plutonium per year—enough to manufacture a single atomic bomb a year. The 50-megawatt and 200-megawatt installations were estimated to produce, after completion, a sufficient amount of plutonium for the annual production of 30 atomic bombs.[36]

The Collapse of the Communist Bloc and Its Aftermath: From the Late 1980s to the Framework Agreement

During this time frame, the aforementioned indicators reflected an overall reduction in North Korea's sense of vulnerability. Though its allies continued to tighten their relationship with its adversaries, those adversaries were initiating conciliatory gestures and acts that conveyed acceptance of the Kim Il-sung regime. Following these developments, North Korea was willing to freeze its nuclear program.

On the verge of its collapse, in September 1990, the Soviet Union established diplomatic relations with the ROK, thus projecting a clear disengagement from Cold War patterns, which had been manifested in a leaning-to-one-side policy on the Korean issue.

The collapse of the communist block, which was followed by the collapse of the Soviet Union, left Moscow with an economic catastrophe to deal with. Thus Russia, then under the control of President Boris Yeltsin, in dire need of economic recovery, put the promotion of its trade relations at the top of its foreign relations agenda and was willing to derogate prior political commitments to achieve this aim. Hence, Russia and South Korea signed a treaty in November 1992 with the purpose of enhancing mutual trade and market economy principles. The warming of Moscow-Seoul relations was followed by a change in Russia's attitude toward the North Korean nuclear program, discouraging rather than encouraging it. Yeltsin preferred to shun the 1961 treaty of friendship between the Soviet Union and North Korea, did not renew it in 1996, and replaced it with a much less obligatory amity pact.[37] Moreover, 20 years after the breakthrough in Chinese-U.S. relations, a similar breakthrough came in Chinese-South Korean relations. The bilateral relationship, established in 1992, put a focus on trade relations, which grew annually during the 1990s at a 20-percent rate, making China South Korea's top trading partner and South Korea one of the major foreign investors in the Chinese economy.[38]

To North Korea's misfortune, its allies' perceived neglect of ideology in favor of trade, as a guide for foreign policy, was only part of a much larger transformation in world politics during the 1990s. The post-Cold War era gave birth to a new structure of the global system. No longer was it a bipolar system in which the Soviet Union and the United States balanced each other. Instead, an emerging uni-multipolar system left the United States as the only superpower with the economic and military clout to play a hegemonic role on the global level and in the multipolar subsystems.[39] The Clinton administration was pursuing an active engagement policy in world affairs with the purpose of enforcing international regimes, improving human rights, and enlarging the liberal-democratic community.[40] From those perspectives, North Korea occupied the center of American attention.

From the Clinton administration's point of view, not only did North Korea disregard the Nuclear Nonproliferation Treaty (NPT) it had signed in December 1985, but it also ignored what Washington saw as U.S. appeasement efforts. Though the United States withdrew all its nuclear warheads from the peninsula, Pyongyang refused to carry out its December 1991 agreement with South Korea for making the peninsula nuclear-free, and it turned its back to the January 1992 Safeguards Agreement it had signed with the International Atomic Energy Agency (IAEA).[41] The picture could look quite different from the North Korean point of view. The withdrawal of U.S. nuclear weapons from the peninsula did not diminish the

American nuclear threat to the North. If Pyongyang was to follow America's lead, it would have had to give up its most valuable strategic asset, required to make up for its conventional inferiority. The war in Iraq clearly illustrated how vulnerable a regime, considered by the United States as a dictatorial one, could be without a sufficient deterrent. Pyongyang's reluctance to carry out its previous obligations was followed by stick-and-carrot diplomacy on the part of Washington, trying to coerce North Korea into giving up the military aspects of its nuclear program.[42]

However, there was another aspect of Pyongyang's relationship with its adversaries that had been absent in previous time frames. Following the ousting of the military junta in South Korea from power and the initiation of an open-door policy to the North in 1988, trade volume between the South and the North increased dramatically, growing from $18.7 million in 1989 to more than $176 million in 1994.[43] Following the South Korean pattern, the George H. W. Bush administration initiated, for the first time since the armistice of 1953, a direct dialogue between American and North Korean diplomats. The two sides first met in Beijing in December 1988 and continued the talks at the consular level for the next 4 years. Eventually, the dialogue led to the first visit of a North Korean top official, party secretary Kim Yong Soon, to the United States, where he met with Under Secretary of State Arnold Kanter for discussions about the nuclear issue.[44] However significant this tacit recognition of the authority of the regime in Pyongyang north of the 38th Parallel was, it did not bring about an immediate reduction in the developmental status of the North Korean nuclear program.

Eventually, it was an increase in North Korea's defiance that brought its American adversary to propose a package deal attractive enough to substantially lower Pyongyang's sense of vulnerability, encompassing the possibility that its American adversary would be transformed into a cooperative partner. North Korea's refusal, on February 10, 1993, to allow the IAEA to inspect two suspected sites, followed by the announcement on March 12, 1993, of its intention to withdraw from the NonProliferation Treaty (NPT),[45] forced President Clinton to consider two options presented to him by the Pentagon and former President Carter, respectively. The Pentagon's operational plan 5027, designed to destroy North Korea's nuclear installations, entailed the probability of a high cost in human lives. Carter's Track II diplomatic efforts focused on breaking the deadlock with North Korea by lowering its sense of vulnerability.[46] Clinton chose the latter.[47] Thus, it was the American guarantee of the safety of the regime in Pyongyang, wrapped up in a series of gestures as manifested in the Framework Agreement, that enabled its signature. Pyongyang "committed itself to give up nuclear-arming in return for replacement of its nuclear reactors (with two light water reactors), a supply of fuel oil, security guarantees, an end to the American economic embargo, and gradual diplomatic normalization."[48]

Following the 1994 Framework Agreement

The high expectations that followed the signing of the Framework Agreement were not fulfilled. The project suffered many setbacks because of mutual suspicions and mistrust. Pyongyang was reluctant and hesitant to accept South Korean modeled light water reactors. The American Congress, for its part, was uncooperative in appropriating the necessary funding for U.S. obligations as agreed upon in the 1994 framework, though Washington's economic role in funding the project was a symbolic one in comparison with Seoul's, which promised to bear the lion's share of the costs, estimated at around $4.5 billion.[49] In 2001, the reactors' project was 5 years behind schedule.[50]

As the Framework Agreement was experiencing major setbacks, another issue inflamed the reemerging mutual mistrust. The American rhetoric surrounding the negotiations that dealt with North Korea's missile development and deployment program and its missile proliferation activity was aggressive and demanding. It conveyed the impression that the United States was interested in scraping off another layer of North Korean strategic defense even before the implementation of the nuclear bargain had marked substantial progress. The 1998 Rumsfeld Report depicted Pyongyang's violations of the Missile Technology Control Regime (MTCR), with an emphasis on its development of the long-range Taepodong I and II missiles, as a national threat. It also pointed out that North Korea's August 1998 ballistic missile test-fire of the Taepodong I over Northeastern Japan "served as a major catalyst for the [U.S.] NMD [National Missile Defense] effort."[51] Pyongyang had a different perspective regarding the NMD, especially after pledging in September 1999 a moratorium on missile tests for as long as the missile negotiations with the United States continued. Scott Snyder points out that:

> The North Korean media has been unusually sensitive to high-level U.S. administration characterizations of North Korea as a threat and as a rationale for NMD. North Korean officials have reacted negatively to the perceived double standard of continued U.S. NMD testing while they have pledged Moratorium on North Korea's Missile tests.[52]

The tension between Washington and Pyongyang was aggravated further with the coming to power of George W. Bush. It did not take long for the new administration, which placed at the center of its foreign policy the active promotion of liberal political institutions and democratic values,[53] to come head to head with the regime in Pyongyang. In his State of the Union address on January 29, 2002, President Bush depicted the North Korean regime in a diabolic manner, alongside the Iraqi and Iranian regimes:

> North Korea is a regime arming with missiles and weapons of mass destruction, while starving its citizens ... States like these, and their terrorist allies, constitute an axis of evil, arming to threaten the peace of the world. By seeking weapons of mass destruction, these regimes pose a grave and growing danger.[54]

Still, both countries continued to comply partially with the 1994 agreement, and North Korea continued to keep its plutonium project in deep freeze. This situation was not to last long. In late 2002, less than a year after the State of the Union address, as a result of U.S. intelligence evidence presented to it by Assistant Secretary of State James Kelly, North Korea was compelled to admit that it had developed in secrecy—probably since 1996[55]—a different nuclear project, one based on enriched uranium. Consequently, the Framework Agreement, already dysfunctional due to the setbacks in its implementation, was put on hold.[56] Nevertheless, Washington had knowledge about Pyongyang's enriched uranium track at least since 1998, as reported to Congress by Larry A. Niksch of the Congressional Research Service on August 27, 2003.[57] Clinton, in his memoirs, denies Niksch's claim that his administration knew about the uranium track since 1998.[58] However, let us presume for a moment that

Niksch[59] reported the truth to Congress. In such a case, why didn't President Clinton deactivate the Agreement? We may find the answer in his memoirs:

> Some people said this development [producing high enriched uranium] called the validity of our 1994 agreement into question. But the plutonium program we ended was much larger than the later [uranium] laboratory effort. North Korea's nuclear program, had it proceeded, would have produced enough weapons-grade plutonium to make several nuclear weapons a year.[60]

Indeed, a data analysis conducted by the Institute for Science and International Security reveals that North Korea stopped discharging plutonium from its 5-megawatt reactor with the coming into force of the Framework Agreement (see Table 1). Moreover, it reveals that, prior to October 1994, Pyongyang had separated less than 20 percent (0-10 kg) of its present stock of separated plutonium (20-53 kg, as of mid-2006). This means that while up to the collapse of the Framework Agreement North Korea did not have any nuclear weapons, or possessed two at most, it might currently hold between four and 13 nuclear bombs.[61] Thus, the mere presence of the Framework Agreement, though mutilated by the setbacks in its implementation, contributed to a significant decrease in the developmental status of North Korea's nuclear program during the late Clinton era.

Table 1. North Korean Plutonium Production and Separation, as of Mid-2006

Plutonium Discharged from 5 M We Reactor		Plutonium Separation		Weapon Equivalents*
Date	Amount (kg)	Date	Amount (kg)	(number)
Before 1990	1-10**	1989-1992	1-10	0-2
1994	27-29	2003-2004	20-28	4-7
Spring 2005	0-15	2005-2006	0-15	0-3
In core of 5 M We Reactor	5-7	-	-	-
Total	43-61		20-53	4-13***

Comments
* It is assumed that each nuclear weapon would require 4-5Kg of separated plutonium.
** This quantity includes up to 1-2 kilograms of plutonium produced in the IRT reactor prior to 1994 service. (See text.)
*** The upper bound of the number of weapons is higher than the sum of the individual upper bounds, because particular periods list more plutonium than needed to give the upper bound for that period.
Source: David Albright and Paul Brannan, "The North Korean Plutonium Stock Mid-2006," Institute for Science and International Security (ISIS), June 26, 2006, p.10.

Though a mechanism known as the Six-Party Talks, which include the United States, China, Russia, Japan, South Korea, and North Korea, was launched in an attempt to resolve the deadlock over the nuclear issue, it has failed so far to persuade North Korea to discontinue its uranium project and its renewed development of the plutonium project. It is only plausible, though, that U.S. efforts would encounter fiercer North Korean resistance, since these talks are overshadowed by an increase in North Korea's sense of vulnerability. North Korea's inclusion in the axis of evil and the breakdown of the Framework Agreement were followed by other proclamations and actions perceived as challenges to its sovereignty. Prominent among these actions is the North Korean Human Rights Act. Passed by the Senate in September 2004, it authorizes funding for programs to promote human rights, democracy, and a market economy inside North Korea and for increasing the availability of information sources that are not controlled by the North's regime. It calls on other countries to join Washington in ensuring that humanitarian aid will be delivered only by way of monitored transparent channels, and it states that any future nonhumanitarian aid will depend on the progress in human rights.[62] The act and its innuendo, the need to change the North Korean regime or its nature, were soon followed by Secretary of State Condoleezza Rice's denouncement of Pyongyang as an, "outpost of tyranny,"[63] and by the appointment of Jay Lefkowitz as a special envoy on human rights in North Korea.

All in all, during George W. Bush's presidency, the renewed increase in North Korea's sense of vulnerability gained much momentum. This increase had started during Clinton's presidency because of the setbacks in implementing the Framework Agreement and the controversy over Pyongyang's missile program. However, although during Clinton's late years in office Pyongyang was secretly initiating a new nuclear project based on uranium enrichment, it refrained from reactivating its larger plutonium project until President Bush deactivated the Framework Agreement.

The time period from 2005 to 2009 demonstrates the dramatic ups and downs of the North Korean nuclear resolution. There were two weddings and two funerals during this period. Hopeful progress had been made with the 2005 Joint Statement and the 2007 Beijing Agreement. In the September 2005 Joint Statement of the Six-Party Talks, North Korea committed to "abandoning all nuclear weapons and existing nuclear programs and returning, at an early date, to the Treaty of the Non-Proliferation of Nuclear Weapons and to IAEA safeguards."[64] At the Six-Party Talks held in Beijing in February 2007, North Korea did pledge to give up its nuclear weapons capabilities. Following this, it provided a U.S. delegation with about 18,000 pages of documentation detailing the operations of two of its primary plutonium-related facilities at Yongbyon in May 2008 and submitted a declaration of its nuclear holdings on June 26, 2008, which indicated that it had extracted a total of around 30kg of plutonium and used 2kg. However, these hopeful promises became immediately overshadowed by North Korea's two nuclear tests in October 2006 and May 2009.

Two changing factors, related to North Korea's two adversaries, had resonated with this North Korean nuclear roller coaster: the Bush administration's ambivalent approaches toward the North Korean nuclear issue and the emergence of the conservative administration in South Korea. With the start of its second term, the Bush administration sought to use its sticks and carrots for North Korea in a more balanced manner. However, with hindsight, this approach was no more than ambivalent. In the face of North Korea's Foreign Ministry announcement on May 11, 2005, that it had finished the retrieval of 8,000 spent fuel rods from its Yongbyon reactor,[65] the United States had an unprecedented number of bilateral talks with North Korea within the Six-Party Talks framework in July 2005, which would eventually lead to the 2005 Joint Statement. On the other hand, the United States used financial sanctions to put more pressure on the North. Under Executive Order 13382, issued on June 29, 2005, by President Bush,[66] the U.S. Treasury Department announced that it was freezing the U.S. assets of three North Korean entities responsible for weapons of mass destruction (WMD) and the missile program and barring its citizens and companies from doing business with them. Just 4 days before the agreement on the 2005 Joint Statement, the United States froze U.S.$25 million in

North Korean accounts in the Banco Delta Asia (BDA), which was accused of helping North Korea launder funds and distribute counterfeit U.S. currency. These and subsequent U.S. financial sanctions increased Pyongyang's sense of vulnerability, deteriorating North Korea's cash-flow problems. They served consequently as a stumbling block for the resolution of the North Korean nuclear problem in general and the Six-Party Talks in particular. Pyongyang boycotted the Six-Party Talks, demanding the lifting of the freeze of the BDA's fund. Just 1 month after the Korean Peninsula Energy Development Organization (KEDO) project to build two light water reactors (LWR) in North Korea was formally terminated in June 2006, Pyongyang test-fired seven ballistic missiles, including its longest-range missile, the Taepodong-2, breaking its voluntary moratorium on flight testing longer-range missiles, which it had observed since 1999. On October 9, 2006, North Korea conducted an underground nuclear test. It is quite reasonable to argue that North Korea conducted missile and nuclear tests to end the U.S. financial sanctions and urge Washington to make a deal with Pyongyang. Kim Yong Nam, President of the Presidium of the Supreme People's Assembly, made sure that North Korea was considering U.S. policy toward the country as the main factor for determining its nuclear testing. He said, "[T]he issue of future nuclear tests is linked to U.S. policy toward our country . . . If the United States continues to take a hostile attitude and apply pressure on us in various forms, we will have no choice but to take physical steps to deal with that."[67]

The United States took the lead in the passage of United Nations Security Council (UNSC) Resolution 1718 against the North, but at the same time it began to take a softer policy toward North Korea. In the 2007 Beijing Agreement, the United States committed to providing, in phase, heavy fuel oil to North Korea in parallel with Pyongyang's gradual dismantling of its nuclear program. It also agreed to remove North Korea from the list of state sponsors of terrorism and not to apply the Trading with the Enemy Act to North Korea. In April 2007, the United States agreed to unfreeze the U.S.$25 million in the North Korean BDA account with the condition that these funds would be used only for humanitarian purposes. With Pyongyang's involvement with a Syrian nuclear facility reinforcing the Bush administration's fundamental mistrust of North Korea, however, the United States demanded excessive verification measures that went beyond the agreed commitments of the Six-Party Talks. This issue of verification had begun to serve as a major cause for U.S.-North Korean conflict and mutual mistrust. With the United States and the North failing to make a breakthrough on this issue, the North launched the so-called Unha-2 rocket, a modified version of its Taepodong-2 ballistic missile, in April 2009 and conducted the second nuclear test in May 2009.

North Korea's rocket launch and nuclear test in 2009 was also catalyzed by the inauguration of the conservative administration in South Korea. After the election of conservative president Lee Myung-Bak in 2007, the South Korean administration immediately denounced the so-called Sunshine Policy of reconciliation with North Korea adopted by its two predecessors and even proclaimed the possibility of not being bound by two declarations made by the North-South Summits in 2000 and 2007. Given the growing importance of the economic relationship with South Korea in the North's economy, this posed a greater threat to the North. Additionally, in March 2009, South Korean Foreign Minister Yu Myung-hwan indicated the country would participate formally in the Proliferation Security Initiative in response to the expected North Korean rocket launch.

CONCLUSION

With little faith in reaching a peaceful and sustainable solution to the nuclear question through engagement and negotiations with the regime in Pyongyang, some scholars argue that nuclear nonproliferation can be enforced on North Korea only through the use of coercive tools within a general framework of containment. On the other hand, other scholars, alarmed by the catastrophe that might result from a vigorous attempt to confront and/or topple the regime in Pyongyang, suggest bypassing it and engaging the North Korean people in the hope that they will gain enough power to transform North Korea into a democratic, nuclear-free country. Indeed, current American policy toward North Korea reflects to a great extent both stances.

However, the problem is that these approaches are built upon the assumption of North Korea's offensive rationale for developing nuclear weapons. North Korean history indicates that Pyongyang's sense of vulnerability has a positive relationship with the developmental status of its nuclear program. This deviates from Eberstadt's claim that the regime's rationale behind the program has been predominantly and persistently offensive since its initiation. On the other hand, this supports Krause and Wenger's claim that the predominant rationale behind Pyongyang's nuclear program is deterring what it perceives as threats to the survivability of its regime—namely, to a large extent, American power. On the basis of this finding, it can be argued that if North Korea's perceived vulnerability can be significantly reduced, it is more likely to give up its nuclear arms program.

Then how can Pyongyang's sense of vulnerability be significantly reduced? The observations of this study suggest that Pyongyang's sense of vulnerability has been more influenced by its perception of its adversaries' hostility than by its perception of its allies' guarantee of its security. During the 1960s, Pyongyang perceived that its allies had strong interests in guaranteeing North Korean security, but its perception of the continuous hostility from its adversaries increased its sense of vulnerability, which resulted in its continuous pursuit of a nuclear program. Despite the decreasing guarantee by Moscow and Beijing for Pyongyang's security since the late 1960s, Washington's progressive approach toward Pyongyang had reduced its sense of vulnerability so significantly during the period from the late 1980s to the mid-1990s that the North was willing to sign the Agreed Framework in 1994. This indicates that the key to reducing North Korea's sense of vulnerability and bringing it back into compliance with international nonproliferation regimes is in the hands of its adversaries rather than those of its traditional allies. In this sense, we may thus assume that China is not bluffing when it claims that it lacks the necessary leverage to push North Korea into an internationally agreed upon solution to the nuclear problem. America's call for China to put more pressure on North Korea may not yield a significant breakthrough for the North Korean nuclear resolution. The key factors to determining Pyongyang's sense of vulnerability and, hence, the future of its nuclear program, are what the United States projects and, more importantly, the manner in which its messages are perceived by North Korea.

In this sense, the two previous U.S. administration's policies towards the North Korean nuclear question can provide invaluable lessons to the contemporary U.S. Government. The 1994 Framework Agreement manifested, among other things, tolerance toward diversity, a theme borrowed from Nixon and Kissinger's foreign policy during the 1970s. President Clinton, who included in the agreement the normalization of relations between Washington and Pyongyang, signaled the *de facto* acceptance of the totalitarian regime in Pyongyang, a clear divergence from his goal of spreading liberalism and democracy, which he had pursued since he came to office. Hence, the reasoning of the 1994 Agreement was not to first wrest from North Korea its strategic deterrent and then proceed with toppling its regime. On the contrary, the purpose was to incorporate North Korea, as it is, into the international community, with the hope that time would yield a change in the nature of the regime as it mingles with the other members of the international community, particularly the United States. In other words, the purpose was not to convey the sense that the United States was planning to topple or coerce the regime in Pyongyang into a change of nature, but to patiently lure it, by its own consent, into such a change.

The Bush administration seemingly took an important step toward reducing Pyongyang's sense of vulnerability by expressing its willingness to give assurances to the security of North Korea, to respect its sovereignty, and to take steps toward the normalization of relations—all in return for North Korea's total nuclear disarmament.[68] Nevertheless, overshadowing and contradicting those promises and guarantees is the North Korean Human Rights Act, which strives to promote democracy in North Korea at the expense of the totalitarian regime, and the ensuing appointment of a special envoy on human rights in North Korea. Without resolving these contradictions, Washington will continue to project ambiguous intentions through its foreign policy, hindering a significant change in North Korea's sense of vulnerability.

From these experiences, the contemporary U.S. Government must learn that engagement with the current regime in Pyongyang and the forgoing of endeavors to promptly and forcefully push democracy in North Korea are inseparable prerequisites to a peaceful and long-lasting solution to the North Korean nuclear question.

End Notes

[1] Michael J. Mazarr, *North Korea and the Bomb: A Case Study in Nonproliferation*, New York: St. Martin's Press, 1995, p. 16.
[2] Leon V. Sigal, *Disarming Strangers: Nuclear Diplomacy with North Korea*, Seoul, Korea: Societal Critics, 1999, p. 4.
[3] Mazarr, p. 16.
[4] Nicholas Eberstadt, "North Korea's Weapons Quest," *The National Interest*, No. 80, Summer 2005, pp. 49-50.
[5] *Ibid*. p. 50.
[6] *Ibid*.
[7] Joachim Krause and Andreas Wenger, eds., *Nuclear Weapons into the 21st Century: Current Trends and Future Prospects*, Bern, Switzerland: Peter Lang AG, European Academic Publishers, 2001, p. 229.
[8] *Ibid*. p. 230.
[9] John G. Stoessinger, *Why Nations Go to War, 2d Ed.*, New York: St. Martin's Press, 1978, pp. 227, 231.
[10] John Lewis Gaddis, *Strategies of Containment: A Critical Appraisal of Postwar American National Security Policy*, New York: Oxford University Press, 1982, pp. 31, 285.
[11] John T. Rourke, *International Politics on the World Stage, 9th Ed.*, Columbus, OH: McGraw-Hill/Dushkin, 2003, p. 20.
[12] Available from *web.mala.bc.ca/davies/H323Vietnam/Acheson.htm*.
13 Bruce Cumings, *Korea's Place in the Sun: A Modern History,* New York: W. W. Norton and Company, 1997, pp. 276-278.
[14] Cumings, p. 266.
[15] *Ibid*.
[16] Cumings, pp. 283-284.

[17] Sergei N. Goncharov, John W. Lewis, and Xue Litai, *Uncertain partners: Stalin, Mao, and the Korean War*, Stanford, CA: Stanford University Press, 1993, p. 216; Shu Guang Zhang, *Mao's military romanticism: China and the Korean War, 1950-1953*, Lawrence, KS: University Press of Kansas, 1995, p. 91.

[18] Cumings, p. 289.

[19] *Ibid*.

[20] Jung-il Kim, *On the Juche Idea of Our Party*, Pyongyang, North Korea: Foreign Languages Publishing House, 1985, p. 53.

[21] Mazarr, pp. 28-29, available from *www.globalsecurity.org/ wmd/world/dprk/nuke.htm*.

[22] Gaddis, pp. 182-185, available from *www.globalsecurity. org/wmd/world/china/nuke.htm*.

[23] Mazarr, pp. 21-24.

[24] Charles W. Kegley, Jr., and Eugene R Wittkopf, *World Politics: Trend and Transformation*, 9th Ed., Belmont, CA: Wadsworth/ Thomson Learning, 2004, p. 118.

[25] Rourke, p. 375.

[26] Gaddis, pp. 274-288.

[27] Gaddis, p. 285.

[28] Aron Shai, *China in International Affairs*, Tel-Aviv, Israel: Zemora-Bitan, 1990, pp. 152-163.

[29] Available from *www.census.gov/foreign-trade/balance/c5700. html*.

[30] Wokhee Shin and Youngho Kim, "Entrapment vs. Abandonment: South Korea-U.S. Alliance in Transition, 1968-1972," unpublished paper, pp. 1-20.

[31] *Ibid*.

[32] Mazarr, p. 26.

[33] Tae-Hwan Kwak and Wayne Patterson, "The Security Relationship between Korea and the United States, 1960-1984," in Yur-Bok Lee and Wayne Patterson, eds., *One Hundred Years of Korean-American Relations, 1882-1982*, Tuscaloosa, AL: University of Alabama Press, 1986, p. 110.

[34] Kwak and Patterson, pp. 110-111.

[35] Mazarr, pp. 28-29, available from *www.globalsecurity.org/ wmd/world/dprk/nuke.htm*; Gavan McCormack, *Target North Korea: Pushing North Korea to the Brink of Nuclear Catastrophe*, New York: Nation Books, 2004, p. 151.

[36] Larry A. Niksch, *CRS Issue Brief for Congress*, August 27, 2003, available from *www.fas.org/spp/starwars/crs/IB91141.pdf*.

[37] Available from *www.missouri.edu/~polswww/papers/pp000 314.pdf*.

[38] Available from *www.apcss.org/Publications/SAS/Asia BilateralRelations/China-SouthRelationsRoy.pdf*.

[39] Aaron L. Friedberg, "Ripe for Rivalry: Prospects for Peace in a Multipolar Asia," in Michael E. Brown, Sean M. Lynn-Jones, and Steven E. Miller, eds., *East Asian Security*, Cambridge, MA: The MIT Press, 1996, pp. 3-4.

[40] Kegley and Wittkopf, pp. 88, 513.

[41] Sigal, p. 5.

[42] *Ibid*.

[43] Suk Hee Kim, *North Korea at a crossroads*, Jefferson, NC: McFarland & Company Inc., 2003, pp. 105-106.

[44] Kyung-Ae Park, "explaining North Korean negotiated cooperation with the U.S.," *Asian Survey*, Vol. 37, No. 7, July 1997, p. 624.

[45] Available from *www.globalsecurity.org/military/ops/dprk_ nuke.htm*.

[46] McCormack, p. 154.

[47] We may learn about Clinton's reasoning regarding this decision from the prior experiences of Presidents Eisenhower and Kennedy. The former rejected the idea of a preventive strike against the Soviet nuclear program "because he feared the Red Army would respond by invading U.S. allies in Europe" and because he feared that even if victorious, the cost of the war would be much more than the United States could handle. Kennedy ruled out a preventive air strike against China's nuclear program, since he feared an outbreak of a colossal war, especially after the Soviets rejected his "secret request for their assistance." Scott D. Sagan, "How to Keep the Bomb From Iran," *Foreign Affairs*, Vol. 85, No. 5. September/October 2006, p. 48.

[48] Sigal, p. 6.

[49] Available from *www.globalsecurity.org/wmd/world/dprk/ nuke-agreedframework.htm*.

[50] Joel S. Wit, "North Korea: The Leader of the Pack," *The Washington Quarterly*, Winter 2001, p. 88.

[51] Scott Snyder, "Pyongyang's Pressure," *The Washington Quarterly*, Vol. 23, No. 3, Summer 2000, p. 165.

[52] Snyder, p. 168.

[53] Jonathan Monten, "The Roots of the Bush Doctrine: Power, Nationalism, and Democracy Promotion in U.S. Strategy," *International Security*, Vol. 29, No. 4, Spring 2005, p. 112.

[54] Transcript of Bush's State of the Union Address, January 29, 2002, available from *archives.cnn.com/2002/ALLPOLITICS/01/29/bush.speech.txt/*.

[55] Hwang Jang-Yop, a senior North Korean official who defected in 2007, revealed a deal struck in the summer of 1996 between Pakistan and North Korea for the supply of highly enriched uranium (HEU) technology to North Korea in return for sharing with Pakistan long-range missile technology. See Larry A. Niksch, *CRS Issue Brief for Congress*, April 7, 2006, pp. 8-9.

[56] Available from *www.armscontrol.org/act/2002_11/nkoreano 02.asp*.

[57] Larry A. Niksch, *CRS Issue Brief for Congress*, August 27, 2003, available from www.fas.org/spp/starwars/crs/IB91141. pdf.

[58] William Jefferson Clinton, *My Life,* New York: Alfred A. Knopf, 2004, p. 625.

[59] American intelligence assessed that only between 2005 to 2007 would North Korea be able to start producing around two nuclear bombs a year from HEU. See Niksch, *CRS Issue Brief for Congress*, April 7, 2006, pp. 8-9. Indeed, according to American examination, North Korea used a plutonium-fueled device in its October 9, 2006, nuclear test. "This suggests to some analysts that the DPRK's uranium enrichment programme . . . has not yet matured enough to produce sufficient fissile material for a nuclear test device." See Robert Karniol and Joseph Bermudez, "UN slaps sanctions on North Korea," *Jane's Defence Weekly,* October 25, 2006, p. 5. However, during Clinton's presidency, it was assessed that North Korea already had an ability to produce nuclear weapons through the plutonium track and indeed might have produced one or two. Moreover, renewed and successful efforts to complete its 50- and 200-megawatt facilities would have enabled North Korea to produce around 30 nuclear bombs a year, 15 times more than it could have produced through HEU.

[60] Clinton, p. 625.

[61] David Albright and Paul Brannan, "The North Korean Plutonium Stock Mid-2006," *Institute for Science and International Security* (ISIS), June 26, 2006, pp. 1-11. See also Table 1.

[62] Available from *www.nautilus.org/DPRKBriefingBook/human itarian/CanKor_VTK_2004_10_18_us_north_korean_human_right_act.pdf*.

[63] "U.S. positive of bilateral contact with N. Korea," *Yonhap News,* May 2, 2005; Kwangtae Kim, "Seoul's allies play down N.K. missile launch," *Yonhap News,* May 2, 2005.

[64] *Joint Statement of the Fourth Round of the Six-Party Talks*, Beijing, China, September 19, 2005, available from *www.fmprc.gov. cn/eng/zxxx/t212707.htm*.

[65] "N.K. completes retrieval of fuel rods from Yongbyon plant," *Yonhap News,* May 11, 2005, Factiva [online].

[66] National Archives and Records Administration, 'The President: Executive Order 13382, "Blocking Property of Weapons of Mass Destruction Proliferators and Their Supporters," *Federal Register*, Vol. 70, No. 126, Friday, July 1, 2005, available from *www. treas.gov/offices/enforcement/ofac/legal/eo/whwmdeo.pdf.*

[67] Naoko Aoki, "N. Korea's No. 2 says more nuke tests up to U.S. policy," *Kyodo News*, October 11, 2006, Factiva [online].

[68] Joo-hee Lee, "N.K. pledges to scrap all nuclear programs," *The Korean Herald*, first page, September 20, 2005.

BIBLIOGRAPHY

Albright, David and Paul Brannan, "The North Korean Plutonium Stock Mid-2006," *Institute for Science and International Security* (ISIS), June 26, 2006.

Baker, Richard W. and Charles E. Morrison, "Regional Overview," *Asia Pacific Security Outlook 2005.* Tokyo: Japan Center for International Exchange, 2005.

Brooke, James, "An Industrial Union," *The New York Times*, October 21, 2004.

Bush, George W., State of the Union Address, January 29, 2002, available from *archives.cnn.com/2002/ALLPOLITICS/01/29/ bush.speech.txt/.*

Carpenter, Ted Galen and Charles V. Pena, "Rethinking Non-Proliferation," *The National Interest*, No. 80, Summer 2005.

Choi, Jang Jip, "Political Cleavages in South Korea," in Hagen Koo, ed. *State and Society in Contemporary Korea.* Ithaca, NY: Cornell University Press, 1993.

Choi, Seung-Whan, "Russia's Foreign Policy toward South Korea: The Cases of the KAL 007 and Spy Expulsion Incidents," available from *www.missouri.edu/~polswww/papers/pp000314.pdf.*

Chun, Hong-Tack, "Economic Conditions in North Korea and Prospects for Reform," in Thomas H. Henriksen and Jongryn Mo, eds. *North Korea After Kim IL Sung: Continuity or Change?* Stanford, CA: The Hoover Institution Press, 1997.

Clinton, William Jefferson, *My Life,* New York: Alfred A. Knopf, 2004.

Cumings, Bruce, *Korea's Place in the Sun: A Modern History*, New York: W. W. Norton and Company, 1997.

"DPRK Ministry of Foreign Affairs Statement," *Korean Central News Agency*, February 10, 2005.

Eberstadt, Nicholas, "North Korea's Weapons Quest," *The National Interest*, No. 80, Summer 2005.

Friedberg, Aaron L., "Ripe for Rivalry: Prospects for Peace in a Multipolar Asia," in Michael E. Brown, Sean M. Lynn-Jones and Steven E. Miller, eds. *East Asian Security.* Cambridge, MA: The MIT Press, 1996.

Fukuyama, Francis, "The End of History?" *The National Interest*, Summer 1989.

Gaddis, John Lewis, *Strategies of Containment: A Critical Appraisal of Postwar American National Security Policy*, New York: Oxford University Press, 1982.

Goncharov, Sergei N., John W. Lewis and Xue Litai, *Uncertain partners: Stalin, Mao, and the Korean War*, Stanford, CA: Stanford University Press, 1993.

Harrison, Selig S., "Did North Korea Cheat?" *Foreign Affairs*, Vol. 84, No. 1, January/February 2005.

Haass, Richard N., *Intervention*, Rev. Ed. Washington, DC: Brookings Institution Press, 1999.

Hassig, Ralph C. and Oh, Kongdan, "The Twin Peaks of Pyongyang," *Orbis*, Winter 2006.

Hoge, Warren, "Security Council Backs Sanctions on North Korea," *The New York Times*, October 15, 2006.

Howard, Michael, *The Causes of Wars, 2nd ed.* Cambridge, MA: Harvard University Press, 1983.

Huntington, Samuel P, "The Clash of Civilizations?" *Foreign Affairs*, Vol. 12, Issue 3, Summer 1993.

Huntington, Samuel P., *The Third Wave: Democratization in the Late Twentieth Century*, Norman, OK: University of Oklahoma Press, 1991.

Hwang, Kyung Moon, "Afterward: Kwangju: the Historical Watershed," in Gi-Wook Shin and Kyung Moon Hwang, eds. *Contentious Kwangju: The May 18 Uprising in Korea's Past and Present*, Lanham, MD: Rowman and Littlefield Publishers, Inc., 2003.

Karniol, Robert and Joseph Bermudez, "UN Slaps Sanctions on North Korea." *Jane's Defence Weekly*, October 25, 2006.

Kegley, Charles W., Jr., and Eugene R. Wittkopf, *World Politics: Trend and Transformation, 9th Ed.*, Belmont, CA: Wadsworth/ Thomson Learning, 2004.

Kim, Hyun, "Roh's Government Urged to Intervene in Hyundai-N.K. Dispute." *Yonhap*, September 13, 2005.

Kim, Jung-il, *On The Juche Idea of Our Party*, Pyongyang, North Korea: Foreign Languages Publishing House, 1985.

Kim, Samuel S., "China and the Future of the Korean Peninsula," in Tsuneo Akaha, ed., *The Future of North Korea*, London: Routledge, 2002.

Kim, Suk Hee, *North Korea at a Crossroads*, Jefferson, NC: McFarland & Company Inc., 2003.

Krause, Joachim and Andreas Wenger, eds., *Nuclear Weapons into the 21st Century: Current Trends and Future Prospects,* Bern, Switzerland: Peter Lang AG, European Academic Publishers, 2001.

Kwak, Tae-Hwan and Wayne Patterson, "The Security Relationship between Korea and the United States, 1960-1984," in Yur-Bok Lee and Wayne Patterson, eds., *One Hundred Years of Korean-American Relations, 1882-1982*. Tuscaloosa, AL: University of Alabama Press, 1986.

Lankov, Andrei, "China Raises its Stakes in North Korea," available from *www.nautilus.org/fora/security/0602Lankov.html.*

Lee, Joo-hee, "N.K. Pledges to Scrap all Nuclear Programs." *The Korean Herald*, September 20, 2005.

Lee, Joo-hee and Ji-hyun Kim, "Roh Cautions Washington Hawks," *The Korea Herald*, January 26, 2006.

Lee, Manwoo, "Double Patronage toward South Korea: Security vs. Democracy and Human Rights," in Manwoo Lee, R.D. Mclaurin, and Chung-in Moon, eds., *Alliance under Tension: The Evolution of South Korean-U.S. Relations,* Seoul, South Korea: Kyungnam University Press, 1988.

Lee, Yur-Bok. "Korean-American Diplomatic Relations, 1882- 1905," in Yur-Bok Lee and Wayne Patterson, eds., *One Hundred Years of Korean-American Relations, 1882-1982,* Tuscaloosa, AL: University of Alabama Press, 1986.

Levitsky, Steven and Lucan A. Way, "International Linkage and Democratization," *Journal of Democracy*, Vol. 16, No. 3, July 2005.

Mazarr, Michael J., *North Korea and the Bomb: A Case Study in Nonproliferation,* New York: St. Martin's Press, 1995.

McCormack, Gavan, *Target North Korea: Pushing North Korea to the Brink of Nuclear Catastrophe,* New York: Nation Books, 2004.

McFaul, Michael, "Iran's Peculiar Election: Chinese Dreams, Persian Realities." *Journal of Democracy*, Vol. 16, No. 4, October 2005.

Monten, Jonathan, "The Roots of the Bush Doctrine: Power, Nationalism, and Democracy Promotion in U.S. Strategy," *International Security*, Vol. 29, No. 4, Spring 2005.

Montgomery, Alexander H., "Ringing in Proliferation: How to Dismantle an Atomic Bomb Network," *International Security*, Vol. 30, No.2, fall 2005.

Niksch, Larry A., *CRS Issue Brief for Congress*, August 27, 2003. Niksch, Larry A., *CRS Issue Brief for Congress,* April 7, 2006.

Oh, John Kie-Chiang, *Korean Politics: The Quest for Democratization and Economic Development*, Ithaca, NY: Cornell University Press, 1999.

Oh, Kongdan and Ralph C. Hassig, *North Korea Through The Looking Glass,* Washington, DC: The Brookings Institution Press, 2000.

Oh, Seung-yul, "North Korea's Economic Development and External Relations," available from *www.keia.com/2-Publications/ 2-2-Economy/Economy2005/Oh.pdf.*

O'Hanlon, Michael and Mike Mochizuki, *Crisis on the Korean Peninsula: How to Deal with a Nuclear North Korea,* New York: McGraw-Hill, 2003.

Park, Kyung-Ae, "Explaining North Korean Negotiated Cooperation with the U.S.," *Asian Survey*, Vol. 37, No. 7, July 1997.

Perry, William J., *Review of United States Policy Toward North Korea: Findings and Recommendations,* Washington, DC: U.S. Department of State, 1999.

Rourke, John T., *International Politics on the World Stage, 9th Ed.*, Columbus, OH: McGraw-Hill/Dushkin, 2003.

Roy, Denny, "China-South Korea Relations: Elder Brother Wins Over Younger Brother," available from *www. apcss. org/ Publications/ SAS/Asia Bilateral Relations/China-South Korea Relations Roy. pdf.*

Sagan, Scott D., "How to Keep the Bomb From Iran," *Foreign Affairs*, Vol. 85, No. 5, September/October 2006.

"Security Council Unanimously Adopts Resolution Sanctioning N.K. for Nuke Test," *Yonhap News*, October 15, 2006.

Shin, Gi-Wook, "Introduction," in Gi-Wook Shin and Kyung Moon Hwang, eds., *Contentious Kwangju: The May 18 Uprising in Korea's Past and Present,* Lanham, MD: Rowman and Littlefield Publishers, Inc., 2003.

Shu, Guang Zhang, *Mao's Military Romanticism: China and the Korean War, 1950-1953,* Lawrence, KS: University Press of Kansas, 1995.

Sigal, Leon V., *Disarming Strangers: Nuclear Diplomacy with North Korea.* Seoul, South Korea: Societal Critics, 1999.

Snyder, Scott, "Pyongyang's Pressure," *The Washington Quarterly*, Vol. 23, No. 3, Summer 2000.

Stoessinger, John G., *Why Nations Go to War, 2nd Ed.,* New York: St. Martin's Press, 1978. *The National Security Strategy Of The United States Of America,* Washington, DC: The White House, March 2006.

Tkacik, John, "North Korea's Bogus Breakthrough," *Far Eastern Economic Review*, Vol. 168, No. 8, September, 2005.

U.S. Census Bureau, Foreign Trade Statistics; available from *www. census.gov/foreign-trade/balance/ c5700.html.*

Weisman, Steven R., "Democracy Push by Bush Attracts Doubters in Party," *The New York Times*, March 17, 2006.

West, James M. and Edward J. Baker, "The 1987 Constitutional Reforms in South Korea: Electoral Process and Judicial Independence," in William Shaw, ed., *Human Rights in Korea,* Cambridge, MA: The East Asian Legal Studies Program of the Harvard Law School, 1991.

Wit, Joel S., "North Korea: The Leader of the Pack," *The Washington Quarterly,* Winter 2001.

Zhang, Shu Guang, *Mao's Military Romanticism: China and the Korean War, 1950-1953.* Lawrence, KS: University Press of Kansas, 1995.

In: North Korea: Nuclear Weapons and the Diplomacy Debate   ISBN: 978-1-62100-450-9
Editor: Brian N. Thompson   © 2012 Nova Science Publishers, Inc.

Chapter 3

NORTH KOREA'S NUCLEAR WEAPONS: TECHNICAL ISSUES[*]

Mary Beth Nikitin

SUMMARY

This report summarizes what is known from open sources about the North Korean nuclear weapons program—including weapons-usable fissile material and warhead estimates—and assesses current developments in achieving denuclearization. Little detailed open-source information is available about the DPRK's nuclear weapons production capabilities, warhead sophistication, the scope and success of its uranium enrichment program, or extent of its proliferation activities. In total, it is estimated that North Korea has between 30 and 50 kilograms of separated plutonium, enough for at least half a dozen nuclear weapons. While North Korea's weapons program has been plutonium-based from the start, in the last decade, intelligence emerged pointing to a second route to a bomb using highly enriched uranium. North Korea openly acknowledged a uranium enrichment program in 2009, but has said its purpose is the production of fuel for nuclear power. In November 2010, North Korea showed visiting American experts early construction of a 100 MWT light-water reactor and a newly built gas centrifuge uranium enrichment plant, both at the Yongbyon site. The North Koreans claimed the enrichment plant was operational, but this has not been independently confirmed. U.S. officials have said that it is likely other, clandestine enrichment facilities exist.Beginning in late 2002, North Korea ended an eight-year freeze on its plutonium production program, expelled international inspectors, and restarted facilities. In September 2005, members of the Six-Party Talks (United States, South Korea, Japan, China, Russia, and North Korea) issued a Joint Statement on the verifiable denuclearization of the Korean Peninsula. On October 9, 2006, North Korea conducted a nuclear test, with a yield of less than 1 kiloton. In February 2007, North Korea and the other members of the Six-Party Talks agreed on steps for phased implementation of the 2005 denuclearization agreement. Phase 1 included the shut-down of plutonium production at the Yongbyon nuclear complex in exchange for an initial heavy fuel oil

---

[*] This is an edited, reformatted and augmented version of a Congressional Research Service publication, CRS Report for Congress RL34256, from www.crs.gov, dated January 20, 2011.

shipment to North Korea. Phase 2 steps included disablement of plutonium production facilities at Yongbyon and a "complete and correct" declaration of DPRK nuclear activities, in exchange for delivery of energy assistance and removal of certain U.S. sanctions. The declaration was submitted in June 2008. Thereafter, President Bush removed North Korea from the Trading with the Enemy Act (TWEA) list and notified Congress of his intent to lift the State Sponsor of Terrorism (SST) designation after North Korea agreed to verification provisions. North Korea did not accept initial U.S. verification proposals, and in September 2008, threatened to restart reprocessing plutonium. U.S. officials announced a verbal bilateral agreement on verification in October 2008, and the Bush administration removed North Korea from the SST List. North Korea soon after said that it had not agreed to sampling at nuclear sites, a key element for verification of plutonium production. The Six-Party Talks have not convened since December 2008.

North Korea's failed satellite launch on April 5, 2009, which used ballistic missile-related technology, led to U.N. Security Council condemnation. In response, North Korea said it would abandon the Six-Party Talks and restart its nuclear facilities, and asked international and U.S. inspectors to leave the country. North Korea claimed it tested a nuclear weapon on May 25, 2009, which is estimated as larger than the 2006 blast, but still modest. Through its official news agency, North Korea claimed in September 2009 that it was conducting "experimental uranium enrichment" and in November 2009 that it had reprocessed spent fuel at the Yongbyon facility and had begun to weaponize the resulting plutonium. Some view the revelations of a uranium enrichment plant and light-water reactor plans in November 2010 as part of a provocative North Korean strategy to draw other states back to the bargaining table, while others view the facilities as evidence that North Korea is determined to advance its nuclear program despite international sanctions. In late 2010, North Korea reportedly offered to allow international nuclear inspectors back into the country and discussed shipping out its stockpile of 12,000 fresh fuel rods.

LATEST DEVELOPMENTS

Efforts toward dismantling North Korea's nuclear weapons program under the Six-Party Talks have been stalled since the spring of 2009.[1] North Korea conducted a second nuclear test in May 2010, which resulted in tougher UN Security Council sanctions. In late 2010, four separate unofficial delegations visited North Korea.[2] During these visits, North Korean officials:

- Revealed that construction had begun on a new 100 megawatt-thermal (approximately 25-30 megawatt electric) light-water reactor at Yongbyon.
- Revealed a previously unknown gas centrifuge uranium enrichment plant at Yongbyon.
- Reportedly offered to invite international inspectors to the enrichment facility to verify it would produce only low-enriched uranium for use as nuclear reactor fuel.
- Told two private U.S. delegations that Pyongyang would be willing to ship out 12,000 fresh nuclear fuel rods currently in storage.

These revelations are potentially significant for several reasons. First, they could indicate a shift in North Korea's stance regarding the Six-Party Talks[3]; some view the revelations of a uranium enrichment plant and light-water reactor plans in November 2010 as part of a North Korean strategy to draw other states back to the bargaining table. Some view these disclosures as evidence that North Korea is determined to advance its nuclear program despite international sanctions. Still others speculate that North Korea may be showing off its advances in nuclear technology in hopes of gaining customers.

Second, an advancement in uranium enrichment technology could give North Korea a second method for producing fissile material for nuclear weapons. U.S. intelligence estimates since 2002 have said that North Korea was pursuing uranium enrichment technology. Gas centrifuges can produce both low-enriched uranium (LEU), which can be made into fuel for nuclear power reactors, or highly enriched uranium (HEU), which is one of two types of material that can be used in nuclear weapons. North Korea has already produced nuclear weapons using plutonium, which is the other type of fissile material used in nuclear weapons.[4] If North Korea's offer to sell the 12,000 fresh fuel rods was realized, this would remove a potential source of plutonium from the country.

BACKGROUND

In the early 1980s, U.S. satellites tracked a growing indigenous nuclear program in North Korea. The North Korean nuclear program began in the late 1950s with cooperation agreements with the Soviet Union on a nuclear research program near Yongbyon. Its first research reactor began operation in 1967. North Korea used indigenous expertise and foreign procurements to build a small nuclear reactor at Yongbyon (5MWe). It was capable of producing about 6 kilograms (Kg) of plutonium per year and began operating in 1986.[5] Later that year, U.S. satellites detected high explosives testing and a new plant to separate plutonium from the reactor's spent fuel. In addition, construction of two larger reactors (50MWe at Yongbyon and 200MWe at Taechon) added evidence of a serious clandestine effort. Although North Korea had joined the Nuclear Nonproliferation Treaty (NPT) in 1985 under Soviet pressure, safeguards inspections began only in 1992, raising questions about how much plutonium North Korea had produced covertly. In 1994, North Korea pledged, under the Agreed Framework with the United States, to freeze its plutonium programs and eventually dismantle them in return for several kinds of assistance.[6] At that time, western intelligence agencies estimated that North Korea had separated enough plutonium for one or two bombs. North Korea complied with the Agreed Framework, allowing International Atomic Energy Agency (IAEA) seals—including the "canning" of spent fuel rods at the Yongbyon reactor—and permanent remote monitoring and inspectors at its nuclear facilities.

When in 2002, U.S. negotiators reportedly presented North Korean officials with evidence of a clandestine uranium enrichment program, the North Korean officials reportedly at first confirmed this, then denied it publicly. The conflict quickly led to the breakdown of the Agreed Framework. The Bush Administration argued that North Korea was in "material breach" of its obligations and, after agreement with South Korea, Japan, and the EU (the other members of the Korean Economic Development Organization, or KEDO), stopped the next shipment of heavy fuel oil.[7] In response, North Korea kicked out international monitors, broke the seals at the Yongbyon nuclear complex, and restarted its reactor and reprocessing plant after an eight-year freeze.

Members of the Six-Party Talks—the United States, South Korea, Japan, China, Russia, and North Korea—began meeting in August 2003 to try and resolve the crisis. In September 2005, the Six Parties issued a Joint Statement on how to achieve verifiable denuclearization of the Korean Peninsula, which formed the basis for future agreements.[8] Negotiations broke down, and North Korea tested a nuclear device in October 2006.

On February 13, 2007, North Korea reached an agreement with other members of the Six-Party Talks to begin the initial phase (60 days) of implementing the Joint Statement from September 2005 on denuclearization. Phase 1 of this agreement included the shut-down of plutonium production at the Yongbyon nuclear complex in exchange for an initial heavy fuel oil shipment to North Korea. Phase 2 steps include the disablement of facilities at Yongbyon and a "complete and correct" declaration of DPRK nuclear activities, in exchange for deliver of heavy fuel oil and equivalent, and removal of the Trading with the Enemy Act (TWEA) and State Sponsors of Terrorism (SST) designations. The United States provided funding and technical assistance for disablement activities in North Korea until April 2009. Energy assistance was divided evenly between the Six Parties in Phase 2 of the agreement. North Korea submitted a declaration of its past plutonium production activities in June 2008 as agreed in an October 3, 2007, joint statement on "Second-Phase Actions."[9] Thereafter, President Bush removed North Korea from the TWEA list and notified Congress of his intent to lift the SST designation after North Korea agreed to verification provisions. North Korea did not accept initial U.S. verification proposals, and in September 2008, threatened to restart reprocessing plutonium. U.S. officials announced a bilateral agreement on verification in October 2008, and the Bush administration removed North Korea from the SST List. The agreement was verbal, and North Korea then said that it had not agreed to sampling at nuclear sites, a key element in verifying past plutonium production. The Six Parties met in December 2008, but did not reach agreement on verification measures. Disablement activities at Yongbyon continued through April 2009, when North Korea expelled international monitors. North Korea then announced it would restart its reprocessing plant and boasted progress in uranium enrichment technology development and soon after tested as nuclear device (see detailed discussions below).

The February 2007 Denuclearization Action Plan did not address uranium enrichment-related activities or the dismantlement of warheads and instead focused on shutting down and disabling the key plutonium production facilities at Yongbyon. A third phase, to have begun after disablement was complete and a declaration accepted by the Six Parties, was expected to deal with all aspects of North Korea's nuclear program, including weapons, using North Korea's declaration as a basis for future action. Understanding the scope of the program and the weapons capability would require transparency and careful verification for the pledged "complete, verifiable, irreversible" disarmament to be achieved.

WEAPONS PRODUCTION MILESTONES

Acquiring fissile material—plutonium-239 or highly enriched uranium (HEU)—is the key hurdle in nuclear weapons development.[10] Producing these two materials is technically challenging; in comparison, many experts believe weaponization to be relatively easy.[11] North Korea has industrial-scale uranium mining and plants for milling, refining, and converting uranium; it also has a fuel fabrication plant, a nuclear reactor, and a reprocessing plant—in short, everything needed to produce Pu-239. In its nuclear reactor, North Korea uses magnox fuel—natural uranium (>99%U-238) metal, wrapped in magnesium-alloy cladding. About 8,000 fuel rods constitute a fuel core for the reactor.

When irradiated in a reactor, natural uranium fuel absorbs a neutron and then decays into plutonium (Pu-239). Fuel that remains in the reactor for a long time becomes contaminated by the isotope Pu-240, which can "poison" the functioning of a nuclear weapon.[12] Spent or irradiated fuel, which poses radiological hazards, must cool after removal from the reactor. The cooling phase, estimated by some at five months, is proportional to the fuel burn-up. Reprocessing to separate plutonium from waste products and uranium is the next step. North Korea uses a PUREX separation process, like the United States. After shearing off the fuel cladding, the fuel is dissolved in nitric acid. Components (plutonium, uranium, waste) of the fuel are separated into different streams using organic solvents. In small quantities, separation can be done in hot cells, but larger quantities require significant shielding to prevent deadly exposure to radiation.[13]

North Korea appears to have mastered the engineering requirements of plutonium production. It has operated its nuclear reactor, is believed to have separated Pu from the spent fuel, and has reportedly taken steps toward weaponization. In January 2004, North Korean officials showed an unofficial U.S. delegation alloyed "scrap" from a plutonium (Pu) casting operation.[14] Dr. Siegfried Hecker, a delegation member, assessed that the stated density of the material was consistent with plutonium alloyed with gallium or aluminum. If so, this could indicate a degree of sophistication in North Korea's handling of Pu metal, necessary for weapons production. But without testing the material, Hecker could not confirm that the metal was plutonium or that it was alloyed, or when it was produced.

Estimating Nuclear Warheads and Plutonium Stocks

Secretary of State Colin Powell in December 2002 stated, "We now believe [the North Koreans] have a couple of nuclear weapons and have had them for years."[15] In February 2005, North Korea officially announced that it had "manufactured nukes for self-defense."[16] Vice Foreign Minister Kim Gye Gwan has previously said that North Korea possesses multiple bombs and was building more.[17]

A key factor in assessing how many weapons North Korea can produce is whether North Korea needs to use more or less material than the IAEA standards of 8kg of Pu and 25kg for HEU per weapon.[18] The amount of fissile material used in each weapon is determined by the design sophistication. There is no reliable public information on North Korean nuclear weapons design.

In all, estimates of North Korea's separated plutonium range between 30 and 50 kg, with an approximate 5 to 6 kg of this figure having been used for the October 2006 test and an additional amount probably used in the May 2009 test.[19] This amounts to enough plutonium for approximately five to eight nuclear weapons, assuming 6 kg per weapon. Taking the nuclear tests into account, North Korean could possess plutonium for four to seven nuclear weapons. A 2007 unclassified intelligence report to Congress says that "prior to the test North Korea could have produced up to 50 kg of plutonium, enough for at least a half dozen nuclear weapons" and points out that additional plutonium is in the fuel of the Yongbyon reactor.[20] North Korea claimed to have reprocessed that fuel in the summer of 2009 (see below).

Questions arise in determining how much plutonium North Korea produced between 2003, when the IAEA monitors were kicked out of the country and the seals were broken at Yongbyon, and 2007, when international monitoring resumed. A South Korean Defense Ministry white paper from December 2006 estimated that North Korea had made 30 kg of weapons-grade plutonium in the previous three years, potentially enough for five nuclear bombs. The white paper also concurred with U.S. estimates that North Korea's total stockpile of weapons-grade plutonium was 50 kg.[21]

The accounting issue was further complicated when North Korea reportedly declared a lower number of 37 kg of separated plutonium in its declaration under the Six-Party Talks.[22] No agreement has been reached on verifying the amount of plutonium stocks through inspections (see discussions on declaration, verification below). In January 2009, an American scholar who had visited Pyongyang said the North Koreans told him that 30.8 kg amount had been "weaponized," possibly meaning that the separated plutonium might now be in warheads. The DPRK officials also told him that they would not allow for warheads to be inspected.[23]

Plutonium Production

Estimates of plutonium production depend on a variety of technical factors, including the average power level of the reactor, days of operation, how much of the fuel is reprocessed and how quickly, and how much plutonium is lost in production processes. North Korean officials claimed to have separated plutonium in hot cells as early as 1975 and tested the reprocessing plant in 1990. North Korea's 5MWe nuclear reactor at Yongbyon operated from 1986 to 1994. It is estimated that North Korea produced and separated no more than 10 kg of plutonium prior to 1994.[24] Its plutonium production program was then frozen between 1994 and 2003 under the Agreed Framework. When this agreement was abandoned, North Korea restarted plutonium production at Yongbyon.

On February 6, 2003, North Korean officials announced that the 5MWe reactor was operating, and commercial satellite photography confirmed activity in March. In January 2004, North Korean officials told an unofficial U.S. delegation that the reactor was operating smoothly at 100% of its rated power. The U.S. visitors noted that the display in the reactor control room and steam plumes from the cooling towers confirmed operation, but that there was no way of knowing how it had operated over the last year.[25]

The same delegation reported that the reprocessing "facility appeared in good repair," in contrast to a 1992 IAEA assessment of the reprocessing plant as "extremely primitive." According to North Korean officials in January 2004, the reprocessing plant's annual throughput is 110 tons of spent fuel, about twice the fuel load of the 5MWe reactor. Officials claimed to have reprocessed all 8,000 fuel rods from the 5MWe reactor between January and June 2003.[26] Reprocessing the 8,000 fuel rods at that time would have yielded between 25 and 30kg of plutonium, perhaps for four to six weapons, but the exact amount of plutonium that might have been reprocessed is unknown. In 2004, North Korean officials stated that the reprocessing campaign was conducted continuously (in four six-hour shifts).

In April 2005, the 5MWe reactor was shut down, this time to harvest fuel rods for weapons.[27] The reactor resumed operations in June 2005.[28] One estimate is that the reactor held between 10 and 15 kg of Pu in April 2005, and that North Korea could have reprocessed all the fuel rods by mid-2006. From August 2005 to 2006, the reactor could have produced another 6 kg of Pu. In total, North Korea could have reprocessed enough separated plutonium for another three weapons (in addition to the estimated 4-6 bomb-worth from reprocessing the 8,000 fuel rods).[29] The 5MWe reactor was again shut down in July 2007, when the IAEA installed containment and surveillance measures and radiation monitoring devices.[30] Its cooling tower was destroyed in June 2008, and it has not been restarted. The IAEA was asked to remove its monitoring equipment and leave the site in April 2009. In early November 2009, the North Korean news agency announced that all 8,000 spent fuel rods in its possession had been reprocessed by the end of August. Reprocessing at that time, is estimated to have produced 7-8 kg of separated plutonium or approximately enough for one nuclear warhead.[31] However, even while the reprocessing facility was shut down, North Korea could have built additional warheads with existing separated plutonium because North Korea's plutonium stocks were not under IAEA safeguards.

No construction has occurred at the 50MWe reactor at Yongbyon or at the 200MWe Taechon reactor since 2002.[32] They were years from completion when construction was halted.[33] The 50 MWe reactor site at Yongbyon is currently being dismantled.[34] The CIA estimated that the two reactors could generate about 275kg of plutonium per year if they were operating.[35] Dr. Hecker estimated that if the 50MWe reactor was functioning, it would mean a tenfold increase in North Korea's plutonium production.[36] North Korea agreed to halt work on reactors as part of the Six-Party Talks. From July 2007 to April 2009, when inspectors were asked to leave, the IAEA was monitoring to ensure that no further construction took place at these sites. Significant future growth in North Korea's plutonium-based arsenal would be possible only if the two larger reactors were completed and operating, and would also depend on progress in the reported uranium enrichment program.

In December 2010, Governor Bill Richardson went to North Korea on an unofficial visit. Press reports and the governor's website say that North Korea is willing to negotiate the sale of the 12,000 fresh fuel rods in storage at Yongbyon to a third party, such as South Korea. These fuel rods were manufactured for the 50 MWe that was never built. These fuel rods could be re-clad to be used in the 5 MWe reactor if North Korea chose to restart it.

Table 1. North Korean Nuclear Power Reactor Projects

Location	Type/Power Capacity	Status	Purpose
Yongbyon	Graphite-moderated Heavy Water Experimental Reactor/5 MWe	Currently shut-down; cooling tower destroyed in June 2009 as part of Six-Party Talks; estimated restart time would be 6 months	Weapons-grade plutonium production
Yongbyon	Graphite-moderated Heavy Water Power Reactor /50 MWe	Never built; Basic construction begun; project halted since 1994	Stated purpose was electricity production; could have been used for weapons-grade plutonium production

Table 1. (Continued)

Location	Type/Power Capacity	Status	Purpose
Yongbyon	Experimental Light-Water Reactor/100 MWT (25-30 MWe)	U.S. observers saw basic construction begun in November 2010	Stated purpose is electricity production; could be used for weapons-grade plutonium production
Taechon	Graphite-moderated Heavy Water Power Reactor/200 MWe	Never built; Basic construction begun; project halted since 1994	Stated purpose was electricity production; could have been used for weapons-grade plutonium production
Kumho District, Sinp'o	4 Light-water reactors/440 MW	Never built; part of 1985 deal with Soviet Union when North Korea signed the NPT; canceled by Russian Federation in 1992	Stated purpose is electricity production; could have been used for weapons-grade plutonium production
Kumho District, Sinp'o [KEDO Project]	2 Light-water reactors (turn-key)/1000 MWe	Never built; part of 1994 Agreed Framework, reactor agreement concluded in 1999; Project terminated in 2006 after North Korea pulled out of Agreed Framework	Electricity production

URANIUM ENRICHMENT

Uranium Enrichment Program: New Facility Unveiled

In November 2010, North Korean officials showed a visiting unofficial U.S. delegation—led by former Los Alamos National Laboratory Director Dr. Siegfried Hecker—what they claimed was an operating gas centrifuge uranium enrichment plant at the Yongbyon nuclear site. In his trip report, Dr. Hecker estimated that the plant had 2,000 centrifuges (most likely P-2 centrifuges)[37] in six cascades, with a capacity of 8,000 kg SWU/year.[38]

North Korea claims the uranium enrichment facility was built to produce enriched uranium for power reactor fuel. The North does not have any functioning nuclear power reactors, but said it is in the process of building a 100 megawatt-thermal (25-30 megawatt-electric) experimental light-water reactor.[39] Satellite images, as well as visitors to the site, confirm initial construction.[40] The reported size of the enrichment plant would match the annual fuel needs for the proposed 100 MWT reactor, which would require 3.5% low-enriched uranium fuel. However, the plant could be altered to produce 40 kg of 90% highly enriched uranium per year.[41] Highly enriched uranium can be used for weapons, while low-enriched uranium cannot.

Subsequently, North Korean representatives reportedly told New Mexican Governor Bill Richardson during an unofficial visit to Pyongyang in December 2010 that they would be willing to invite International Atomic Energy Agency (IAEA) inspectors back into the country to monitor the enrichment plant at Yongbyon, and presumably verify that it was not producing highly enriched uranium.[42] In April 2009, the North Korean government expelled all U.S. and IAEA inspectors that were monitoring nuclear disablement activities agreed to in the Six-Party Talks at the Yongbyon nuclear site. A return of the inspectors to Yongbyon would need to be negotiated between North Korea and the IAEA. To date, there are no reports that North Korea has directly invited the IAEA. Some countries might be opposed to sending monitors to observe activities at the enrichment plant absent North Korea's return to a denuclearization process. Others might argue that any transparency on this new facility would be worthwhile.

While it was known prior to Dr. Hecker's visit that North Korea was pursuing a uranium enrichment capacity, many analysts were surprised at the size and sophistication of the plant.[43] Although North Korea's weapons program has been plutonium-based from the start, in the past decade, intelligence had emerged pointing to it pursuing a second route to a nuclear bomb using highly enriched uranium. Even before North Korea unveiled the facility in November 2010, there was some certainty that North Korea has parts and plans for such a program, but far less certainty over how far this program had developed.

In particular, this revelation raises questions about North Korea's domestic capability to manufacture components, as well as how and when Pyonyang obtained any equipment or materials for the facility. Analysts point to a history of cooperation with Pakistan, particularly through the A. Q. Khan network, and multiple reports of transshipments through China.[44] The scale of the plant at Yongbyon could suggest North Korea possesses research level facilities elsewhere in the country. Another concern is that a clandestine facility might exist that is configured to produce HEU for the North Korean nuclear weapons program. U.S. Ambassador to the IAEA Glyn Davies told the IAEA Board of Governors in December 2010 that the United States believes it is likely that other, clandestine uranium enrichment facilities exist in locations other than Yongbyon.[45] It is not known where North Korea develops or manufactures centrifuges.

Pakistani President Musharraf revealed in his September 2006 memoir, *In the Line of Fire*, that Abdul Qadeer Khan—chief scientist in Pakistan's nuclear weapons program who proliferated nuclear weapons technology for profit—"transferred nearly two dozen P-1 and P-2 centrifuges to North Korea. He also provided North Korea with a flow meter, some special oils for centrifuges, and coaching on centrifuge technology, including visits to top-secret centrifuge plants."[46] However, the United States has not been able to get direct confirmation from Khan. According to press reports, North Korea said it had imported 150 tons of high-strength aluminum tubes from Russia that could be used in a uranium enrichment program.[47]

Previous North Korean Statements on its Enrichment Program

Until May 2009, North Korea denied the existence of a highly enriched uranium program for weapons. North Korea had threatened in April 2009 that it would build a light-water reactor if the UN Security Council did not apologize for its condemnation of the North's missile test. Following the June 12 UN Security Council Resolution condemning North Korea's nuclear test, Pyongyang issued a statement: "The process of uranium enrichment will be commenced." The statement also said that "pursuant to the decision to build its own light-water reactor, enough success has been made in developing uranium enrichment technology to provide nuclear fuel to allow the experimental procedure."[48] In the June statement, North Korea was apparently saying it would, at a minimum, start the experimental enrichment of uranium for fuel.[49] Pyongyang offered a further statement in September 2009: "experimental uranium enrichment has successfully been conducted to enter the completion phase." However, it was unclear what a "completion phase" meant in technical terms. After showing the plant at Yongbyon to visiting American scientists in November 2010, North Korea issued a statement saying that "a modern factory for uranium enrichment equipped with thousands of centrifuges is operating to supply fuel" [to the light-water reactor].[50]

U.S. Intelligence Assessments

A 2002 CIA report to Congress said, "In 2001, North Korea began seeking centrifuge-related materials in large quantities. It also obtained equipment suitable for use in uranium feed and withdrawal systems. North Korea's goal appears to be a plant that could produce enough weapons-grade uranium for two or more nuclear weapons per year when fully operational."[51] A 2002 unclassified CIA working paper on North Korea's nuclear weapons and uranium enrichment estimated that North Korea "is constructing a plant that could produce enough weapons-grade uranium for two or more nuclear weapons per year when fully operational—which could be as soon as mid-decade."[52] Such a plant would need to produce more than 50kg of HEU per year, requiring cascades of thousands of centrifuges.[53]

Questions have been raised about whether the 2002 estimates were accurate.[54] In a hearing before the Senate Armed Services Committee on February 27, 2007, Joseph DeTrani, the mission manager for North Korea from the Office of the Director of National Intelligence and former chief negotiator for the Six-Party Talks, was asked by Senator Jack Reed whether he had "any further indication of whether that program has progressed in the last six years, one; or two, the evidence—the credibility of the evidence that we had initially, suggesting they had a program rather than aspirations?" DeTrani responded that "the assessment was with high confidence that, indeed, they were making acquisitions necessary for, if you will, a production-scale program. And we still have confidence that the program is in existence—at the mid-confidence level." In a clarification of his response, DeTrani issued a DNI press release that said there was a high level of confidence in 2002 that North Korea had a uranium enrichment program, and "at least moderate confidence that North Korea's past efforts to acquire a uranium enrichment capability continue today."[55] Assistant Secretary of State Christopher Hill said in February 2007 that the United States is not sure if North Korea has mastered "some considerable production techniques," although they have acquired some technology for an enrichment program.[56]

A DNI unclassified report of August 2007 stated,

> We continue to assess with high confidence that North Korea has pursued efforts to acquire a uranium enrichment capability, which we assess is intended for nuclear weapons. All Intelligence Community agencies judge with at least moderate confidence that this past effort continues. The degree of progress towards producing enriched uranium remains unknown, however.[57]

In testimony to Congress on February 2008, Director of National Intelligence Michael McConnell confirmed this assessment. The confidence level of these assessments may have changed because of a decrease in international procurement by North Korea. Uranium enrichment-related imports would be more easily detected by intelligence agencies than activities inside North Korea itself. Uranium enrichment facilities can be hidden from aerial surveillance more easily than plutonium facilities, making it more difficult for intelligence agencies to even detect—thus, "degree of progress" in turning the equipment into a working enrichment program is "unknown." Furthermore, there are significant differences between assembling a small-scale centrifuge enrichment program and operating a large-scale production plant, and reportedly little evidence of procurement for a large-scale plant has emerged.[58] Dr. Siegfried Hecker has assessed that it is "highly likely that North Korea had a research and development uranium enrichment effort, but there is little indication that they were able to bring it to industrial scale."[59]

In 2007, North Korea gave the United States a sample of the aluminum tubing in an effort to prove that it never intended to produce highly enriched uranium for weapons, and that the imported materials were for conventional weapons or dual-use projects. However, when U.S. scientists analyzed the aluminum tubing provided as sample "evidence," they found traces of enriched uranium on the tubing. Analysts argue that in addition to the possibility that this is proof of a North Korean uranium enrichment program, it is also possible that the uranium traces could have been on the tubing when North Korea received it.[60]

In 2008, U.S. personnel found traces of highly-enriched uranium on the documents submitted as part of North Korea's nuclear declaration, raising new doubts about the extent of North Korea's uranium enrichment program.[61] Ambassador Hill told Congress that North Korea included as part of its June 2008 "declaration package" a letter that says that "they do not now and will not in the future have a highly enriched uranium program."[62]

The Section 721 Unclassified Report to Congress covering the period January 1 to December 31, 2008, said that

> Although North Korea has halted and disabled portions of its plutonium production program, we continue to assess North Korea has pursued a uranium enrichment capability at least in the past. Some in the IC have increasing concerns that North Korea has an ongoing covert uranium enrichment program.

Uranium Enrichment and Nuclear Negotiations

The uranium enrichment issue was central to denuclearization negotiations since October 2002, when the Bush Administration accused North Korea of having a clandestine uranium enrichment program. U.S. lead negotiator James Kelly told North Korean First Deputy Foreign Minister Kang Sok-chu that the United States had evidence of a uranium enrichment program for nuclear weapons in violation of the Agreed Framework and other agreements. James Kelly said that Kang acknowledged the existence of such a program at that meeting. However, Kang later denied this, and Foreign Minister Paek Nam Sun said that Kang had told Kelly that North Korea is "entitled" to have such a program or "an even more powerful one" to deter a preemptive U.S. attack.[63]

U.S. Special Representative for North Korea Policy Ambassador Stephen Bosworth said after a bilateral meeting in North Korea that the subject of a uranium enrichment program will be "on the agenda" when the Six-Party Talks resume.[64] After the November 2010 revelations of a small-scale centrifuge uranium enrichment facility, negotiators will be faced with decisions over how to address this plant, which the North Koreans say is for the peaceful production of power plant fuel, and how to verify the dismantlement of any other plants as part of any future denuclearization process.

U.S. official statements have downplayed North Korea's new enrichment facility and related offers, saying they are not surprising, and are not sufficient for a return to talks. For example, State Department Spokesman P. J. Crowley said in late December 2010, "If they meet their international obligations, take affirmative steps to reduce tensions in the region and take affirmative steps to denuclearize, we will respond accordingly."[65] Neither the offer to sell the fresh fuel or to invite international monitors to the uranium enrichment plant demonstrates a commitment to denuclearization steps by North Korea, demanded by the U.S. and South Korean governments as a condition for reconvening the Six-Party Talks. Officials from both governments have said they want to avoid falling into the diplomatic "trap" of being drawn into a lengthy negotiating process in which Pyongyang does not take concrete steps to denuclearize. However, North Korea's offers may have some intrinsic value on technical grounds: removal of the fresh fuel could reduce the amount of ready material to produce plutonium if the 5 MWe reactor was restarted (it would take only six months to do so); the presence of international inspectors at the newly built uranium enrichment site, depending on the degree of access given, could shed light on the extent and type of technical capability of the North Korean enrichment program.

The October 9, 2006, Nuclear Test[66]

The U.S. Director of National Intelligence confirmed that North Korea conducted an underground nuclear explosion on October 9, 2006, in the vicinity of P'unggye.[67] However, the sub-kiloton yield of the test suggests that the weapon design or manufacturing process likely needs improvement.[68] North Korea reportedly told China before the test that it expected a yield of 4 kilotons (KT), but seismic data confirmed that the yield was less than 1 KT.[69] Radioactive debris indicates that the explosion was a nuclear test, and that a plutonium device was used.[70] It is widely believed that the warhead design was an implosion device.[71] Uncertainties remain about when the plutonium used for the test was produced and how much plutonium was in the device, although a prominent U.S. nuclear scientist has estimated that North Korea likely used approximately 6 kg of plutonium for the test.[72]

The test's low yield may not have been a failure. Another possibility is that the test's low yield was intentional—a sophisticated device designed for a Nodong medium range missile. Alternatively, a low yield could have been intended to avoid radioactive leakage from the test site or to limit the amount of plutonium used.[73]

The May 25, 2009, Nuclear Test

The DPRK announced on May 25, 2009, that it had successfully conducted another underground nuclear test. An official North Korean news release said that this test was "on a new higher level in terms of its explosive power and technology of its control and the results of the test helped satisfactorily settle the scientific and technological problems arising in further increasing the power of nuclear weapons." This may be a reference to design problems associated with the low yield of the 2006 test. A North Korean official statement had threatened on April 29, 2009, that it would conduct "nuclear tests" to bolster its deterrent.[74]

The U.S. Geologic Survey registered an underground blast on May 25 with a seismic magnitude of the event as 4.7 on the Richter scale.[75] The Directorate of National Intelligence released a statement on June 15 saying, "The U.S. Intelligence Community assesses that North Korea probably conducted an underground nuclear explosion in the vicinity of P'unggye on May 25, 2009. The explosion yield was approximately a few kilotons. Analysis of the event continues."[76] Additional analysis will also be needed to determine the device's design and how much nuclear material was used. In contrast to 2006, no radioactive noble gases have been detected by international monitoring stations and no national governments have announced such data.[77] It is possible that North Korea may have been able to contain the release of these gases and particles from the test site. This data can provide not only evidence of a test, but potentially also information on the type of weapon detonated.[78]

Delivery Systems

Although former Defense Intelligence Agency (DIA) Director Lowell Jacoby told the Senate Armed Services Committee in April 2005 that North Korea had the capability to arm a missile with a nuclear device, Pentagon officials later backtracked from that assessment. A DNI report to Congress says that "North Korea has short and medium range missiles that could be fitted with nuclear weapons, but we do not know whether it has in fact done so."[79] North Korea has several hundred short-range Scud-class and medium range No Dong-class ballistic missiles, and is developing an intermediate range ballistic missile. The Taepo-Dong-2 that was tested unsuccessfully in July 2006 would be able to reach the continental United States if it becomes operational. DNI assessed in 2008 that the Taepo-Dong-2 has the potential capability to deliver a nuclear-weapon-sized payload to the United States, but that absent successful testing the likelihood of this is low.[80] A launch of a Taepo-Dong 2 missile as part of a failed satellite launch in April 2009 traveled further than earlier unsuccessful launches but still did not achieve a complete test.

It is possible that Pakistani scientist A.Q. Khan may have provided North Korea the same Chinese-origin nuclear weapon design he provided to Libya and Iran. Even though that design was for an HEU-based device, it would still help North Korea develop a reliable warhead for ballistic missiles—small, light, and robust enough to tolerate the extreme conditions encountered through a ballistic trajectory. Learning more about what is needed for miniaturization of warheads for ballistic missiles could have been the goal of North Korea's testing a smaller nuclear device.[81]

Doctrine and Intent

U.S. officials in their threat assessments have described the North Korean nuclear capabilities as being more for deterrence and coercive diplomacy than for war fighting, and assess that Pyongyang most likely would "not attempt to use nuclear weapons against U.S.

forces or territory unless it perceived the regime to be on the verge of military defeat and risked an irretrievable loss of control."[82] Statements by North Korean officials emphasize that moves to expand their nuclear arsenal are in response to perceived threats by the United States against the North Korean regime.[83] Nuclear weapons also give North Korea leverage in diplomatic negotiations, and threatening rhetoric often coincides with times of crisis or transitions in negotiations. In January 2008, a North Korean media report stated that the country "will further strengthen our war deterrent capabilities in response to U.S. attempts to initiate nuclear war," to express its displeasure that it had not yet been removed from the U.S. terrorism list.[84] Statements from Pyongyang in January 2009 may also be part of a strategy to increase leverage in nuclear talks,[85] or could indicate an increasing role for the North Korean military in nuclear policy making.[86] A spokesman for North Korea's General Staff said on April 18, 2009 that the revolutionary armed forces "will opt for increasing the nation's defense capability including nuclear deterrent in every way."[87] At the same time, the DPRK issues periodic statements, such as its 2010 New Year's address stating its dedication to achieving a nuclear-free Korean Peninsula through negotiations.

STEPS TOWARD DENUCLEARIZATION UNDER THE SIX-PARTY TALKS (2005-2009)

In September 2005, North Korea agreed to abandon "all nuclear weapons and existing nuclear programs," but implementation of this goal was stalled.[88] The October 9, 2006, nuclear test is seen as a catalyst in uniting the other members of the Six-Party Talks to toughen their stance towards North Korea, and as a turning point in Pyongyang's attitude. UN Security Council Resolution 1718 calls on North Korea to abandon its nuclear weapons in a "complete, verifiable, and irreversible manner."[89] In February 2007, as part of implementation of the September 2005 Joint Statement, North Korea committed to disable all nuclear facilities and provide a "complete and correct" declaration of all its nuclear programs.[90]

Disablement

The October 2007 Six-Party joint statement said the United States would lead disablement activities and provide the initial funding for those activities.[91] Disablement indicates a physical measure to make it difficult to restart operation of a facility while terms are being worked out for its eventual dismantlement. U.S. officials said that their aim was a disablement process that would require a 12-month time period to start up the facility again.[92] The Six Parties agreed to 11 discrete steps to disable the three main Yongbyon facilities related to North Korea's plutonium program (nuclear fuel fabrication plant, plutonium reprocessing plant, and 5-megawatt experimental nuclear power reactor).[93] The disablement process began in early November 2007 and continued through April 2009. The most time-consuming step was the removal of the irradiated fuel from the reactor to storage in an adjacent cooling pond.[94] A reported eight out of eleven steps were completed (see Table 2).[95]

Table 2. Disablement Steps at Yongbyon, DPRK

Step	Facility	Status
Discharge of 8000 spent fuel rods to the spent fuel pool	5-megawatt reactor	6,400 completed as of April 2009
Removal of control rod drive mechanisms	5-megawatt reactor	To be done after spent fuel removal completed
Removal of reactor cooling loop and wooden cooling tower interior structure	5-megawatt reactor	Tower demolished June 26, 2008
Disablement of fresh fuel rods	Fuel fabrication facility	Not agreed to by North Korea; consultations held Jan. 2009 with South Korea on possibility of purchase
Removal and storage of 3 uranium ore concentrate dissolver tanks	Fuel fabrication facility	Completed
Removal and storage of 7 uranium conversion furnaces, including storage of refractory bricks and mortar sand	Fuel fabrication facility	Completed
Removal and storage of both metal casting furnaces and vacuum system, and removal and storage of 8 machining lathes	Fuel fabrication facility	Completed
Cut cable and remove drive mechanism associated with the receiving hot cell door	Reprocessing facility	Completed
Cut two of four steam lines into reprocessing facility	Reprocessing facility	Completed
Removal of drive mechanisms for the fuel cladding shearing and slitting machines	Reprocessing facility	Completed
Removal of crane and door actuators that permit spent fuel rods to enter the reprocessing facility	Reprocessing facility	Completed

Source: "North Korean Disablement Actions," *Arms Control Today*, October 2008; "Disablement Actions," National Committee on North Korea website; Siegfried Hecker, "Denuclearizing North Korea," Bulletin of the Atomic Scientists, May/June 2008.

North Korea periodically slowed the pace of spent fuel rod removal at Yongbyon to show its displeasure over other aspects of the Six-Party agreements.[96] For example, in June 2008, Pyongyang said that while 80% of the disablement steps had been completed, only 36% of energy aid had been delivered.[97] North Korea again delayed disablement work in August, September, and October 2008, and those instances appear to have been linked to disputes over when the U.S. would remove the DPRK from its State Sponsors of Terrorism List and negotiations over verification measures. After the U.S. removed the SST designation, disablement work resumed in October 2008, and continued until North Korea halted the process in April 2009.

The steps that were not completed in disabling the Yongbyon facilities as part of phase 2 of the Six-Party Talks are: completing the removal of the spent fuel rods from the 5 megawatt reactor; removing the control rod drive mechanism (after all rods are removed); and disabling or removing from the country the fresh fuel rods at the site. As of early April 2009, approximately 80% or 6,400 of the 8,000 spent fuel rods had been moved from the reactor to the cooling pond.[98] Pyongyang subsequently issued statements saying it had itself removed the remaining fuel rods from the reactor and completed reprocessing all 8,000 spent fuel rods by August 2009.[99]

In addition, North Korea possesses 2,400 5-MWt fresh fuel rods and 12,000 50-MWt fresh fuel rods in storage at Yongbyon. A technical delegation from South Korea visited the facility in January 2009 to consider possibilities for removing the fuel rods. Another option discussed was to bend them so they could not be readily used in the reactor.[100] It is not clear whether North Korea had agreed to disablement or removal of the fresh fuel, and then balked, or whether it never had agreed to this measure. North Korea told visiting unofficial American delegations in late 2010 that the North would consider shipping out (and selling) the 12,000 fresh fuel rods, most likely to South Korea, if the United States reaffirmed a 2000 Joint Statement which said the U.S. held no hostile intent toward the North.[101]

Reversing Disablement

The North Korean Foreign Ministry said on April 25, 2009, that it had restarted its reprocessing facility, but there has been no way to independently verify this. North Korea said in November 2009 that it had reprocessed the 8,000 spent fuel rods in its possession by the end of August.

The extent to which the Yongbyon facilities had been disabled was first tested in September 2008 when North Korea halted international monitoring at the reprocessing facility, moved some equipment out of storage, and threatened to begin reprocessing again.[102] This temporary reversal was corrected and equipment moved back to storage by November 2008. Taking into account the need to test the facility (e.g., for leaks and cracks in the piping) and introduce chemicals, experts estimated that restarting the reprocessing plant could take approximately six to eight weeks, although this timeline might be shorter since some initial work may have been done in September 2008. It would then take approximately three to four months to reprocess the spent fuel rods now in storage at Yongbyon, resulting in 7 kg to 8 kg of plutonium. This would be enough for at least one nuclear weapon.[103] According to reports, disablement was limited to the "front-end," where spent fuel is loaded, at the reprocessing facility for technical reasons related to the safe disposal of the high-level waste in the facility.[104]

In order to produce additional plutonium, the North Koreans would need to restore their 5-MWt reactor or build a new reactor. Timelines for restoring the 5-MWt reactor are uncertain, although experts estimate between six months and one year. Rebuilding the cooling tower, which was destroyed in June 2008, could take approximately six months, but other venting solutions for the reactor could be possible. Additionally, this aging reactor may be in need of additional parts or repair. The fuel fabrication facility would have to be restored to produce additional fuel. Former Director of the Los Alamos National Laboratories, Siegfried Hecker, has said that while significant work is needed to do so, North Korea could restore operations at the 5 megawatt reactor and fuel fabrication facility without foreign equipment or materials, and could do so in approximately six months. After the facilities were operating, they could produce approximately 6 kg of plutonium per year.[105] Dr. Hecker confirmed this estimate again after his visit to North Korea in November 2010.[106] Significant future growth in North Korea's arsenal would be possible only if larger reactors were completed and operating, and would also depend on any progress in the reported uranium enrichment program.

Declaration

The required content of a "complete and correct" declaration as promised under the Six-Party negotiations evolved over time. Bush administration officials in fall 2007 said they expected the declaration to include a full declaration of the separated weapons-grade plutonium that has already been produced, as well as full disclosure of uranium enrichment activities.[107] The North Korean Foreign Ministry said on January 4, 2008 that it had notified the United States of the content of its declaration in November 2007. However, Assistant Secretary Hill said that the two sides had discussed what was expected to be in a declaration, and "it was clearly not a complete and correct declaration."[108] At that time, North Korea reportedly suggested it would declare 30 kg of separated plutonium in its declaration, a lower number than U.S. officials have alluded to (see above) but in the range of some analyses.[109] The United States has said that "materials, facilities and programs" need to be included in a declaration. In addition to plutonium stocks, North Korea agreed to "address concerns about a uranium enrichment program but denies that it has one" (see below). Other outstanding issues are nuclear proliferation activities and warhead information. North Korea has said it would not include warhead information at this stage. Once the original December 31 deadline for submission of the declaration had passed, U.S. officials emphasized that the completeness of the document was more important than its timing. U.S. officials also made statements in early 2008 that removal from sanctions lists would only happen after a complete declaration was submitted to the six parties.

According to press reports,[110] at a bilateral meeting in Singapore in April 2008, the United States and North Korea agreed to a formulation in which North Korea would include its plutonium production activities in a formal declaration, and the enrichment and proliferation issues would be dealt with separately in a secret side agreement in which North Korea would "acknowledge" the U.S. concerns over North Korean proliferation to Syria without confirming or denying them. This agreement is also supposed to have included a pledge by North Korea that it would not engage in any future nuclear proliferation. Administration officials in spring 2008 emphasized that ending plutonium production and tallying the plutonium stockpile were the highest priorities. However, concerns were raised in the Congress and elsewhere by those skeptical of this approach, with some observers wanting assurance that the North Korean declaration of its plutonium stockpile would be adequately verified before the United States removed them from the State Sponsors of Terrorism List.

On May 8, 2008, North Korean officials gave State Department Korean Affairs Director Sung Kim approximately 19,000 pages of documentation related to its nuclear program.

According to a State Department fact sheet, the documents consist of operating records for the five-megawatt reactor [5-MW(e)] and fuel reprocessing plant at the Yongbyon nuclear complex, dating back to 1986. They reportedly include reactor operations and information on all three reprocessing campaigns undertaken by North Korea.[111] As referenced above, press reports indicated that U.S. personnel had found traces of highly-enriched uranium on these documents, raising new doubts about the extent of North Korea's uranium enrichment program at a sensitive juncture in the negotiations.[112]

On June 26, 2008, North Korea submitted a declaration of its nuclear programs to China, the Chair of the Denuclearization Working Group. Ambassador Christopher Hill said in testimony to Congress that the "declaration package" addresses "its plutonium program, and acknowledged our concerns about the DPRK's uranium enrichment and nuclear proliferation activities, specifically with regard to Syria."[113] Press reports have said that North Korea submitted a list of nuclear sites and declared 37 kg of plutonium in the 60-page document. The confidential message acknowledging U.S. concerns about uranium enrichment and proliferation activities was received days earlier.[114] In response, also on June 26, 2008, President Bush announced that the Trading with the Enemy Act (TWEA) would no longer apply to North Korea and notified Congress of his intent to remove North Korea's designation as a State Sponsor of Terrorism (SST) after the required 45-day wait period.[115] The day after the declaration was submitted the U.S. assisted North Korea in destroying the cooling tower at the 5-megawatt reactor at Yongbyon. Subsequent verification issues are discussed below.

Verification

IAEA inspectors returned to North Korea in July 2007 to monitor and verify the shut-down, install seals, and monitor facilities at the Yongbyon nuclear complex, and had a continuous presence there until mid-April 2009.[116] In his September 10, 2007, statement to the IAEA Board of Governors, Director General Mohamed ElBaradei stated that the IAEA was able to verify the shutdown of nuclear facilities, including the nuclear fuel fabrication plant, radio-chemical laboratory (reprocessing plant), and the 5MWe experimental nuclear power reactor. Inspectors were also monitoring the halt in construction of the 50-megawatt nuclear power plant at Yongbyon and the 200-megawatt nuclear power plant in Taechon.[117] The United States has contributed $1.8 million as the U.S. voluntary contribution and Japan has contributed $500,000 to the IAEA for their work in North Korea.[118] In the future, the IAEA may be called on to investigate North Korea's past nuclear program in addition to monitoring activities; however, to date, its role was limited to monitoring the shut-down of Yongbyon facilities. The IAEA's role in disablement and future dismantlement efforts was not clearly determined. Some analysts recommended an observer role for the IAEA during disablement steps and continued IAEA monitoring to boost international confidence in the process.[119] The United States and North Korea reportedly agreed on an "consultative and support" role for the IAEA in future verification in October 2008.[120]

After IAEA inspectors were expelled from North Korea in 2002, information about North Korea's nuclear weapons production depended on remote monitoring and defector information, with mixed results. Satellite images correctly indicated the start-up of the 5MWe reactor, but gave no details about its operations. Satellites also detected trucks at Yongbyon in late January 2003, but could not confirm the movement of spent fuel to the reprocessing plant;[121] imagery reportedly detected activity at the reprocessing plant in April 2003, but could not confirm large-scale reprocessing;[122] and satellite imagery could not peer into an empty spent fuel pond, which was shown to U.S. visitors in January 2004. North Korean officials stated in 2004 that the reprocessing campaign was conducted continuously (four six-hour shifts). U.S. efforts to detect Krypton-85 (a by-product of reprocessing) reportedly suggested that some reprocessing had taken place, but were largely inconclusive. Even U.S. scientists visiting Pyongyang in January 2004 could not confirm North Korean claims of having reprocessed the spent fuel or that the material shown was in fact plutonium. These are some of the uncertainties verification measures will seek to answer.

Verification received increased attention in the Six-Party process beginning in spring 2008. Statements made by President Bush and Secretary of State Rice in June 2008 further demonstrated that the U.S. administration was linking SST removal with progress on verification issues.[123] U.S. officials have said there have been spoken agreements with the North Koreans saying that the only way the declaration can be deemed "complete and correct" is if it verifiable.

The State Department said in a June 26 fact sheet that by submitting the declaration, North Korea had "begun to fulfill its declaration commitment." The fact sheet also stated that a comprehensive verification regime would include "short notice access to declared or suspect sites related to the North Korean nuclear program, access to nuclear materials, environmental and bulk sampling of materials and equipment, interviews with personnel in North Korea, as well as access to additional documentation and records for all nuclear related facilities and operations." It also said that the actual rescission of North Korea's designation as a State Sponsor of Terrorism will occur only after "the Six Parties reach agreement on acceptable verification principles and an acceptable verification protocol; the Six Parties have established an acceptable monitoring mechanism; and verification activities have begun."[124]

On July 12, 2008, the Six Parties agreed unanimously to principles for a "verification mechanism" for the denuclearization of the Korean Peninsula, to be detailed by the denuclearization working group.[125] Thereafter, U.S. negotiators submitted a proposed verification protocol to North Korea called the "Verification Measures Discussion Paper" which outlined extensive measures to verify all aspects of North Korea's nuclear programs, including plutonium production, uranium enrichment, weapons, weapons production and testing, and proliferation activities.[126] North Korea reportedly submitted a counter-proposal that objected to provisions related to inspections at undeclared facilities and the taking of samples.

The 45-day wait period for the SST List removal ended on August 11, 2008, but the administration did not take action. On August 26, the North Korean news agency announced it had suspended disablement activities at Yongbyon as of August 14 since the United States had not removed it from the terrorism list. The North Korean Foreign Ministry statement said that the agreement had been to delist North Korea once it had submitted a declaration of its nuclear programs, not once verification measures had been agreed upon. It said, "As far as the verification is concerned, it is a commitment to be fulfilled by the six parties at the final phase of the denuclearization of the whole Korean Peninsula according to the September 19 joint statement.... All that was agreed upon at the present phase was to set up verification and monitoring mechanisms within the framework of the six parties."[127] The statement also threatened to restore facilities at Yongbyon.

On Monday, September 22, 2008, North Korea asked the International Atomic Energy Agency (IAEA) personnel monitoring the shut-down of facilities at the Yongbyon nuclear complex to remove the seals and surveillance equipment from the plutonium reprocessing plant. North Korea informed the IAEA that inspectors would no longer have access to that facility. IAEA inspectors and U.S. Department of Energy personnel located at Yongbyon were not expelled from the Yongbyon site, and other monitoring and inspection activities related to disablement continued. However, North Korea told the IAEA that it planned to "introduce nuclear material to the reprocessing plant in one week's time."[128]

These actions were reversed when, in early October, the US and North Korea agreed on a "verification mechanism" to determine the accuracy of the DPRK's declaration of its plutonium production. Ambassador Hill traveled to Pyongyang October 2-3 for further bilateral talks on the verification agreement. As a result of these talks, the US and DPRK reached agreement on verification measures. Although the document has not yet been made public, according to State Department officials North Korea has agreed to: the US taking samples out of country for review; visits to all declared sites and to undeclared sites by mutual consent; participation of South Korea and Japan in verification; and a consultative role for the IAEA.[129] They also agreed that "all measures contained in the Verification Protocol will apply to the plutonium-based program and any uranium enrichment and proliferation activities." According to the State Department's fact sheet on the agreement, the measures are "codified in a joint document between the United States and North Korea and certain other understandings." Many observers interpret "other understandings" as referring to verbal agreements or separate documents, but neither the United Stats nor North Korea have made this clear. The United States removed North Korea from the State Sponsors of Terrorism List on October 11.

Then-Presidential candidate Barack Obama issued a statement after the October 11, 2008 SST list removal that emphasized strong verification measures:

> If North Korea refuses to permit robust verification, we should lead all members of the Six Party talks in suspending energy assistance, re-imposing sanctions that have recently been waived, and considering new restrictions. Our objective remains the complete and verifiable elimination of North Korea's nuclear weapons programs. This must include getting clarity on North Korea's efforts to enrich uranium and its proliferation of nuclear technology abroad.[130]

Key concerns about the details of the tentative verification agreement as well as whether North Korea had actually agreed to the provisions surfaced soon after the announcement. For example, while State Department officials said that North Korea agreed to removal of samples from the country for analysis, North Korea statements in press reports contradicted this.[131] The Six Parties were unable to reach agreement on a codified version of the verification measures in their December 2008 meeting, as North Korea appeared to reject inclusion of sampling provisions.

As described above, verification and monitoring activities in North Korea ended when Pyongyang asked U.S. and international inspectors to leave the country on April 14, 2009.[132] North Korea reportedly told Bill Richardson in December 2010 that it would allow IAEA inspectors into the country to verify that the uranium enrichment plant built at Yongbyon was for peaceful purposes and was not producing highly enriched uranium (which could be used for weapons).[133]

Future Considerations

The DPRK committed in 2005 to abandoning "all nuclear weapons and existing nuclear programs" and to returning to the Non-Proliferation Treaty and IAEA safeguards at an early date.[134] If the DPRK decides to return to the Six-Party Talks and uphold these commitments, there will be a number of issues that have not yet been resolved.

The next stage, after disablement, was to have been the decommissioning and dismantlement of the weapons production facilities. The terms for this work still need to be negotiated. This stage may include a return of IAEA monitoring of nuclear material stocks (including weapons-usable separated plutonium) and verification of actual weapons dismantlement. The question of dismantling North Korea's nuclear warheads has not yet been addressed directly, although the September 2005 joint statement commits North Korea to abandon all nuclear weapons. Critics have raised concerns about the lack of clear verification provisions for these steps and the omission of specific references to key issues such as fissile materials, warheads, the reported uranium enrichment program, the nuclear test site, and nuclear proliferation activities and history (such as possible nuclear transfers to Syria).

Some analysts have proposed that the United States should be ready to implement cooperative threat reduction (CTR)-style programs in North Korea, as were created for the former Soviet Union.[135] These might include the redirection of North Korean nuclear weapon scientists to peaceful work.[136] North Korean officials have said that they are interested in eventually reorienting the Yongbyon workforce to the peaceful use of nuclear energy.[137] This could include research, medical and industrial applications, and not necessarily a nuclear power program.

PROLIFERATION ISSUES[138]

Concerns persist that North Korea will continue its proliferation of missile and nuclear technology for a variety of motivations, including financial profit, joint exchange of data to develop its own systems, and as part of the general provocative trend. According to DNI Admiral Dennis Blair's testimony to Congress in 2009, North Korea is known to have sold in the past ballistic missiles and associated materials to "several Middle Eastern countries, including Iran, and, in our assessment, assisted Syria with the construction of a nuclear reactor."[139] On the likelihood of nuclear proliferation from the DPRK, the DNI assessed that

> Pyongyang is less likely to risk selling nuclear weapons or weapons-quantities of fissile material than nuclear technology or less sensitive equipment to other countries or non-state actors, in part because it needs its limited fissile material for its own deterrent. Pyongyang probably also perceives that it would risk a regime-ending military confrontation with the United States if the nuclear material was used by another country or group in a nuclear strike or terrorist attacks and the United States could trace the material back to North Korea. It is possible, however, that the North might find a nuclear

weapons or fissile material transfer more appealing if its own stockpile grows larger and/or it faces an extreme economic crisis where the potentially huge revenue from such a sale could help the country survive.

- Due to concerns of proliferation and North Korea's past track record, the Security Council deliberations on a resolution condemning the May 2009 North Korean test focused on ways to interdict North Korean shipments of missile and WMD-related technologies and prevent their financing. U.N. Security Council Resolution 1874 calls on all states to "inspect, in accordance with their national legal authorities and consistent with international law, all cargo to and from the DPRK, in their territory, including seaports and airports," if that state has information that the cargo is prohibited by UN Security Council Resolutions. This would include cargo related to heavy arms (see UNSCR 1718 (8)(a)) and nuclear-related, ballistic missile-related, or other WMD-related programs. The resolution also calls on states to inspect suspect vessels on the high seas, with the consent of the flag state, and prohibits "bunkering services" for such shipments such as refueling or servicing. This is significant because North Korea reportedly ships most goods under its own flag, and typically uses small vessels that would need refueling. Reportedly due to objections by Russia and China, the resolution does not authorize the use of force if a North Korean vessel resists inspection.[140] The resolution also has strict provisions regarding financial services and transfer of funds through third parties, measures that may also help prevent proliferation-related transfers. Resolution 1874 bans all arms transfers from North Korea, and all arms transfers to North Korea except for small arms and light weapons (which require notification).

In addition, the Proliferation Security Initiative is a U.S.-led coordinating mechanism that is meant to guide international cooperation in carrying out interdictions of proscribed WMD and missile-related goods, including to or from North Korea.[141] China does not participate in PSI.

Therefore, a key question for implementation of the Security Council resolution will be China's commitment to actual interdiction measures and willingness of others to share sensitive information, particularly if Chinese firms are implicated, as has been the case in the past. Also, there is little emphasis on airspace interdictions, which would be relevant, for example, in the case of North Korean shipments passing over Chinese airspace on their way to the Middle East. However, questions remain about the true commitment of China and others to preventing WMD and missile-related transfers to and from North Korea, in particular because North Korea has stated it views any interdiction as an "act of war."

ISSUES FOR CONGRESS

Funding[142]

Congress will have a clear role in considering U.S. funding for any future dismantlement of North Korea's nuclear facilities, as well as other inducements for cooperation as agreed in the Six-Party Talks. U.S. assistance to nuclear disablement activities at Yongbyon was funded through the State Department's Nonproliferation and Disarmament Fund (NDF). The State Department paid the North Korean government for the labor costs of disablement activities, and also paying for related equipment and fuel. Approximately $20 million was approved for this purpose. NDF funds may be used "notwithstanding any other provision of law" and therefore may be used to pay North Korea. DOE's National Nuclear Security Administration (NNSA) has been contributing its personnel as technical advisors to the U.S. Six-Party delegation and as technical teams on the ground at Yongbyon overseeing disablement measures. NNSA has estimated it spent approximately $15 million in support of Phase Two (Yongbyon disablement) implementation.[143] Congress has also provided funding for energy assistance to North Korea under the Six-Party Talks through the State Department's Economic Support Fund.

Authority

Congress also plays a role in establishing legal authority for assistance to nuclear disablement and dismantlement in North Korea. Section 102 (b) (the "Glenn Amendment" *U.S.C. 2799aa-1*) of the Arms Export Control Act prohibits assistance to a non-nuclear weapon state under the NPT that has detonated a nuclear explosive device. Due to this restriction, DOE funds cannot be spent in North Korea without a waiver. Congress passed language in the FY2008 Supplemental Appropriations Act (P.L. 110-252) that would allow the President to waive the Glenn Amendment restrictions and that stipulates that funds may only be used for the purpose of eliminating North Korea's WMD and missile-related programs.[144] If the President had exercised the Glenn Amendment waiver authority, then DOE "will be able to procure, ship to North Korea, and use equipment required to support the full range of disablement, dismantlement, verification, and material packaging and removal activities that Phase Three will likely entail."[145] NNSA estimated that this would cost over $360 million in FY2009 if verification proceeded and North Korea agreed to the packaging and disposition of separated plutonium and spent fuel at Yongbyon. Because North Korea conducted an underground nuclear test on May 25, 2009, the waiver may no longer be issued under P.L. 110-252. The law stipulated that a nuclear test after the date of enactment would nullify the waiver authority.[146]

Congress had expressed concern that the Department of Energy have enough funds available to support the disablement of North Korea's nuclear weapons arsenal and production capability. In the FY2008 Consolidated Appropriations Act, the Committees on Appropriations provided DOE's NNSA with funding discretion to provide up to $10 million towards its activities in North Korea. It also directs the Department to submit a supplemental budget request if additional resources are required during FY2008.[147] However, due to North Korean withdrawal from the Six-Party Talks, Congress did not fund administration requests in the FY2009 Supplemental Appropriations or the FY2010 Consolidated Appropriations Act. The State Department's NDF, which did receive funding, could be used for denuclearization assistance in the case of a breakthrough in the talks.

Beyond the Glenn amendment restrictions, Department of Defense funds must be specifically appropriated for use in North Korea. Section 8045 of the FY2008 Defense Appropriations Act says that "None of the funds appropriated or otherwise made available in this Act may be obligated or expended for assistance to the Democratic People's Republic of Korea unless specifically appropriated for that purpose." Section 8044 of the FY2009 Consolidated Security, Disaster Assistance, and Continuing Appropriations Act, 2009 (P.L. 110-329) also contains this language. However, authorization was given for CTR funds to be used globally. The FY2008 Defense Authorization Act specifically encourages "activities relating to the denuclearization of the Democratic People's Republic of Korea" as a potential new initiative for CTR work. Senator Richard Lugar has proposed that the CTR program be granted "notwithstanding authority"[148] for this work since the Defense Department's experience in the former Soviet Union, expertise and resources could make it well-positioned to conduct threat reduction work in North Korea and elsewhere. The Department of Defense did not work on recent disablement efforts, but there may be a future role for DOD if North Korea in the future agrees to dismantlement work.

Policy Guidance

Congress may choose to influence the course of negotiations with North Korea through legislation that limits or places requirements on U.S. diplomatic actions. For example, the North Korean Counter-Terrorism and Non-Proliferation Act (H.R. 3650) introduced in the 110th Congress called for certification by the President that North Korea has met a range of nonproliferation and political benchmarks before the administration could lift any U.S. sanctions.[149] Congress could establish reporting requirements on progress, or condition appropriations or disbursement to North Korea upon verification measures.[150] Congress could also be involved in other aspects of potential changes in U.S. relations with Pyongyang, such as the monitoring of human rights issues, funding for further denuclearization steps including verification provisions, and establishment of normalized ties once nuclear dismantlement has been achieved. Congress also plays a role in setting sanctions policies, as in the bill Security through Termination of Proliferation Act of 2009 (H.R. 485).

Congress also sometimes gives its sense of what actions North Korea should take. House Resolution 1735, passed by the House on December 1, 2010, calls upon North Korea to

> immediately cease any and all uranium enrichment activities and take concrete steps to dismantle, under international verification and assistance, all sensitive nuclear facilities, in accordance with United Nations Security Council Resolutions 1695 (2006), 1718 (2006), and 1874 (2009);

This resolution was passed following North Korea's unveiling of a uranium enrichment plant at Yongbyon in November 2010 and its attack on Yeonpyeong Island.

End Notes

[1] See CRS Report R41259, North Korea: U.S. Relations, Nuclear Diplomacy, and Internal Situation, by Emma Chanlett-Avery and Mi Ae Taylor.

[2] Amb. Charles "Jack" Pritchard and Nicole M. Finneman of the Korea Economic Institute and Jean Pritchard traveled to North Korea from November 2-6, 2010. The next delegation from Stanford University included Dr. Siegfried Hecker and Professors John Lewis and Robert Carlin, who were at Yongbyon on November 12, 2010. A third unofficial delegation included U.S. academics Leon Sigal, Joel Wit and Morton Abramovitz in late November 2010. Then-Governor of New Mexico Bill Richardson traveled to North Korea on an unofficial visit with CNN correspondent Wolf Blitzer in mid-December 2010.

[3] The Six-Party Talks include the United States, South Korea, Japan, China, Russia and North Korea. See CRS Report R41259, North Korea: U.S. Relations, Nuclear Diplomacy, and Internal Situation, by Emma Chanlett-Avery and Mi Ae Taylor.

[4] Plutonium must be obtained by separating it from spent nuclear reactor fuel—a procedure called "reprocessing." See also CRS Report RL34256, North Korea's Nuclear Weapons: Technical Issues, by Mary Beth Nikitin.

[5] 5MWe is a power rating for the reactor, indicating that it produces 5 million watts of electricity per day (very small). Reactors are also described in terms of million watts of heat (MW thermal).

[6] See CRS Report RL33590, North Korea's Nuclear Weapons Development and Diplomacy, by Larry A. Niksch and CRS Report R40095, Foreign Assistance to North Korea, by Mark E. Manyin and Mary Beth Nikitin.

[7] "Adherence To and Compliance With Arms Control, Nonproliferation and Disarmament Agreements and Commitments," U.S. Department of State, August 2005.

[8] "Joint Statement of the Fourth Round of the Six-Party Talks, Beijing," September 19, 2005, at http://www.state.gov/r/ pa/prs/ps/2005/53490.htm.

[9] Second-Phase Actions for the Implementation of the September 2005 Joint Statement, October 3, 2007 http://www.state.gov/r/pa/prs/ps/2007/oct/93223.htm.

[10] Highly enriched uranium (HEU) has 20% or more U-235 isotope; 90% U-235 is weapons-grade.

[11] The physical principles of weaponization are well-known, but producing a weapon with high reliability, effectiveness, and efficiency without testing presents significant challenges.

[12] Plutonium that stays in a reactor for a long time (reactor-grade, with high "burn-up") contains about 20% Pu-240; weapons-grade plutonium contains less than 7% Pu-240.

[13] Hot cells are heavily shielded rooms with remote handling equipment for working with irradiated materials. For background, see Jared S. Dreicer, "How Much Plutonium Could Have Been Produced in the DPRK IRT Reactor?"Science and Global Security, 2000, vol. 8, pp. 273-286, at http://www.princeton.edu/sgs/publications/sgs/pdf/8_3Dreicer.pdf.

[14] Alloying plutonium with other materials is "common in plutonium metallurgy to retain the delta-phase of plutonium, which makes it easier to cast and shape" (two steps in weapons production). Hecker, January 21, 2004, testimony before SFRC.

[15] Transcript of December 29, 2002, Meet the Press.

[16] James Brooke, "North Korea says it has atom arms It will boycott talks on ending program; arsenal called self-defense against Bush," The New York Times, February 11, 2005.

[17] "We have enough nuclear bombs to defend against a U.S. attack. As for specifically how many we have, that is a secret." "North Korea Admits Building More Nuclear Bombs," ABC News, June 8, 2005, at http://abcnews.go.com/ WNT/story?id=831078&page=1.

[18] IAEA Safeguards Glossary: http://www-pub.iaea.org/MTCD/publications/PDF/nvs-3-cd/PDF/NVS3_scr.pdf.

[19] Siegfried Hecker estimates 40-50 kg of separated plutonium and 6 kg for the 2006 test; David Albright and Paul Brannan's study says 33-55 kg of separated plutonium and roughly 5 kg for the 2006 test. U.S. Assistant Secretary of State Christopher Hill cites 50 kg in his comments. Hecker, ibid. David Albright and Paul Brannan, "The North Korean Plutonium Stock February 2007," Institute for Science and International Security, February 20, 2007. Christopher Hill, "Interview on PBS NewsHour," October 3, 2007, at http://www.state.gov/p/eap/rls/rm/2007/93274.htm.

[20] Unclassified Report to Congress on Nuclear and Missile Programs of North Korea, Office of the Director of National Intelligence, August 8, 2007.

[21] "North Korea 'serious threat' to South," BBC News, http://news.bbc.co.uk/2/hi/asia-pacific/6216385.stm.

[22] Warren Strobel, "North Korean nuclear documents challenge CIA assertions," McClatchyNewspapers, May 28, 2008.

[23] "N.K. says plutonium 'weaponized' and off-limits," The Korea Herald, January 19, 2009.

[24] David Albright and Paul Brannan, "The North Korean Plutonium Stock February 2007."

[25] Siegfried Hecker, January 21, 2004, testimony before Senate Foreign Relations Committee.

[26] "North Korea Says It Has Made Fuel For Atom Bombs," New York Times, July 15, 2003.

[27] "North Koreans Claim to Extract Fuel for Nuclear Weapons," New York Times, May 12, 2005.

[28] David Albright and Paul Brannan, "The North Korean Plutonium Stock February 2007," Institute for Science and International Security, February 20, 2007.

[29] Technical difficulties associated with the fuel fabrication facility may have slowed how often the fuel was unloaded from the reactor, limiting production to at most one bomb per year. Siegfried Hecker, "Report on North Korean Nuclear Program," Center for International Security and Cooperation, Stanford University, November 15, 2006.

[30] IAEA Team Confirms Shut Down of DPRK Nuclear Facilities, http://www.iaea.org/NewsCenter/PressReleases/2007/prn200712.html.

[31] Siegfried Hecker, "The Risks of North Korea's Nuclear Restart," Bulletin of the Atomic Scientists, May 12, 2009, http://www.thebulletin.org/web-edition/features/the-risks-of-north-koreas-nuclear-restart

[32] Report by the Director General to the IAEA Board of Governors, "Applications of Safeguards in the Democratic People's Republic of Korea (DPRK)," GOV/2007/45-GC(51)/19, August 17, 2007.

[33] Siegfried Hecker, "Report on North Korean Nuclear Program," Center for International Security and Cooperation, Stanford University, November 15, 2006.

[34] Hecker January 21, 2004, testimony before SRFC.

[35] CIA unclassified point paper distributed to congressional staff on November 19, 2002.

[36] Siegfried Hecker, "A Return Trip to North Korea's Yongbyon Nuclear Complex," Center for International Security and Cooperation, Stanford University, November 20, 2010. http://iis-db.stanford.edu/pubs/23035/HeckerYongbyon.pdf

[37] Hecker's assumption is based on the chief process engineer's comment that the rotors were made of "iron". P-2 centrifuges use rotors made of maraging steel (vs. high-strength aluminum for the P-1 centrifuges). See Siegfried Hecker, "A Return Trip to North Korea's Yongbyon Nuclear Complex," Center for International Security and Cooperation, Stanford University, November 20, 2010. http://iis-db.stanford.edu/pubs/23035/HeckerYongbyon.pdf

[38] Ibid. A SWU is a "separative work unit", and refers to the thermodynamic work needed to produce nuclear fuel. For a description of SWU and comparison chart for SWU capacities at enrichment facilities worldwide, see page 13 of CRS Report RL34234, Managing the Nuclear Fuel Cycle: Policy Implications of Expanding Global Access to Nuclear Power, coordinated by Mary Beth Nikitin.

[39] Preliminary construction was shown to an earlier unofficial U.S. delegation from the Korea Economic Institute, led by Amb. Charles "Jack" Pritchard.

[40] ISIS Imagery Brief, "New Satellite Imagery of Yongbyon Shows Construction Progress on Experimental Reactor," Institute for Science and International Security web-site, November 18, 2010. http://isis-online.org/uploads/isis-reports/documents/Yongbyon_Light_Water_Reactor_Construction_18November 2010_200PM.pdf

[41] Siegfried Hecker, Comments at the Korean Economic Institute, November 23, 2010. The International Atomic Energy Agency estimates the amount of HEU needed to make a nuclear explosive device ("significant quantity") is 25kg of uranium enriched at 20% or more. http://www-pub.iaea.org/MTCD/publications/PDF/nvs-3-cd/PDF/ NVS3_prn.pdf

[42] Chris Buckley, "North Korea to allow in IAEA inspectors—Richardson," Reuters, December 21, 2010.

[43] David Albright and Paul Brannan, Taking Stock: North Korea's Uranium Enrichment Program, The Institute for Science and International Security, October 8, 2010. http://www.isis-online.org/uploads/isis-reports/documents/ ISIS_DPRK_UEP.pdf

[44] David Albright and Paul Brannan, Taking Stock: North Korea's Uranium Enrichment Program, The Institute for Science and International Security, October 8, 2010. http://www.isis-online.org/uploads/isis-reports/documents/ ISIS_DPRK_UEP.pdf

[45] Amb. Glyn Davies, "U.S. Statement to the IAEA: DPRK," IAEA Board of Governors Meeting, December 2-3, 2010, http://vienna.usmission.gov/101202dprk.html

[46] Pervez Musharraf, In the Line of Fire: A Memoir, (New York: Free Press, September 2006), p. 296.

[47] "NK Admits to Buying Aluminum Tubes," KBS World News, September 27, 2007, and Takashi Sakamoto, "DPRK Admits To Importing Aluminum Tubes From Russia for Uranium Enrichment," Yomiuri Shimbun, in Japanese, Translated by BBC Monitoring Asia Pacific, October 26, 2007.

[48] http://www.kcna.co.jp/item/2009/200906/news13/20090613-10ee.html.

[49] Hui Zhang, "Assessing North Korea's Uranium Enrichment Capabilities," Bulletin of the Atomic Scientists, June 28, 2009.

[50] "North Korean paper reports plans for uranium enrichment," BBC Monitoring Asia-Pacific, November 30, 2010.

[51] Unclassified Report to Congress January-June 2002, Central Intelligence Agency, https://www.cia.gov/library/reports/archived-reports-1/jan_jun2002.html#5

[52] http://www.fas.org/nuke/guide/dprk/nuke/cia111902.html.

[53] North Korea would first have to convert uranium "yellowcake" into uranium hexafluoride to feed into the centrifuges. The centrifuges would "enrich" the uranium, or increase the portion of U-235. Weapons-grade enriched uranium according to the IAEA needs to have an enrichment level of at least 20%. See CRS Report

RL34234, Managing the Nuclear Fuel Cycle: Policy Implications of Expanding Global Access to Nuclear Power, coordinated by Mary Beth Nikitin.

[54] Paul Kerr, "News Analysis: Doubts Rise on North Korea's Uranium-Enrichment Program," Arms Control Today, April 2007, at http://www.armscontrol.org/act/2007_04/NewsAnalysis.asp.

[55] "There has been considerable misinterpretation of the Intelligence Community's view of North Korean efforts to pursue a uranium enrichment capability. The intelligence in 2002 was high quality information that made possible a high confidence judgment about North Korea's efforts to acquire a uranium enrichment capability. The Intelligence Community had then, and continues to have, high confidence in its assessment that North Korea has pursued that capability. We have continued to assess efforts by North Korea since 2002. All Intelligence Community agencies have at least moderate confidence that North Korea's past efforts to acquire a uranium enrichment capability continue today." ODNI News Release 04-07, March 4, 2007, at http://www.dni.gov/press_releases/20070304_release.pdf.

[56] "Update on the Six Party Talks," Brookings Institution, February 22, 2007, at http://www.brookings.edu/events/2007/0222south-korea.aspx.

[57] Unclassified Report to Congress on Nuclear and Missile Programs of North Korea, Office of the Director of National Intelligence, August 8, 2007.

[58] See David Albright, "North Korea's Alleged Large-Scale Enrichment Plant: Yet Another Questionable Extrapolation Based on Aluminum Tubes," The Institute for Science and Security, February 23, 2007, at http://www.isis-online.org/ publications/dprk/DPRKenrichment22Feb.pdf.

[59] Siegfried Hecker, "Denuclearizing North Korea," Bulletin of the Atomic Scientists, May/June 2008.

[60] Glenn Kessler, "Uranium Traces Found on N. Korean Aluminum Tubes," Washington Post, December 21, 2007, at http://www.washingtonpost.com/wp-dyn/content/article/2007/12/20/AR2007122002196_pf.html.

[61] Glenn Kessler, "New Data Found On North Korea's Nuclear Capacity; Intelligence on Enriched Uranium Revives Questions About Weapons," The Washington Post, June 21, 2008.

[62] Senate Armed Services Hearing on the North Korean Six-Party Talks and Implementation Activities, July 31, 2008.

[63] Selig Harrison, "Did North Korea Cheat?" Foreign Affairs, vol. 84, no. 1, January/February 2005.

[64] Department of State, "Briefing on Recent Travel to North Korea," December 16, 2009, http://www.state.gov/p/eap/ rls/rm/2009/12/133718.htm

[65] "North Korea to Allow Nuclear Inspectors as Tension Eases, Richardson Says," Bloomberg News, December 21, 2010.

[66] See also CRS Report RL33709, North Korea's Nuclear Test: Motivations, Implications, and U.S. Options, by Emma Chanlett-Avery and Sharon Squassoni.

[67] "Analysis of air samples collected on October 11, 2006 detected radioactive debris which confirms that North Korea conducted an underground nuclear explosion in the vicinity of P.unggye on October 9, 2006. The explosion yield was less than a kiloton." ODNI News Release No. 19-06, at http://www.dni.gov/announcements/20061016_release.pdf.

[68] By comparison, a simple plutonium implosion device normally would produce a larger blast, perhaps 5 to 20 kilotons (KT). The first nuclear tests conducted by other states range from 9 KT (Pakistan) to 60 KT (France), but tests by the United States, China, Britain, and Russia were in the 20 KT range.

[69] Mark Mazzetti, "Preliminary Samples Hint at North Korean Nuclear Test," New York Times, October 14, 2006, at http://www.nytimes.com/2006/10/14/world/asia/14nuke.html.

[70] Thom Shanker and David Sanger, "North Korean fuel identified as plutonium," New York Times, October 17, 2006, at http://www.nytimes.com/2006/10/17/world/asia/17diplo.html. A debate on this issue can be found in the November 2006 issue of Arms Control Today, at http://armscontrol.org/act/2006_11/tech.asp#Sidebar1.

[71] Implosion devices, which use sophisticated lenses of high explosives to compress fissile material, are generally thought to require testing, although the CIA suggested in 2003 that North Korea could validate a simple fission nuclear weapons design using extensive high explosives testing. CIA response to questions for the record, August 18, 2003, submitted by the Senate Select Committee on Intelligence, at http://www.fas.org/irp/congress/2003_hr/021103qfrcia.pdf.

[72] Siegfried Hecker, "Report on North Korean Nuclear Program," Center for International Security and Cooperation, Stanford University, November 15, 2006.

[73] Ibid. Also see Peter Hayes, Jungmin Kang, "Technical Analysis of the DPRK Nuclear Test," Nautilus Institute, October 22, 2006, http://www.nautilus.org/fora/security/0689HayesKang.html.

[74] "UNSC Urged to Retract Anti-DPRK Steps," KCNA, April 29, 2009, http://www.kcna.co.jp/item/2009/200904/news29/20090429-14ee.html.

[75] http://earthquake.usgs.gov/eqcenter/recenteqsww/Quakes/us2009hbaf.php.

[76] Statement by the Office of the Director of National Intelligence on North Korea's Declared Nuclear Test on May 25, 2009, http://www.dni.gov/press_releases/20090615_release.pdf.

[77] http://www.ctbto.org/press-centre/highlights/2009/experts-sure-about-nature-of-the-dprk-event/.

[78] See also "Factfile: underground nuclear testing," BBC News, May 26, 2009, http://news.bbc.co.uk/2/hi/asia-pacific/ 6033893.stm.

[79] Unclassified Report to Congress on Nuclear and Missile Programs of North Korea, Office of the Director of National Intelligence, August 8, 2007. Also see CRS Report RS21473, North Korean Ballistic Missile Threat to the United States, by Steven A. Hildreth.

[80] Annual Threat Assessment of the Director of National Intelligence for the Senate Select Committee on Intelligence, February 5, 2008, at http://www.dni.gov/testimonies/20080205_testimony.pdf.

[81] "Technical Perspective on North Korea's Nuclear Test: A Conversation between Dr. Siegfried Hecker and Dr. GiWook Shin," Stanford University website, October 10, 2006, at http://aparc.stanford.edu/news/technicaljerspective_on_north_koreas_nuclear_test_a_conversation_between_dr_siegfried_hecker_and_dr_gi wook_s hin_20061010//.

[82] Annual Threat Assessment of the Director of National Intelligence for the Senate Select Committee on Intelligence, February 5, 2008, at http://www.dni.gov/testimonies/20080205_testimony.pdf.

[83] See, for example, North Korea's statement of February 10, 2005, at http://news.bbc.co.uk/2/hi/asia-pacific/ 4252515.stm.

[84] "North Korea says nuclear declaration submitted," Reuters, January 4, 2008.

[85] Blaine Harden, "With Obama in the White House, North Korea Steps Up Big Talk," Washington Post, February 3, 2009.

[86] See "North Korea" section of CRS Report R40439, Nuclear Weapons R&D Organizations in Nine Nations, coordinated by Jonathan Medalia.

[87] "DPRK military warns against sanctions for rocket launch," Xinhua, April 18, 2008.

[88] Joint Statement of the Fourth Round of Six Party Talks, Beijing, September 19, 2005, at http://www.state.gov/r/pa/ prs/ps/2005/53490.htm.

[89] United Nations Security Council Resolution 1718, October 14, 2006, at http://daccessdds.un.org/doc/UNDOC/GEN/ N06/572/07/PDF/N0657207.pdf?OpenElement.

[90] "Denuclearization Action Plan," February 13, 2007, at http://merln.ndu.edu/archivepdf/northkorea/state/80479.pdf.

[91] Second Phase Actions for the Implementation of the September 2005 Joint Statement, October 3, 2007, at http://www.state.gov/r/pa/prs/ps/2007/oct/93223.htm.

[92] On-the-Record-Briefing, U.S. Assistant Secretary of State Christopher Hill, October 3, 2007, at http://www.state.gov/p/eap/rls/rm/2007/93234.htm.

[93] "North Korea 'Agrees to Nuclear Disablement Procedure,'" Chosun Ilbo, October 27, 2007.

[94] David Albright and Paul Brannan, "Disabling DPRK Nuclear Facilities," United States Institute of Peace Working Paper, October 23, 2007.

[95] See charts at "North Korean Disablement Actions," Arms Control Today, October 2008; "Disablement Actions," National Committee on North Korea website.

[96] "N. Korea 'Slowing Disablement of Nuclear Facilities," Chosun Ilbo, January 29, 2008.

[97] Lee Chi-dong, "N Korea Complains About Slow Provision of Energy Aid," Yonhap News, June 5, 2008.

[98] "N. Korea can produce plutonium for 1.5 bombs in 6 months: expert," Kyodo News, April 25, 2009.

[99] Kim So-hyun, "N.K. says it reprocessed 8,000 spent fuel rods," The Korea Herald, November 4, 2009.

[100] "MOFAT Reveals North Korean Fuel Rod Images," Daily North Korea, February 4, 2009. http://www.dailynk.com/ english/read.php?cataId=nk03100&num=4516.

[101] John Pomfret, "North Korea suggests discarding one of its nuclear arms programs in deal," The Washington Post, November 22, 2010.

[102] IAEA Press Release, "IAEA Removes Seals at Yongbyon," September 24, 2008.

[103] Peter Crail, "North Korea Moves to Restart Key Nuclear Plant," Arms Control Today, October 2008.

[104] For a discussion of the pro's and con's see sidebar "A Diplomatic and Technological Cocktail," Bulletin of the Atomic Scientists, May/June 2008, p.49.

[105] "North Korea can produce plutonium for 1.5 bombs in 6 months," Japan Economic Newswire, April 25, 2009.

[106] Siegfried Hecker, "A Return Trip to North Korea's Yongbyon Nuclear Complex," Center for International Security and Cooperation, Stanford University, November 20, 2010. http://iis-db.stanford.edu/pubs/ 23035/HeckerYongbyon.pdf.

[107] On-The-Record Briefing: Assistant Secretary of State for East Asian and Pacific Affairs and Head of the U.S. Delegation to the Six-Party Talks Christopher R. Hill, October 3, 2007, at http://www.state.gov/p/eap/rls/rm/2007/ 93234.htm.

[108] Joint Press Availability, Assistant Secretary of State Christopher R. Hill, January 7, 2008. http://www.state.gov/p/ eap/rls/rm/2008/01/98756.htm.

[109] David Albright, Paul Brannan, and Jacqueline Shire, "North Korea's Plutonium Declaration: A Starting Point for an Initial Verification Process," The Institute for Science and International Security, January 10, 2008. http://www.isisonline.org/publications/dprk/NorthKoreaDeclaration10Jan2008.pdf.

[110] See, for example, Helene Cooper, "Past Deals by N. Korea May Face Less Study," The New York Times, April 18, 2008. http://www.nytimes.com/2008/04/18/washington/18diplo.html?_r= 2&adxnnl=1&oref=slogin&ref=world& adxnnlx=1208545358-9gpsLj35wtiPmoT8RHM6mQ and Glenn Kessler, "U.S. Ready to Lift Sanctions on North Korea," The Washington Post, April 11, 2008. http://www.washingtonpost.com/wp-dyn/content/article/2008/04/10/ AR2008041004082.html?nav=emailpage.

[111] "Update on the Six-Party Talks," State Department Fact Sheet, May 10, 2008. http://www.state.gov/r/pa/prs/ps/2008/may/104558.htm.

[112] Glenn Kessler, "New Data Found On North Korea's Nuclear Capacity; Intelligence on Enriched Uranium Revives Questions About Weapons," The Washington Post, June 21, 2008.

[113] Statement of Christopher R. Hill, Assistant Secretary of State, Bureau of East Asian and Pacific Affairs, U.S. Department of State, to the Senate Committee on Armed Services, July 31, 2008.

[114] Glenn Kessler, "Message to US Preceded North Korean Nuclear Declaration," The Washington Post, July 2, 2008.

[115] http://www.whitehouse.gov/news/releases/2008/06/20080626-4.html; http://www.state.gov/r/pa/prs/ps/2008/jun/ 106281.htm.

[116] "IAEA Team Confirms Shut Down of DPRK Nuclear Facilities," IAEA press release, July 18, 2007, at http://www.iaea.org/NewsCenter/PressReleases/2007/prn200712.html.

[117] GOV/2007/45-GC(51)/19, August 17, 2007.

[118] Statement of Christopher R. Hill Assistant Secretary, Bureau of East Asian and Pacific Affairs, Department of State before the House Committee on Foreign Affairs, Subcommittee on Asia, the Pacific and the Global Environment and Subcommittee on Terrorism, Nonproliferation and Trade, Joint Hearing on the North Korea Six-Party Process, October 25, 2007.

[119] North Korea reportedly did not want the IAEA involved and wanted the United States to do the disabling. Albright and Brannan, ibid.

[120] "U.S.-North Korea Understandings on Verification," October 11, 2008. http://2001-2009.state.gov/r/pa/prs/ps/2008/ oct/110924.htm.

[121] "Reactor Restarted, North Korea Says," Washington Post, February 6, 2003.

[122] "US Suspects North Korea Moved Ahead on Weapons," New York Times, May 6, 2003.

[123] "President Bush Discusses North Korea," White House press release, June 26, 2008; Condoleezza Rice, "U.S. Policy Toward Asia," Heritage Foundation speech, June 18, 2008.

[124] "North Korea: Presidential Action on State Sponsor of Terrorism (SST) and the Trading with the Enemy Act (TWEA)," State Department Fact Sheet, June 26, 2008. http://www.state.gov/r/pa/prs/ps/2008/jun/106281.htm.

[125] Press Communique of the Heads of Delegation Meeting of the Sixth Round of the Six-Party Talks, Beijing, July 12, 2008. http://www.mofa.go.jp/region/asia-paci/n_korea/6party/press0807.html.

[126] This paper was made public by the Washington Post. Glenn Kessler, "Far-Reaching U.S. Plan Impaired North Korea Deal," The Washington Post, September 26, 2008.

[127] "Foreign Ministry's Spokesman on DPRK's Decision to Suspend Activities to Disable Nuclear Facilities," KCNA, August 27, 2008. http://www.kcna.co.jp/index-e.htm.

[128] http://www.iaea.org/NewsCenter/PressReleases/2008/prn200813.html.

[129] See October 11, 2008 State Department Press Statement http://2001-2009.state.gov/r/pa/prs/ps/2008/oct/110924.htm and Fact Sheet http://2001-2009.state.gov/r/pa/prs/ps/2008/oct/110924.htm.

[130] Statement of Senator Barack Obama on the Agreement with North Korea, October 11, 2008.

[131] "SKorea to press for sampling at NKorean nuke plants," Agence France Presse, November 14, 2008. http://news.yahoo.com/s/afp/20081113/wl_asia_afp/nkoreanuclearweaponsskoreaus.

[132] "IAEA Inspectors Asked to Leave the Democratic People's Republic of Korea," IAEA Press Release, April 14, 2009, http://www.iaea.org/NewsCenter/PressReleases/2009/prn200903.html.

[133] Chris Buckley, "North Korea to allow in IAEA inspectors—Richardson," Reuters, December 21, 2010.
[134] http://2001-2009.state.gov/r/pa/prs/ps/2005/53490.htm.
[135] Joel Wit, Jon Wolfsthal, Choong-suk Oh, "The Six Party Talks and Beyond: Cooperative Threat Reduction in North Korea," CSIS Press, December 2005. http://www.csis.org/media/csis/pubs/051216_ctr.pdf.
[136] David Albright, "Phased International Cooperation with North Korea's Civil Nuclear Programs," Institute for Science and International Security, March 19, 2007. http://www.isis-online.org/publications/dprk/CivilNuclearNK.pdf.
[137] "North Korea and Its Nuclear Program—A Reality Check," A Report to Members of the Committee on Foreign Relations, United States Senate, October 2008, S. Prt. 110-50.
[138] Also see "Nuclear Collaboration with Iran and Syria" in CRS Report RL33590, North Korea's Nuclear Weapons Development and Diplomacy, by Larry A. Niksch, and "Clandestine Nuclear Program and the IAEA Investigation" in CRS Report RL33487, Syria: Issues for the 112th Congress and Background on U.S. Sanctions, by Jeremy M. Sharp.
[139] http://intelligence.senate.gov/090212/blair.pdf.
[140] Blaine Harden, "North Korea Says It Will Start Enriching Uranium," Washington Post, June 14, 2009.
[141] For background on PSI, see CRS Report RL34327, Proliferation Security Initiative (PSI), by Mary Beth Nikitin.
[142] For a detailed discussion, see CRS Report R40095, Foreign Assistance to North Korea, by Mark E. Manyin and Mary Beth Nikitin.
[143] Statement of William H. Tobey, National Nuclear Security Administration, U.S. Department of Energy, to the Senate Committee on Armed Services, July 31, 2008.
[144] Similar language appeared in the Senate version of the FY2009 Duncan Hunter National Defense Authorization Act (P.L. 110-417), but was not included in the House version. The final act includes it under "legislative provisions not adopted" under Title XII, since the waiver authority was passed earlier in the FY2008 Supplemental. See joint explanatory note: http://armedservices.house.gov/pdfs/fy09ndaa/FY09conf/FY2009NDAAJointExplanatoryStatement.pdf.
[145] Tobey testimony, ibid.
[146] In P.L. 110-252 Sec. 1405 (b)(3), there is an exception for activities described in Subparas A or B of section102(b)1 of AECA. This includes "transfers to a non-nuclear weapon state a nuclear explosive device," and "is a non-nuclear-weapon state and either (i) receives a nuclear explosive device, or (ii) detonates a nuclear explosive device."
[147] See p. 50 of http://www.rules.house.gov/110/text/omni/jes/jesdivc.pdf.
[148] So that funds may be used "notwithstanding any other provision of law." Senator Richard Lugar, Remarks to National Defense University, October 2, 2008. http://lugar.senate.gov/record.cfm?id=304026&&.
[149] This bill was introduced and referred to the House Committee on Foreign Affairs. H.R. 3650, September 25, 2007.
[150] For example, see S.Res. 399.

In: North Korea: Nuclear Weapons and the Diplomacy Debate   ISBN: 978-1-62100-450-9
Editor: Brian N. Thompson   © 2012 Nova Science Publishers, Inc.

Chapter 4

NORTH KOREA'S 2009 NUCLEAR TEST: CONTAINMENT, MONITORING, IMPLICATIONS*

Jonathan Medalia

SUMMARY

On May 25, 2009, North Korea announced that it had conducted its second underground nuclear test. Unlike its first test, in 2006, there is no public record that the second one released radioactive materials indicative of a nuclear explosion. How could North Korea have contained these materials from the May 2009 event and what are the implications?

As background, the Comprehensive Nuclear-Test-Ban Treaty (CTBT) would ban all nuclear explosions. It was opened for signature in 1996. Entry into force requires ratification by 44 states specified in the treaty, including the United States and North Korea. As of November 2010, 153 states, including 35 of the 44, had ratified. North Korea has not signed the CTBT. President Clinton signed it in 1996; in 1999, the Senate voted not to consent to its ratification. In 2009, President Obama pledged to press for its ratification.

The treaty establishes a verification mechanism, including an International Monitoring System (IMS) to detect nuclear tests. Three IMS technologies detect waves that pass through the oceans (hydroacoustic), Earth (seismic), or atmosphere (infrasound); a fourth detects radioactive material from a nuclear test. Scientists concur that only the latter proves that an explosion was nuclear. Some believe that deep burial and other means can contain radioactive effluents. Another view is that containment is an art as much as a science. The United States learned to improve containment over several decades. Yet by one estimate, North Korea contained over 99.9% of the radioactive effluents from its 2009 test. It might have done so by application of lessons learned from its 2006 test or the U.S. nuclear test experience, use of a higher-yield device, release of material below the detection threshold, good luck, or some combination. Alternatively, the 2009 event may have been a nonnuclear explosion designed to simulate a nuclear test.

Containment could be of value to North Korea. It could keep radioactive fallout from China, Japan, Russia, or South Korea, averting an irritant in relations with them. It could

---

* This is an edited, reformatted and augmented version of a Congressional Research Service publication, CRS Report for Congress R41160, from www.crs.gov, dated November 24, 2010.

prevent intelligence services from gathering material that could reveal information about the weapon that was tested. It could permit North Korea to host nuclear tests by other nations, such as Iran; while such tests would be detected by seismic means, they could not be attributed to another nation using technical forensic means if effluents, especially particles, were contained.

An issue for Congress is how containment could affect CTBT prospects. Supporters might argue that explosion-like seismic signals without detected radioactive material would lead to calls for an onsite inspection. Opponents might claim that only detection of radioactive material proves that a nuclear explosion occurred. Both would note inspections could not be required unless the treaty entered into force, supporters to point to a benefit of the treaty and opponents to note that North Korea could block inspections by not ratifying the treaty. Congress may wish to consider ways to improve monitoring capability, such as supporting further research on test signatures, improving monitoring system capability, and deploying more monitoring equipment. This update reflects developments in the North Korean uranium program and prospects for another nuclear test.

BACKGROUND

On May 25, 2009, North Korea announced that it had conducted a nuclear test.[1] The test produced seismic signals characteristic of an explosion, indicating that they were generated by human activity. They were detected by at least 61 seismic stations. However, no radioactive materials were reportedly detected, in contrast to the first North Korean test on October 9, 2006. Such materials could confirm that the test was nuclear. Although a sample size of one is not sufficient to draw conclusions with high confidence, the possible ability of North Korea to contain radioactive materials from a nuclear test could be of value for that nation. This report presents what is known publicly about the tests, discusses detection and containment of nuclear tests, explores the possible significance of containment for North Korea, and raises, as issues for Congress, implications for the Comprehensive Nuclear-Test-Ban Treaty (CTBT) and possible means of improving U.S. and international ability to monitor nuclear testing.

States currently possessing nuclear weapons would probably need to conduct nuclear tests to develop more advanced designs and, some argue, to ensure that existing weapons are safe, secure, and reliable. States with fledgling nuclear weapon programs could design and deploy the simplest type of nuclear weapon without testing,[2] but such weapons make very inefficient use of scarce fissile material and are heavy and bulky. To develop small, rugged, powerful warheads for long-range missiles, these states would need to conduct nuclear tests.

Nonnuclear experiments can answer some questions important to the design of nuclear weapons, but many processes essential to the functioning of a nuclear weapon can only be studied under the conditions of an actual nuclear test. Each test not only shows whether a device "works" or "fails," but also provides much more data. Many technical disciplines contribute to a test, and each gains data from it. Weapon designers learn how the design might be improved, physicists gain data on the science underlying nuclear explosions, metallurgists gain data on how uranium or plutonium deforms under pressure, engineers can discover unanticipated flaws arising from manufacturing processes, physicists who design computer models of nuclear weapon performance gain data to refine their models, electrical engineers gain data to improve the instrumentation for collecting nuclear test data, radiochemists can analyze radioactive samples from the test for data on the yield and performance of the device, and those involved in preventing radioactive material from escaping from the test gain data to improve containment.

Because testing is crucial for developing weapons, efforts to ban nuclear tests have been underway for decades as an arms control measure.[3] The multilateral 1963 Limited Test Ban Treaty banned atmospheric, space, and underwater tests. The U.S.-Soviet Threshold Test Ban Treaty and Peaceful Nuclear Explosions Treaty, signed in 1974 and 1976, respectively, limited underground nuclear explosions to a yield of 150 kilotons.[4] Both entered into force in 1990.

In an attempt to extend these bans to cover all nuclear tests, negotiations on the CTBT were completed in 1996. The treaty's basic obligation is to ban all nuclear explosions. It establishes an International Monitoring System (IMS) to monitor signs of an explosion. The treaty contains procedures for authorizing and conducting on-site inspections (OSIs), which would search the site of a suspected nuclear test for evidence of the test, and permits data from national technical means of verification as well as from the IMS to be used to support a request for an OSI.

As of November 2010, 182 nations had signed the treaty and 153 of them had ratified.[5] To enter into force, 44 specified nations, basically those with a nuclear reactor in 1995 or 1996, must all ratify. As of November 2010, 35 had done so; the others are China, Egypt, India, Indonesia, Iran, Israel, North Korea (the Democratic People's Republic of Korea, DPRK), Pakistan, and the United States. The U.S. Senate voted not to give its advice and consent to ratification of the treaty, 48 for, 51 against, and 1 present, in 1999. Two uncertainties that led to its defeat concerned U.S. ability to verify compliance with the treaty and U.S. ability to maintain its nuclear stockpile without testing. In April 2009, President Obama pledged to pursue U.S. ratification of the CTBT "immediately and aggressively."[6]

THE NORTH KOREAN NUCLEAR TESTS

The 2006 Test

North Korea conducted its first nuclear test on October 9, 2006. It was clearly nuclear because it released radioactive materials. The U.S. Office of the Director of National Intelligence (ODNI) released this statement: "Analysis of air samples collected on October 11, 2006 detected radioactive debris which confirms that North Korea conducted an underground nuclear explosion in the vicinity of P'unggye on October 9, 2006. The explosion yield was less than a kiloton."[7] (ODNI declined to state whether "debris" referred to particulates, gases, or both.[8]) According to a press report, "American intelligence agencies have concluded that North Korea's test explosion last week was powered by plutonium that North Korea harvested from its small nuclear reactor, according to officials who have reviewed the results of atmospheric sampling since the blast."[9] In a similar vein, the Comprehensive Nuclear-Test-Ban Treaty Organization (CTBTO) Preparatory Commission (PrepCom) stated, "Two weeks after the event, the radionuclide noble gas station at Yellowknife, Canada, registered a higher concentration of Xenon 133. Applying atmospheric transport models to backtrack the dispersion of the gas, its registration at Yellowknife was found to be consistent with a hypothesized release from the event in the DPRK."[10] The Swedish Defence Research Agency (FOI) used atmospheric models at a much shorter distance. It flew mobile xenon analysis equipment to South Korea and began collecting samples within three days of the test. "All the samples were found to contain radioactive xenon and, in combination with meteorological information, FOI were able to conclude that the gas did, with a relatively high level of probability, originate from the area in North Korea where the explosion took place."[11]

The 2009 Test

North Korea announced on May 25, 2009, that it had conducted a second nuclear test. ODNI stated: "The U.S. Intelligence Community assesses that North Korea probably conducted an underground nuclear explosion in the vicinity of P'unggye on May 25, 2009. The explosion yield was approximately a few kilotons. Analysis of the event continues."[12] The lack of certainty as to whether the test was nuclear arises because seismic signals, including those detected by 61 stations of the IMS,[13] were consistent with a nuclear test, and seismic signals from the 2006 and 2009 events were very similar,[14] but open sources did not report the detection of physical evidence that would provide conclusive proof of a nuclear test, such as certain radioactive isotopes of noble gases or radioactive particulates (i.e., fallout). For example, the CTBTO PrepCom stated,

> The detection of radioactive noble gas, in particular xenon, could serve to corroborate the seismic findings. Contrary to the 2006 announced DPRK nuclear test, none of the CTBTO's noble gas stations have detected xenon isotopes in a characteristic way that could be attributed to the [2009] DPRK event so far, even though the system is working well and the network's density in the region is considerably higher than in 2006.
> ...
> Nor have CTBTO Member States using their own national technical means reported any such measurements. Given the relatively short half-life of radioactive xenon (between 8 hours and 11 days, depending on the isotope), it is unlikely that the IMS will detect or identify xenon from this event after several weeks.[15]

It would be desirable to establish if the event was nuclear because the possibility that chemical explosives caused the seismic waves could undermine confidence in the ability to verify compliance with the CTBT. Earthquakes can be differentiated from explosions (whether chemical or nuclear) because their seismic waves have different characteristics. But while seismic signals from the 2009 event were consistent with a nuclear test, it is very difficult to differentiate between seismic signals generated by a nuclear test and a chemical explosion of comparable energy, so it is conceivable that the test was nonnuclear. Geoffrey Forden, a scientist at MIT, posits a scenario in which a room could be filled with 2,500 tons of TNT, enough to create an explosion within the yield range estimated for the 2009 North Korean test, in two months using about four 10-ton truckloads per day. He finds this scenario "quite doable and to be potentially undetectable by the West."[16] The United States conducted large aboveground[17] and underground[18] tests using chemical explosives to simulate some effects of nuclear explosions.

The CTBTO PrepCom cites analysis that rejects the chemical-explosive possibility:

Verification technology experts such as Professor Paul Richards from the Lamont-Doherty Earth Observatory, Columbia University, USA, considered the scenario of a "bluff", i.e. the creation of a nuclear explosion-like seismic signal using conventional explosives. While technically possible, he stated that it was highly implausible. As CTBTO seismic data have clearly indicated an explosion of a yield many times greater than that of 2006, it would have required several thousand tons of conventional explosives to be fired instantaneously. Richards explained that such a massive logistical undertaking would have been virtually impossible under the prevailing circumstances and would not have escaped detection.[19]

Specifically, satellite imagery might have detected preparations for a large chemical explosion, and if the explosives did not detonate instantaneously, they could have caused a seismic signal with characteristics of a chemical explosion.[20]

Questions about whether the May 25 event was nuclear or nonnuclear remain unresolved. Onsite inspections could prove conclusively that a test was nuclear, but they could only be conducted if the CTBT were to enter into force, or if North Korea gave its permission outside the treaty. Other ways to establish (but not necessarily prove) that an explosion was nuclear are nonseismic means, such as communications intercepts and satellite imagery; note that high-quality commercial satellite imagery is available for purchase. The CTBT envisions that some monitoring technologies not part of the IMS could be added (Article IV, paragraphs 11, 23) to that system if agreed pursuant to the treaty's amendment process (Article VII).

The apparent absence of radioactive material released from the May 25 event raises several questions: How can such material be detected? How might North Korea have contained its second test? What are some implications of successful containment for North Korea? What issues do detection and containment raise for Congress? This report now turns to these questions.

MONITORING AND CONTAINING NUCLEAR TESTS

Monitoring, Verification, Intelligence

Central concerns in negotiating an arms control agreement are to establish a regime that facilitates detection of cheating and to ensure, insofar as possible, that a state party to the treaty cannot gain an advantage by cheating. To this end, the CTBT, the CTBTO, and individual nations would take several interlocking steps. The first is monitoring, which provides technical data on suspicious events. The treaty establishes the IMS, which is one of several components in the verification regime established by Article IV of the treaty. Verification refers to determining whether a nation is in compliance with its treaty obligations, which in this case means determining whether a suspicious event was a nuclear test. The treaty establishes the verification regime in great detail: Article IV takes up nearly half the treaty, and the Protocol, which provides details on the verification regime, is nearly as long as the treaty itself. The verification regime, in addition to the IMS, includes provisions for consultation and clarification of suspicious events; an International Data Center (IDC) to analyze IMS data and distribute the results to states parties to the treaty; detailed provisions for on-site inspections; and confidence-building measures. As one of its functions, the Provisional Technical Secretariat of the CTBTO PrepCom operates the verification regime.[21]

The treaty (Article IV, paragraph 14) does not direct the Technical Secretariat to determine that a particular nation has cheated. But while some IMS sensors (e.g., seismic) can only provide evidence that a nuclear test may have occurred, IMS radionuclide sensors would prove that a nuclear test had occurred if they found certain types of radioactive debris, and an OSI would prove that a nuclear test had occurred at a particular location if it found the radioactive cavity left by an underground nuclear test. Once the verification regime provides data and analysis of suspected or actual nuclear tests to the states parties, the role of the Technical Secretariat would end. In the event of a suspected violation, the Conference of the States Parties, pursuant to Article V, paragraphs 3 and 4, "may recommend to States Parties collective measures which are in conformity with international law," or the conference or the Executive Council "may bring the issue ... to the attention of the United Nations."[22]

In judging how to respond, nations would use various means to determine whether the event was a nuclear test, combining data and analysis from multiple sources, such as the International Data Center; national technical means of verification; non-technical means, such as information from people and open sources; and other governments and nongovernmental organizations. But because of background noise, limitations of detectors, etc., it is almost a truism that there will always be some threshold below which a nuclear test cannot be unambiguously identified by seismic and other IMS technologies. As a result, a decision on a nation's response to a suspected nuclear test would depend not on perfect verification but on effective verification. In 1988, Paul Nitze offered a widely-used definition: by effective verification, "[w]e mean that we want to be sure that, if the other side moves beyond the limits of the treaty in any militarily significant way, we would be able to detect such violation in time to respond effectively, and thereby deny the other side the benefit of the violation."[23] Judgments on the effectiveness of verification have been crucial in consideration of past nuclear testing treaties; this is likely to be the case for any future CTBT debate as well.

Beyond that, some nations can be expected to use their intelligence capabilities to learn more than whether an event was a nuclear test. They will want to know such details as weapon yield, weapon fuel (uranium or plutonium), and weapon design to understand how quickly a nation's weapons program is advancing, what problems it is encountering, and what development path it is following. In some cases, such as a nuclear detonation in a remote ocean area or by terrorists, technical analysis may support attribution of the detonation to a specific nation.

Monitoring Nuclear Tests

Because a nuclear test generates immense amounts of energy and radioactive material, it presents many signatures by which it can be detected, some at a distance of thousands of miles, others only on site. Atmospheric tests are easy to detect because of their radioactive fallout. China conducted the most recent atmospheric nuclear test in October 1980.[24] Underwater tests are also easy to detect, though attribution may be a problem. Satellites (not part of the IMS) can detect nuclear tests in space, though some evasion scenarios have been suggested. A particularly difficult environment in which to detect clandestine tests is underground, and is the one relevant to North Korean nuclear testing, since both of its tests were conducted in that manner.

When completed,[25] the IMS will have 321 monitoring stations, 16 laboratories, and an International Data Center to process data. A Global Communications Infrastructure will link IMS facilities, the data center, and member states. As of November 2010, 248 monitoring stations and 10 laboratories were operational.[26] The IMS uses four technologies to detect nuclear tests:[27]

Seismic: Seismographs detect various types of waves (e.g., pressure waves) moving through the Earth.[28] The science of seismology has made great progress over the last half-century in filtering out seismic signals characteristic of explosions from other seismic signals, such as by using more sensitive instruments and more elaborate data-processing algorithms. However, there are some scenarios for concealing the seismic signals from low-yield tests that have been hotly debated for many years, as discussed later. Analysis of seismic and other waves cannot by itself prove that an explosion was nuclear; for example, it is difficult if not impossible to distinguish by seismic means between a nuclear explosion and a large (e.g., 1,000-ton) chemical explosion that is designed to mimic a nuclear explosion and is successfully conducted.

Hydroacoustic: Hydrophones can detect a very small underwater chemical explosion at distances of thousands of miles as pressure waves generated by the explosion move through the water, so an underwater nuclear explosion would be readily detected.[29] While this method might detect some nuclear tests conducted on land, such as on a small island, there were no reports that it was of use in detecting the 2009 North Korean test.

Infrasound: Sensors measure very small changes in atmospheric pressure caused by very low frequency acoustic waves. Infrasound sensors are not at present intended for monitoring of underground nuclear explosions, though they did detect the 2009 North Korean test.[30] The observed magnitude of the infrasound signal, approximately three tons of TNT equivalent[31] vs. several kilotons for the seismic signal,[32] indicated the explosion was not at the Earth's surface.[33]

Radionuclides: To gain direct physical evidence that an explosion was nuclear, the IMS monitors for radioactive particles and gases. When complete, it will have 80 stations that can detect radioactive particulates, of which 40 will also have equipment to detect radioactive forms of xenon, which are of particular value for detecting a nuclear explosion. The resulting data are sent to the IDC and national data centers for analysis. As of November 2010, 59 particulate stations, of which 25 had radioxenon collection capability, were operational.

Many technological advances made in recent years improve the ability to detect nuclear explosions. These include techniques to image the Earth's inner structure to better understand how that structure affects seismic waves,[34] use of satellite-borne "radar imaging technology to detect near-vertical surface deformations measuring less than 1 centimeter caused by underground disturbances,"[35] development of equipment to detect extremely low levels of radioactive noble gases,[36] development of computer models of wind patterns, use of seismic waves detected at regional as well as longer distances to improve the ability to discriminate between earthquakes and explosions,[37] and the rollout of the IMS.[38]

To resolve uncertainties over whether suspicious events—such as any that generate explosion-like seismic signals but do not release radioactive material—are nuclear, the CTBT provides for onsite inspections (OSIs). OSIs would search for signatures that can only be detected at a test site, such as small amounts of several radioactive noble gases, certain non-gaseous radioactive materials,[39] physical signs of a test (e.g., melted snow, changes to vegetation, pebbles thrown in bushes by ground shock), and the underground cavity formed by a nuclear test (found by drilling) that would have tell-tale radioactive debris. The treaty and its Protocol include great detail on authorization and conduct of an inspection. Article IV (verification), paragraph 56, of the treaty requires each state party to permit OSIs.[40] Of course, OSIs pursuant to the treaty could only occur after the treaty had entered into force, though it is possible that OSIs could be done outside the treaty regime, such as if requested by one country before the treaty enters into force to prove that it had not conducted a nuclear test, or pursuant to a bilateral agreement permitting one state to monitor another state's nuclear test site.

The United States has its own technical means of detecting nuclear explosions, which the Air Force Technical Applications Center (AFTAC) operates. AFTAC "operates and maintains a global network of nuclear event detection sensors called the U.S. Atomic Energy Detection System.

Once the USAEDS senses a disturbance underground, underwater, in the atmosphere or in space, the event is analyzed for nuclear identification and findings are reported to national command authorities through Headquarters U.S. Air Force."[41] USAEDS predates the CTBT, and in the course of negotiations for that treaty, some USAEDS monitoring stations were included as contributing stations to the IMS. Similarly, in addition to performing independent analyses of events as the operator of USAEDS, AFTAC has a formal role under the CTBT as the U.S. National Data Center to receive data from the International Data Center.

What Radioactive Materials Can a Nuclear Test Release into the Atmosphere and How Can They Be Detected at a Distance?

An underground nuclear test may be fully contained, or it may release two types of material, particulates and gases, into the atmosphere. Either may prove that a nuclear test occurred. Gases include radioactive isotopes of noble gases (gases that are chemically inert), such as krypton-85, argon-37, and several xenon isotopes.

Krypton-85 is of little value for nuclear detection at a distance because a substantial background of this isotope is present in the atmosphere. Most of it is generated by nuclear power plants and is released when the spent fuel is reprocessed, but since its half-life is 10.76 years, some remains from past atmospheric nuclear tests.[42]

Argon-37 (half-life 35.04 days) is of value for onsite inspections and is not—but perhaps could be—used for long-range detection. It is produced when neutrons interact with calcium-40 in soil or rock.[43] While naturally-occurring neutrons produce a background of argon-37,[44] that mechanism would not produce a local concentration of the isotope. Therefore, finding a local concentration of it at the site of a suspected underground nuclear explosion would be an indicator of a nuclear explosion, making it of value for OSIs; one source calls it "a definitive and unambiguous indicator of a nuclear underground explosion."[45] Some believe that argon-37 could be detected at long range. Professor Roland Purtschert, Department of Climate and Environmental Physics, University of Bern, Switzerland, an expert on argon-37, states,

> I am very confident that instruments could be developed that could operate automatically at remote locations to detect argon-37 from underground nuclear tests. At present, radioxenon detection equipment used by the International Monitoring System concentrates xenon isotopes from a large volume of air. It should be possible to separate

argon from this same air sample, keep the argon sample as a backup, and measure the fraction of argon-37 when xenon isotopes indicate a possible nuclear explosion. The amount of argon-37 from a nuclear test that is detected would depend on the bomb yield, the rate at which the isotope is released from the underground explosion cavity to the atmosphere, and the sensitivity of the detection system.

I also think that it would be desirable to develop such instruments and deploy them as part of the International Monitoring System. The atmospheric background for argon-37 is very low and constant (about 0.5 to 1 nuclei decaying per second per 1000 cubic meters of air). Civilian sources generate large quantities of xenon and krypton isotopes. As a result, elevated xenon concentrations, for example, become unambiguous indicators of a nuclear explosion only in combination with atmospheric transport modeling. In contrast, there are virtually no civilian sources for argon-37, and the background is low due to argon-37's short half-life. At the same time, the half-life is long enough to allow for the isotope to be transported from the cavity of a nuclear explosion to the atmosphere.[46]

Since argon-37 is produced from neutron reactions on calcium in the soil, neutrons from a nuclear explosion will produce that isotope if calcium is present. It appears that calcium is present almost everywhere. For example, one text states that calcium "is the fifth most abundant element in the earth's crust.... Vast sedimentary deposits of [calcium carbonate], which represent the fossilized remains of earlier marine life, occur over large parts of the earth's surface."[47] It makes up some 4% of the Earth's crust.[48] Even if there were a potential test site devoid of calcium, it would be difficult for a would-be evader to find that site and then to be certain that no calcium was present. In addition, the soil would need to be free of potassium as well because a reaction of a neutron with a potassium atom can produce argon-39, which would be detected in the same way as argon-37.

One value of long-range detection of argon-37 from a nuclear test is that it has a longer half-life than radioxenons, enabling detection at a distance for a longer time. A second value is that ensuring that no argon-37 seeps out, in addition to making sure no other effluents leak out, would increase the difficulty of conducting a nuclear test clandestinely. A third value, pointed out by Charles Carrigan, a geophysicist at Lawrence Livermore National Laboratory, is that detection of a seismic signal characteristic of an explosion followed by simultaneous detection of a spike in radioxenons and in argon-37 would be a compelling indicator of a nuclear explosion.[49]

While the radiation emitted when argon-37 decays has a much lower energy than gamma rays produced by radioactive decay of many other elements, that energy "can be detected with special techniques with relative ease," according to Ted Bowyer, a physicist at Pacific Northwest National Laboratory who specializes in atmospheric detection of radioactive isotopes of noble gases.[50]

There are several uncertainties regarding the use of argon-37 for long-range detection of nuclear explosions. First, what is the background level of that isotope from natural and human sources? While the background appears to be low, a definitive conclusion would require further study. Second, can an automated system for detecting this isotope be designed and fielded? While it can be detected in the laboratory, or in the field using manual equipment, an automated system would be needed if detectors are to be placed at remote locations, such as IMS radionuclide stations. Carrigan notes a third uncertainty: the detectability of argon-37 would depend on the rate at which it reaches the surface. If a nuclear test released a large quantity promptly, the isotope would be much easier to detect at long range than if it were released over days or weeks.

Radioactive isotopes of xenon ("radioxenons") are of great value for long-range detection, and the noble gas detection equipment deployed at some IMS radionuclide stations monitors only for them.[51] They are produced by nuclear explosions and nuclear reactors. Nuclear explosions also generate iodine-133 (half-life, 20.8 hours) and iodine-135 (half-life, 6.6 hours), which decay into xenon-133 and xenon-135, respectively. Radioxenons can be detected in minute quantities at great distances, but such detection must be accomplished soon after a nuclear test because of short half-lives. The half-life of xenon-133, an isotope of particular value for identifying nuclear explosions, is 5.24 days, so long-range detection can only be done within about 3 weeks of a test.[52] The other radioxenons of use for monitoring nuclear tests are xenon-135 (half-life, 9.14 hours), xenon-133m (half-life, 2.19 days), and xenon-131m (half-life, 11.84 days).[53]

Several techniques and technologies have greatly improved the ability to detect radioxenons worldwide over the past several decades. As a result, it is possible to detect and identify a particular form of radioxenon thousands of miles from its source within a few weeks of a nuclear test, during which time it will have been reduced to a minute concentration through radioactive decay and mixing with air. IMS equipment takes in large quantities of air, separates and collects any xenon, and compresses the latter to a small volume. Various techniques then acquire data for transmission to the IDC for analysis. One is gamma-ray spectroscopy.[54] Gamma rays are high-energy photons emitted by atomic nuclei when they undergo radioactive decay. Each radioxenon emits gamma rays in a pattern, or spectrum, of energies that uniquely identifies its source. Figure 1 illustrates the combined spectra of four radioxenons. The horizontal axis has a range of energies measured in keV, or thousands of electron volts; the vertical axis records the number of gamma rays detected at each energy from a sample of a specified mass in a specified time. For example, the spectrum for xenon-133m in Figure 1 has a peak at 233 keV. Another technique, known as beta-gamma coincidence counting, relies on the simultaneous emission of a beta particle (an electron or positron) and an 81-keV gamma ray when an atom of xenon-133 decays. This signature is unique to xenon-133 and is insensitive to background radiation, so it can be detected even in minute concentrations of xenon-133.[55] Improved sensitivity of radioxenon detection instruments enhances such techniques.

Once radioxenons are detected and identified, the data can be used for long-range detection of nuclear tests in at least three ways. One is to use atmospheric transport modeling (ATM). ATM can help determine the region (as opposed to a precise location) where a nuclear test was conducted by calculating the path of air masses that may be carrying radioactive materials. It uses a computer model to assemble millions of pieces of data collected in near real time by weather satellites, World Meteorological Organization stations,[56] and the IMS network. The model then generates wind speed and direction at many points across a wide area. It can then be "put in motion." Like a movie, the model can be run forward to show the movement of air masses in order to predict the future path of radionuclides released at a precise location. Alternatively, it can be run in reverse to backtrack radionuclides from a specific point (e.g., an IMS radionuclide station) to a region where they may have originated, a process called source region attribution. Source region data may be fused with other data, e.g., IMS seismic observations, using a software graphics tool to narrow the location of a suspected nuclear explosion.

In 2006, IMS noble gas equipment at Yellowknife, Canada, detected xenon-133 some two weeks after the North Korean nuclear test. The measurement could not be traced back to known releases at nuclear facilities (e.g., a nuclear reactor at Chalk River, Canada, used in part to produce radiopharmaceuticals[57]). Instead, ATM showed that the detection was consistent with a hypothesized release of radionuclides taking place in North Korea at the place and time of the event.[58]

Combining this fact with the level of sensitivity of the detectors,[59] IDC staff concluded that "the containment of any generated xenon (under the hypothesis that this was a nuclear test) was above 99.9 percent" for the 2009 event.[60]

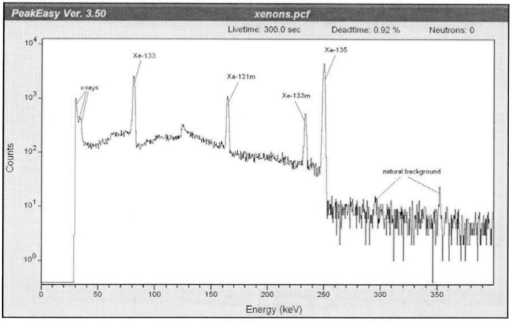

Source: Provided by Scott Garner, Technical Staff Member, Los Alamos National Laboratory, October 15, 2009.

Notes: Radioactive isotopes of xenon emit gamma rays when they decay. Each of these isotopes emits gamma rays in a particular pattern, or spectrum, with a peak at a particular energy. The gamma rays can be counted, and the number of counts at each energy plotted on a graph. This graph and its peak can be used to differentiate one xenon isotope from another.

Figure 1 shows the lower-energy part of a gamma-ray spectrum taken with a "Detective," a small, commercially-available high-purity germanium detector. The source is a small sample (less than a billionth of a gram each) of xenon-131m, -133, -133m, and -135. According to Garner, "The relative quantities I have displayed here do not even remotely represent the relative quantities seen in actual samples, but were chosen to make it obvious that the different isotopes are easy to tell apart from each other when a strong enough signal is present."

Technical details: The sample is composed of 2.45E-10 grams (7.66E+05 Becquerels) of Xe-131m, 1.50E-11 grams (1.0E+05 Becquerels) of Xe-133, 6.22E-12 grams (1.0E+05 Becquerels) of Xe-133m, and 1.07E-12 grams (1.0E+05 Becquerels) of Xe-135. ("E" is an abbreviation for exponent; one Becquerel is one decay per second.) The source is located 25 centimeters in front of the detector and the data were taken for 300 seconds.

Figure 1. Gamma-ray Signatures of Four Radioactive Isotopes or Isomers of Xenon.

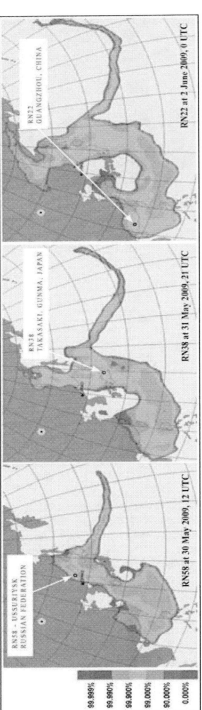

Source: Robert Pearce et al., "The Announced Nuclear Test in the DPRK on 25 May 2009," *CTBTO Spectrum*, September 2009, p. 28.

Notes: (modified from text of source report) This figure shows the distribution of a hypothetical radioactive xenon plume at the time of its highest concentration at the IMS radioxenon station indicated in each image. These stations were operational at the time of the 2009 North Korean test. Only those parts of the plume above the minimum detectable concentration are shown. The plume was calculated assuming (1) immediate venting at the time and place of the 2009 North Korean test and (2) zero containment corresponds to the full release of the xenon-133 generated by a four-kiloton nuclear explosion. The key on the left shows the degree of containment of the test. (The online version of this report shows the graphic in color.) For 90% containment, the detectable plume would cover only the areas in green, yellow, and orange. For 99.9% containment, the detectable plume would cover the areas in green, yellow, and orange. The fact that these stations did not record xenon-133 signals at the time each would have experienced the maximum concentration of that isotope is the basis on which the authors, who are past or current employees of the International Data Center, "concluded that the containment of any generated xenon (under the hypothesis that this was a nuclear test) was above 99.9 percent." The yellow circle at the upper left of each image is a radioxenon station in Mongolia, the only such station operating in this region at the time of the 2006 North Korean nuclear test.

Figure 2. Atmospheric Transport Modeling; Basis for Concluding 2009 North Korean Test Was >99.9% Contained.

Second, "most of the environmentally occurring radio-xenon has been produced with nuclear reactors producing radiopharmaceutical materials."[61] Monitoring releases of such reactors can rule out particular reactors as the source of radioxenons at a specific time, as was the case in analyzing the Yellowknife data following the 2006 test. The ratio of certain radioactive xenon isotopes may also prove whether the xenon came from a nuclear test or a nuclear reactor.[62]

Third, if samples are collected and analyzed within hours of a nuclear test, the ratio of xenon-135 to xenon-133 may indicate whether the nuclear explosive was fueled by uranium or plutonium.[63] This information is of interest for analyzing characteristics of the nuclear device, but is not needed to determine whether the test would violate the CTBT if that treaty were to enter into force, which requires only knowing if the test was nuclear. Don Barr, a retired Los Alamos radiochemist with over 50 years of nuclear testing and related experience, calculates that the window for such determination is only an hour or two.[64] Another ratio, xenon-133m/xenon-131m, may enable differentiation between these fuels for a longer time.[65] The IMS could not perform ratio analysis for the 2006 North Korean test because the station at Yellowknife detected only xenon-133 two weeks after the event; xenon-135 was presumably not detected because of its shorter half-life. Jungmin Kang, Frank von Hippel, and Hui Zhang explain a further reason why ratio analysis is of value for only a short time:

> Most of the xenon isotopes released into the atmosphere during the first few hours after a test would have been produced directly from the nuclear fission. In this period, therefore, the ratios of different xenon isotopes could be used to discriminate between plutonium and HEU explosives. Within two days after an explosion, however, most of the xenon isotopes would come indirectly from the decay of radioactive iodines that are produced in almost the same ratio from plutonium-239 and uranium-235 fission.[66]

Thus "while it is true that there is some possibility of determining fuel type from xenon ratios, it would likely be a slim chance."[67]

Nuclear tests may also release particulates, which may contain fission products from the weapon,[68] unfissioned atoms of uranium and plutonium, and melted bits of soil or rock. They range in size from a centimeter in diameter or larger to 0.1 mm or smaller,[69] often less than 0.001 mm. The smaller they are, the farther they can travel before "falling out" to the ground. For decades, particulates have provided not only evidence of a test but other details as well. For example, in 1949, U.S. Air Force "sniffer" aircraft flying over the Pacific Ocean collected particulate samples on filters. A commercial laboratory "dissolved [the filters], chemically separated a selection of fission products such as radioactive isotopes of barium, cerium, molybdenum, zirconium and lead, carefully measured the rates of radioactive decay of the isotopes and counted back to establish when each isotope had been created—its radioactive birthday. Only if all the birthdays were identical could the isotopes have been created in an atomic bomb."[70] Analysis of this sort enabled the United States to conclude that the Soviet Union had conducted its first atomic bomb test on August 29, 1949. According to one report, "During the first 50 years of the nuclear weapons era, radiochemistry techniques were developed and used to determine the characteristics (such as yield, materials used, and design details) of nuclear explosions carried out by the United States and by other countries."[71] As another example of the capability to analyze particulate samples, several researchers, in a 010 report, analyzed a 7.5- gram sample of debris from "Trinity," the first U.S. nuclear test (1945), and were able to reach several conclusions on the characteristics of the test device.[72] IMS radionuclide stations collect particles on a filter, analyze the gamma-ray spectra on location, and transmit the results to the International Data Center. If a station's filter collects two or more types of particulates that are relevant to CTBT verification, the sample would be shipped to an IMS laboratory to confirm detection and to conduct more detailed investigation. Figure 3 shows the IMS radionuclide stations closest to North Korea. As it shows, some are not yet in service, some are planned to have radionuclide monitoring stations but not noble gas monitoring equipment prior to entry into force of the CTBT, and there are gaps of many hundreds of kilometers or more between stations.

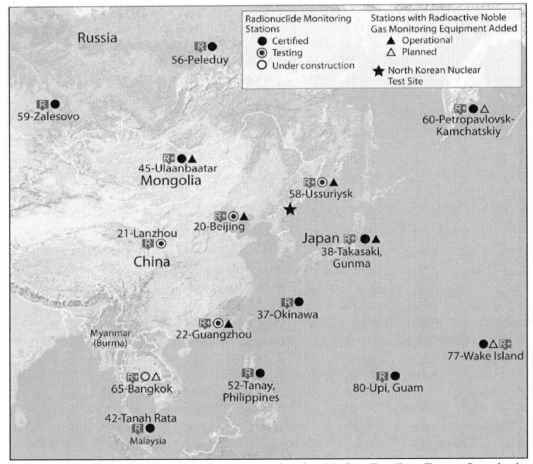

Source: Map with station locations from Comprehensive Nuclear-Test-Ban Treaty Organization Preparatory Commission, station names and symbols by CRS.

Notes: Numbers are those assigned to the stations by Annex 1 to the Protocol of the Comprehensive NuclearTest-Ban Treaty. "Certified" stations have been certified by the Provisional Technical Secretariat as meeting its technical standards and are fully operational.

Figure 3. Radionuclide Monitoring Stations of the International Monitoring System; As of February 2010.

Background levels of radionuclides in the atmosphere can vary at radionuclide stations due to patterns of weather, season, or climate, and to sources of radioactive material other than current nuclear tests, such as iodine-131 and technetium-99m from hospitals and cesium-137 from past atmospheric nuclear tests. Because of this background variation from place to place and time to time, a single measurement may not mean anything unless placed in context with this variation. Accordingly, the Provisional Technical Secretariat, in collaboration with other organizations, measures and characterizes background levels at each radionuclide station to help determine whether an elevated level of radioxenons may have come from a nuclear test.

Releases of radionuclides from an underground nuclear test can occur in any of three ways. One is referred to as "vents." They generally occur promptly, and vary in size from very small (and undetectable at long distances) to large (and easily detectable at long distances). Figure 4 depicts large vents from two U.S. tests. Vents occur when high-pressure gas generated by an explosion finds a path to the surface, often by a leak in the sealing, or "stemming," of the excavated hole or tunnel, or by a natural fracture in the rock that reaches the ground surface. Unfavorable geology of the test site can contribute to venting in other ways. Certain geologic formations tend to have more preexisting fractures, raising the probability of vent paths. Carbonates in rock produce carbon dioxide when heated by an explosion, raising the pressure of gas in the cavity left by the explosion and thus the probability of venting.

Source: "Des Moines," Lawrence Livermore National Laboratory; "Baneberry," U.S. Department of Energy.

Figure 4. Venting of Nuclear Tests; "Des Moines" 1962 (left), "Baneberry" 1970 (right).

A nuclear explosion turns water in rocks into steam, adding pressure in the explosion cavity that can lead to venting. The Soviet Union found that, at least in some instances, a significant amount of water and carbonate rock led to seeps (discussed next) and venting at its Novaya Zemlya test site, while the opposite conditions at its Semipalantinsk (Kazakhstan) test site did not.[73] Noble gases, being less chemically reactive than other gases and particulates, will always be released by a large vent; seeps and smaller vents release predominantly noble gases, with very little or no particulate matter.[74] It is likely that the first North Korean test vented, since it apparently released enough radioxenon to be detected two weeks later at Yellowknife.

A second class of release from an underground nuclear test is known as a "seep." Seeps tend to release much smaller amounts of radioactive material, and the released material is generally limited to noble gases and possibly volatile elements, notably radioactive iodine. Seeps do not occur promptly, but instead release at much lower rates, potentially over periods of weeks to months. Seepage can occur through porous rock or small fractures in the rock. Seeps are potentially detectable at the test site by an OSI, offering confirmation of a test. However, seeps occurring more than a few weeks after the detonation are unlikely to release amounts in quantities that could be detected hundreds of miles away by IMS or other monitoring systems.

Seeps and vents both result when high-pressure gases generated by a nuclear explosion escape from the explosion-generated cavity by way of pathways in the surrounding geology or stemming material. When pressure drops sufficiently, seeps and vents cease.

A third class of release, "barometric pumping," relies on a different mechanism that enables gases to reach the surface even after gas pressure in the cavity has dropped to a level of equilibrium with its surroundings. A decrease in atmospheric pressure, such as occurs during a storm, lowers the pressure in fractures terminating near the surface so that the relative pressure in the cavity end of a fracture becomes greater. This pressure differential draws noble gases upward toward the Earth's surface. As gases flow upward in a fracture, they also diffuse into the porous walls of the fracture and are temporarily stored there even when increased atmospheric pressure causes gases in a fracture to flow downward. The stored gases are available to diffuse from the porous walls into the next upward flow of gases in the fracture. Thus barometric pumping creates a ratcheting effect that eventually can transport noble gases to the surface after seeps and vents induced by pressure within the cavity have ceased.[75] Barometric pumping would probably not aid long-range detection because quantities of radioactive noble gases released through this mechanism are small and can take many weeks to reach the surface, during which time most of these gases will have undergone radioactive decay, but it can produce enough of these gases to be detected by an OSI.

How Can Radioactive Material Be Contained?

Containment is no simple matter. According to a National Academy of Sciences report, "Recent Russian papers documenting Soviet nuclear testing state that all underground tests at Novaya Zemlya and about half the underground tests at the Semipalatinsk test site in Kazakhstan resulted in release of radioactivity."[76] While fewer U.S. nuclear tests released radioactivity, containment failures did occur. For example, Figure 4 shows the "Des Moines" nuclear test. It was conducted in June 1962 at the Nevada Test Site, and had an explosive yield of 2.9 kilotons, comparable to the "few kilotons" of yield that the U.S. Office of the Director of National Intelligence assessed for the North Korean event of May 2009. Figure 4 also shows "Baneberry," a 10-kiloton test conducted at the Nevada Test Site in December 1970.

The United States went to great lengths to contain nuclear tests. Containment relies on a detailed understanding of how well the geology around the nuclear device may contain the explosion and an ability to engineer containment, such as by sealing the test shaft. Barr said, "Deep burial of a nuclear device, combined with gas blocking techniques, virtually eliminates the seepage of noble gases to the surface, though some such gases might occasionally be detected, but only at the surface above the detonation point."[77] On the other hand, knowledge of the geology surrounding a nuclear explosive is imperfect, so there may be hidden pathways for vents and seeps. As a result, there is an element of art and chance to containment:

> The earth, from the surface to the mile or so in depth that has been used in underground nuclear testing is an inhomogeneous body of materials ... it is not possible to know all, or even most, of the details of the medium where the detonation takes place.
> So, empirical rules are developed, approximations are made and are used in computer codes to model the behavior of the earth materials following a detonation, but there is a further complication. Important processes occur during a time span that ranges from fractions of a microsecond to hours....
> In such a situation experience and empirical evidence from previous detonations assumes a considerable importance when trying to judge what will happen when a particular detonation takes place in some specific location. The experience and evidence that there is has been gathered over the years, sometimes in a costly fashion.[78]

The unclassified U.S. literature contains information on containing a test. A 1977 publication by the Departments of Defense and Energy provides data on how deeply to bury a nuclear explosive device to contain radioactive gases.[79] A 1989 Office of Technology Assessment (OTA) report provides technical details. It notes that containment properties of rock depend on its type, structure, and water content; lists some U.S. procedures used to evaluate containment; and provides diagrams of mechanisms used to contain various types of nuclear tests.[80] A 1995 report sponsored by Lawrence Livermore National Laboratory and the Defense Nuclear Agency provides further details.[81]

Better techniques can greatly improve containment. For the United States, improvement occurred in two major steps. The Limited Test Ban Treaty, which bans nuclear tests in the atmosphere, in space, and under water, was signed on August 5, 1963. Before that date, "no specific test containment design criteria existed. Therefore, while radioactive effluents released from underground tests conducted during this period [September 15, 1961, to August 5, 1963] were not always expected, any effluent releases that did occur were not considered accidental, or even unexpected."[82] After August 5, 1963, "all tests (except four Plowshare cratering tests) were designed to be completely contained underground."[83] Following Baneberry, the Atomic Energy Commission instituted new containment practices.[84] In consequence, while the Department of Energy reported that 101 of 335 U.S. nuclear tests conducted from August 5, 1963, through 1970 accidentally released radiation, it reported that 6 of 388 tests conducted from 1971 through the most recent U.S. nuclear test, in 1992, did so.[85] In addition, small amounts of noble gases seeped into the atmosphere and were detected, onsite only, days to years after five tests from 1984 to 1989,[86] and radioactive material was released intentionally after quite a few post-1970 tests, such as by drilling back into the cavity to collect samples for analysis.[87] The 1989 OTA report provided another view of the effectiveness of post-Baneberry containment: "If the same person had been standing at the boundary of the Nevada Test Site in the area of maximum concentration of radioactivity for every test since Baneberry (1970), the person's total exposure would be equivalent to 32 extra minutes of normal background exposure (or the equivalent of 1/1000 of a single chest x-ray)."[88] Some U.S. nuclear tests that were not reported as releasing radioactive material might have done so, but the amount released may have been below the detection threshold for instruments available at the time.

While there is no publicly-available information on whether North Korea attempted to contain its second test, and if so what methods it used, containment could have resulted from one of the following factors, or a combination of several:

Lessons learned from the first test: As noted, a nuclear test provides data for many disciplines
involved with the test. North Koreans involved in containment would have learned lessons from the first test applicable to the second test, including how such factors as stemming methods, depth of burial, and type of rock affect containment.

Lessons learned from the experience of other nations: These lessons deal with such factors as depth of burial, type of stemming, and geologic considerations, as discussed previously.

Use of a higher-yield nuclear device: It can be harder to contain lower-yield underground nuclear explosions than higher-yield ones. The latter produce more energy, which pushes outward against the surrounding rock, which then rebounds toward its original position. OTA states, "the rebounded rock locks around the cavity forming a stress field that is stronger than the pressure inside the cavity. The stress 'containment cage' closes any fractures that may have begun and prevents new fractures from forming."[89] A nuclear explosion melts rock, forming a glass-like substance. These effects can seal leak paths, especially fractures in the rock through which noble gases or particulates might escape. Sealing is more likely for a higher-yield test. While both North Korean tests were of low yield, the second reportedly had several times the yield of the first.

Good luck: North Korea may have, by chance, selected a test site with solid rock having no fissures, or with another geology favorable to containment, and may have used enough material to seal the test shaft or tunnel solidly enough to contain radioactive material. As noted, even in the period before 1963, when there was no particular effort made to contain U.S. underground nuclear tests, quite a few of them did not have measured releases of radioactivity.

Venting below the detection threshold: The standard for IMS radioxenon equipment is the ability to detect one atom of xenon-133 decaying per second per thousand cubic meters of air (the minimum detectable concentration).[90] In practice, the equipment is more sensitive than that.[91] While this threshold has become lower over the years, it is greater than zero. It is thus possible that the test vented, but that the quantity of material released was below the detection threshold.

Nonnuclear explosion: The May 25 event may not have been a nuclear test, which would explain the lack of radioactive effluents.

While evidently not the case for the 2009 test, as Figure 2 implies, attention to atmospheric conditions could impede detection of radionuclides and thus contribute to the appearance of containment. Waiting to conduct a test until wind currents were blowing away from IMS or national radionuclide stations could prevent these stations from collecting radionuclides.

Given the learning curve, potential failure modes of containment, and the sensitivity of detection equipment, it would be a significant achievement if North Korea had, by design, been able to hold venting of its second test to below the current detection threshold. At the same time, one test that apparently did not release radioactive effluents is too small a sample size from which North Korea, the United States, or other nations could draw firm conclusions as to North Korea's containment capability. That nation's ability to contain any future tests thus bears close watching.

POTENTIAL VALUE OF CONTAINMENT FOR NORTH KOREA

The ability to contain radioactive material from the 2009 test offers several potential benefits for North Korea. First, careful attention to containment should reduce the likelihood of a major venting of fallout similar to Baneberry. Venting would arguably not be in North Korea's interests. Fallout reaching China could harm North Korea's relationship with its major ally, perhaps leading China to increase pressure on North Korea to halt nuclear testing or even its nuclear weapons program. Fallout reaching Russia could have a similar effect. Fallout on Japan or South Korea would likely antagonize them. Fallout on North Korea could contaminate land. Avoiding fallout is reason enough for North Korea to try to improve its containment capabilities.

Second, if particulates containing uranium or plutonium vented and could be collected at a distance, other nations could analyze them in an attempt to gain data on weapon characteristics, helping to track problems and progress of North Korea's nuclear weapons program. This is another reason for North Korea to focus on containment of its underground explosions.

Third, absence of radionuclides from a nuclear test, as a result of containment, could make it harder to muster the 30 votes in the 51-member CTBTO Executive Council needed to authorize an OSI by providing scientific cover to nations that wanted to deny a request for an OSI on political grounds. This approach could be more significant for a nation with more allies than North Korea has. On the other hand, a lack of radioactive noble gases combined with a nuclear explosion-like seismic signal and other technical evidence would provide a compelling technical case for requesting an OSI. Of course, the surer way for North Korea to avert OSIs would be for that nation not to ratify the CTBT, keeping it from entering into force.

Fourth, and more speculatively, successful containment could enable other nations to conduct nuclear tests in North Korea. This does not appear to have happened, but Iran is a possible candidate. The two have a record of conventional arms trade and missile cooperation.[92] Events in 2009, such as the discovery of a covert facility for uranium enrichment, increased suspicions that Iran is pursuing nuclear weapons. It is not unprecedented for one nation to "host" another's nuclear tests: the United Kingdom conducted 24 tests jointly with the United States at the Nevada Test Site between 1962 and 1991.[93]

Iranian testing in North Korea would aid the latter by providing data for weapons development and giving the impression that its nuclear weapons program was proceeding rapidly. Such testing would aid Iran by helping it develop nuclear weapons while potentially avoiding consequences of a test in Iran, such as an attack on its nuclear facilities. In particular, an extremely low yield test (e.g., 0.5 kilotons) conducted in Iran might be interpreted as a failure, inviting attack before the weapons program developed further, while a larger test (e.g., 20 kilotons) in Iran might deter attack. Conducting one or two tests in North Korea might avert the former contingency. This arrangement would demand high confidence in North Korea's containment ability so as to deny radioactive samples by which the test could be attributed to its partner. Analysis of these samples might reveal if the bomb fuel was uranium or plutonium, details of the bomb design, and perhaps which reactor produced the fuel. While particulate samples convey more data than do gases, the ability to contain gases would imply a strong ability to contain particulates.

Several factors argue against this scenario. Iran might use nuclear tests in Iran to demonstrate its nuclear capability as a deterrent, to gain leverage in the Middle East, and to show its people that other nations could not dictate its nuclear policies. Iran might believe it could deter a U.S. strike on its nuclear facilities by its nuclear threat or the prospect of retaliation against U.S. forces in the area. Iran might discount the threat of an Israeli strike if it felt that Israel could only inflict a temporary setback to its nuclear program. North Korea might halt nuclear tests if it thought it could make major gains in the Six-Party Talks. North Korea and Iran might not have high confidence in North Korea's ability to contain nuclear tests. There are questions about the reliability of media reports on Iranian-North Korean cooperation in the nuclear area.

Developments of late 2010 may soon render this scenario overtaken by events. According to a report of November 2010, North Korea is pursuing uranium enrichment but not plutonium reprocessing. As a result, it would be difficult to use uranium debris collected from a nuclear test to determine whether the test device was manufactured by North Korea, Iran, or another nation. Details are as follows.

Siegfried Hecker, Co-Director, Center for International Security and Cooperation, Stanford University, and Director Emeritus of Los Alamos National Laboratory, reported on a visit to North Korea's nuclear complex at Yongbyon. North Korean officials showed him and other U.S. visitors "a new facility that contained a modern, small industrial-scale uranium enrichment facility with 2,000 centrifuges that was recently completed." Further, "we were told that they began construction in April 2009 and completed the operations a few days ago." Hecker reported that the chief process engineer told him that the centrifuges were not of a first-generation P-1 design, and inferred that they were most likely of the more advanced P-2 design. He wrote, "I expressed surprise that they were apparently able to get cascades of 2,000 centrifuges working so quickly, and asked again if the facility is actually operating now—we were given an emphatic, yes." He stated that "the greatest concern is that a facility of equal or greater capacity, configured to produce HEU, exists somewhere else. Such a facility would be difficult to detect as demonstrated by the fact that this facility was undetected in the middle of the Yongbyon fuel fabrication site."[94] Another analysis also raised the possibility that the enrichment facility at Yongbyon "may not be the first gas centrifuge plant that North Korea has built. It is possible that North Korea built another plant previously and either transferred it to Yongbyon or simply built another one based on its experience of bringing the first, perhaps smaller, one into operation."[95]

North Koreans told Hecker that the centrifuges were being used to produce low-enriched uranium (LEU) as fuel for a nuclear power plant. (LEU cannot be used for a nuclear weapon.) However, Hecker stated that the centrifuges could be rearranged to produce up to 40 kg of highly-enriched uranium (HEU) per year; HEU can be used in a nuclear weapon. Regarding plutonium, he saw no activity at the facility for reprocessing plutonium; that and other data led him to conclude that "Pyongyang has apparently decided not to make more plutonium or plutonium bombs for now. My assessment is that they could resume all plutonium operations within approximately six months and make one bomb's worth of plutonium per year for some time to come."[96]

It might in theory be possible to determine the provenance of a weapon from analysis of particulate debris, but this could be difficult in practice. For example, detecting uranium in debris from a nuclear test conducted inside North Korea would not be proof that the weapon was North Korean, even if it could be determined that the uranium was of North Korean manufacture: "David Asher, who helped direct efforts to counter North Korea's proliferation activities in the George W. Bush administration ... [said] 'My fear is that just as Iran's demands for enriched uranium for a bomb are expanding, North Korea may be in the position to begin supplying.'"[97]

ANOTHER NORTH KOREAN TEST?

Prospects for Another Test: Reports Are Mixed

Many press reports of late 2010 speculated on whether DPRK was preparing another nuclear test and when such a test might occur:

- "Unification Minister Hyun In-taek on [October 22] said the government is watching North Korea closely for signs that the Stalinist country is preparing another test.... But Hyun added the chances are 'low' at the moment."[98]
- "A U.S. reconnaissance satellite has detected signs of North Korea preparing for a nuclear test in North Hamgyong Province, where it had conducted two earlier tests in October 2006 and May 2009. A South Korean government source on [October 20] said 'brisk movement' of vehicles and people has been detected in Punggye-re recently.... However, it seems unlikely that the North will conduct a third nuclear test in the immediate future since current activities there suggest it will take 'about three months' to prepare, the source added."[99]
- The Defense Minister of the Republic of Korea, Kim Tae-Young, "told lawmakers the North is 'constantly seeking to make its nuclear weapons smaller' for possible future delivery by ballistic missiles or bombers.... But Kim said he sees 'no clear signs' so far that the communist country is preparing for another test."[100] (Nuclear testing is one way to reduce the size of nuclear weapons.)
- "A government official says Seoul has yet to find substantial evidence that suggests that North Korea is seeking to conduct another nuclear test."[101]
- "New satellite imagery shows renewed activities in northeastern North Korea where Pyongyang conducted its second nuclear test in May 2009, but it is too early to say whether another test is imminent, a U.S. analyst told Kyodo News on Wednesday. Images captured by DigitalGlobe Inc., an American company specializing in geographical imagery, suggest work is being carried out at the site in North

Hamgyong Province, according to Allison Puccioni, an image analyst for the defense intelligence group Jane's. She said one of the images taken on Oct. 16 shows at least six vehicles or pieces of equipment at the site's operation base. There also appears to be a 12-meter-wide pile of excavated debris in the base's staging area, indicating that tunneling is under way."[102]

- "A Japanese government official said ... 'the timing cannot be specified, but a nuclear test could happen any time.'"[103]
- "A Cheong Wa Dae official said, 'North Korea is up to something, but we don't expect anything to happen right now.' Judging from the depth of the shaft that has been dug so far, it will apparently take three to six more months before a nuclear test can be conducted."[104]
- "A South Korean government official says that it has yet to confirm detailed proof that North Korea is preparing for another nuclear test at a nuclear testing site in Gilju County, North Hamgyeong Province."[105]

From the foregoing and similar reports, it appears that as of late November 2010, North Korea is conducting work at its nuclear test site, that this work is consistent with preparations for a nuclear test, and that the site is not ready for a nuclear test. It is not clear if the work is farther along than the reports imply; or if the apparent excavation is a ruse, with no actual work done; or if preparations for a nuclear test are underway at another site elsewhere in North Korea.

What to Look for in the Event of Another Test

The material presented earlier in this report indicates many data points that Congress may wish to look for in government and media reports on a future North Korean test. The data can be used to improve an understanding of the test and its significance:

- Could the event have been nonnuclear? Was the evidence seismic only? Was there evidence of a large quantity of conventional explosives being brought to the test site?
- Was the test nuclear? What was the evidence of the test, and how reliable is it? Were radionuclides detected in addition to seismic signals? If radionuclides were detected, were they only in the form of gases, or were particulates detected as well? If gases were collected, were they collected soon enough to analyze the ratio between xenon isotopes?
- What was the estimated yield of the test? What is the range of credible estimates?
- Is there any evidence of advanced design, such as increased yield, boosting, or steps toward a thermonuclear weapon (hydrogen bomb)? For example, a mixture of deuterium and tritium gases (isotopes of hydrogen) is used to boost the yield of modern nuclear weapons. Tritium must be manufactured. Is there any evidence (whether from the test or other intelligence sources) of production or use of tritium?
- How well did the IMS and other sensors detect the event? How quickly were seismic signals detected, analyzed, and distributed? How many IMS seismic stations detected the event? What other stations (hydroacoustic, infrasound, radionuclide) detected it?

Did the projected path of the air mass over the test site at the time of the test and for several days thereafter coincide with the actual path?
- Was there any reporting on how well U.S. national technical means of verification, such as aircraft to detect debris, satellites, and seismic stations not part of IMS, performed?
- Conversely, how effectively did North Korea contain the test? Was there evidence of containment techniques or, if the test was well contained, did containment appear to be mainly a function of deep burial?
- Was there any indication of foreign assistance to, or observation of, the test? Was there any indication that the test was conducted for a nation other than North Korea?

ISSUES FOR CONGRESS

The 2009 North Korean test raises at least two issues for Congress. What does the test imply for U.S. ability to verify compliance with the CTBT? And what unilateral and multilateral steps might Congress mandate or encourage to improve monitoring and verification capability?

Implications for the CTBT

Supporters and opponents of the CTBT will likely draw opposing conclusions on what the absence of detectable radionuclides from the 2009 test indicates. Here are points they might raise in a future debate.

Opponents might argue that without detection of radionuclides there is no proof that North Korea conducted a nuclear test. For example, the May 2009 event might have been a large conventional explosion conducted to inflate the appearance of progress in North Korea's weapons program.

The treaty's supporters might respond that the ability of the IMS seismic component to pick out signals characteristic of an explosion originating in the area of the suspected test from the many seismic signals occurring each day shows the capability of the IMS. As another example, the IMS detected the 2009 event seismically, and identified it as an explosion, before North Korea announced it.[106] More generally, the 2009 test shows that an attempt to evade detection would also have to contain radionuclides and suppress other signatures, a more difficult task than suppressing only one signature. Suspicious seismic signals and an absence of radionuclides, it is argued, would surely lead to calls for an OSI.

Opponents might counter that OSIs could not happen unless the treaty entered into force, and that North Korea is unlikely to ratify the treaty, thereby preventing entry into force, as long as it has any interest in future nuclear tests. Even if North Korea ratified the treaty, it could bar inspections of its territory, and if it allowed them, inspectors might not find proof that a test occurred. While the case could be referred to the United Nations, CTBT opponents would see only a slim likelihood of that body taking effective action.[107]

Supporters recognize that OSIs could not be conducted under the treaty without entry into force, and see that as a benefit of entry into force. They believe that OSIs have a good chance of finding a "smoking gun," and that the U.N. would adopt stringent sanctions on North Korea in response to nuclear tests conducted after the treaty had entered into force. They see a refusal by a state party to permit inspections as *prima facie* evidence of a violation.

One generally-accepted means of evading detection of nuclear tests, especially low-yield tests, is "decoupling," testing in a large underground cavity to muffle the seismic signal. Opponents could argue that a decoupled test conducted in a manner that prevented release of radionuclides, such as deep under a mountain, might go undetected by radionuclide sensors as well as seismographs, and that the other two IMS technologies, infrasound and hydroacoustic, would not be expected to detect a test of this sort, so all IMS technologies might be circumvented simultaneously. Opponents might argue further that the ability of the IMS to detect the 2006 and 2009 tests does not show that that system can detect clandestine tests because neither test was conducted evasively. (North Korea announced both of them.) In this view, any cheater would use evasive methods, so the IMS has merit only insofar as it can detect evasive tests.[108]

Supporters question the feasibility of decoupling, or otherwise hiding, a test of more than 1 or 2 kilotons. They note that the IMS has detected seismic signals down to a small fraction of a kiloton; that it is difficult to hide the rock that must be removed to create an underground cavity; and that, despite precautions, an evader cannot count on near-perfect containment. The merits of various evasion techniques have been debated for decades.[109]

Entry into force requires ratification by North Korea, among others, yet that nation's ratification may be difficult to obtain. To circumvent the problem, some CTBT supporters have suggested bringing the treaty into force provisionally.[110] This apparently would mean that states that had ratified the treaty would behave among themselves as if the treaty had entered into force, permitting OSIs among these states and formal operation of the structures of the CTBTO. But there are problems with provisional entry into force. First, a state not party to provisional entry into force might conduct a large conventional explosion designed to simulate a nuclear explosion so as to give the impression of progress on its nuclear program. Since the IMS is designed to detect nuclear tests only, it would not detect signatures that would identify a test as nonnuclear. Second, since a state could conduct a test in a host state that was not party to provisional entry into force, it would be important to attribute the test to learn if a state party to provisional entry into force had conducted the test; that would be difficult to do if the test were well contained. "Regular" entry into force would address both concerns. OSIs could reveal if the test was nuclear or conventional, and attribution would not matter for the treaty's verification regime because any nuclear test would violate the CTBT.

Improving Monitoring and Verification Capability

Key problems for analyses of the 2009 North Korean event were determining whether it was a nuclear explosion and learning more about it. In examining budgets and programs, Congress may wish to consider various means of improving U.S. and international ability to monitor nuclear testing by North Korea and other nations. The preceding sections of this report lead to several possible means to do this. They fall into several categories: (1) conduct research to better characterize nuclear explosions and containment, (2) deploy more monitoring equipment, (3) improve the performance of monitoring systems, and (4) look for new signatures to help determine if a test is nuclear. Note that government agencies that conduct programs to improve monitoring and verification capability develop strategic plans for their work and update them annually; the options presented here would need to be prioritized against existing programs.[111]

Conduct Research to Better Characterize Nuclear Explosions and Containment

Conduct Basic Research on Containment

Radioactive gases, and especially radioactive noble gases, are an important sign of a nuclear explosion. Yet Raymond Jeanloz, Professor of Earth and Planetary Science, University of California at Berkeley, said: "The science underlying the containment of gases in the Earth's crust is poorly understood. The U.S. nuclear test program focused on containment of particulates. The program did not try to gain a full understanding of what determines how or when gases are contained, but instead developed practical solutions to containment."[112] A better understanding of the science of how the Earth contains gases, especially in the case of nuclear tests, should help evaluate North Korean containment efforts.

Evaluate the Adequacy of Monitoring of North Korean Containment

Given the potential significance of North Korean efforts to contain radioactive material from nuclear tests, it may be of value to have the Intelligence Community analyze the first two North Korean nuclear tests to see what containment methods were used, and in what ways, if any, North Korea modified those methods for its second test. Similarly, it may be of value for that community to pay particular attention to containment methods in monitoring North Korean preparations for any future nuclear test. The Intelligence Community could report its findings on a classified basis to the congressional committees of jurisdiction.

Conduct Research to Improve Atmospheric Transport Modeling

Improving atmospheric transport modeling could improve the accuracy with which it could track radionuclides back to their location of origin, or predict the path of an air mass carrying radioactive materials.

Provide Fellowships

Breakthroughs in analysis could enable seismologists to extract more information from seismic data and lead to improved concepts for future seismic networks.[113] However, such advances, as well as maintaining long-term monitoring capability more generally, will require training of graduate students in nuclear explosion monitoring disciplines. One expert stated,

> The past decade has seen sharp fluctuations in funding of programs in this area by two key sources, the Air Force Research Laboratory and the National Nuclear Security Administration, and funding has been far below the level recommended by a 1997 National Research Council report. Low and erratic funding has disrupted graduate student training. As a result, it is becoming hard to sustain adequate numbers of experts in nuclear explosion monitoring, as evidenced by recent difficulties in replacing seismologists who retired.[114]

To address this issue, the United States could support, at a steady level, fellowships and programs adequate to produce enough experts in nuclear explosion monitoring to meet national needs. Similarly, Congress, in P.L. 111-140, Nuclear Forensics and Attribution Act, found, "The number of radiochemistry programs and radiochemists in United States National Laboratories and universities has dramatically declined over the past several decades."[115] In response, this act would establish a National Nuclear Forensics Expertise Development Program.

Deploy More Monitoring Equipment

Add Radionuclide Stations and Radioxenon Equipment

Since venting or seepage of radioxenons is more likely than venting of particulates, many agree that it would be desirable for the IMS to have radioxenon equipment at all 80 radionuclide stations instead of the 40 currently planned. The treaty (Protocol, paragraph 10) provides for this expansion once it enters into force: "At its first regular meeting, the Conference [of the States Parties] shall consider and decide on a plan for implementing noble gas monitoring capability throughout the network." The CTBTO PrepCom indicates that adding radioxenon equipment to the remaining 40 particulate stations would not be technically difficult, but is more a matter of political will and financial resources.[116] The PrepCom also states, "there has been a strong interest in building up and strengthening the noble gas capability since the 2006 DPRK declared test within the CTBTO PrepCom."[117] The European Union has made voluntary contributions for this purpose,[118] and the United States has made technical contributions to this effort.[119] It may also be desirable to equip all 80 stations with radioxenon equipment, or to increase the number of radionuclide stations with radioxenon equipment beyond 80, *before* the treaty enters into force. Additional stations in Japan and South Korea, and in areas of China and Russia close to North Korea, would be of particular value for monitoring any testing by that nation.

Procure Mobile Radionuclide Collection Equipment for Rapid Deployment

Even completing the IMS and having radioxenon equipment at all 80 radionuclide stations would leave gaps in coverage, as Figure 2 shows for North Korea. These gaps pose a problem for monitoring and verification. For example, a test might release radioactive material that wind currents blow away from IMS stations, or the wind might loft such material high above these stations, which are at ground level. Mobile detection systems ready to deploy immediately after detecting a nuclear test would help address this problem. These systems could include ships and radionuclide collection aircraft to deploy on or over international waters, and land-mobile systems to deploy in nations near the suspected test. These systems might or might not be part of the IMS depending on how they were handled pursuant to Article IV (verification), paragraphs 23-25 of the treaty, "Changes to the International Monitoring System." Even if these systems were not included in the IMS, states could still share the resulting data with the International Data Center pursuant to Article IV, paragraphs 27 and 28, "Cooperating National Facilities."

Mobile systems offer many advantages. The ability to collect over broad ocean areas would close some gaps in the IMS. Since mobile systems could collect data close to and soon after a suspected detonation, they might be able to collect particulates before they dropped back to Earth. Particulates can provide high confidence that the material originated from a nuclear test; they can also provide data on certain weapon characteristics. Gathering radioxenons quickly is of particular value for analyzing the ratio of xenon-135 to xenon-133, which can also provide high confidence that a test was nuclear. The rapid decay of xenon-135 (half-life, 9.14 hours), plus the decay of iodine-133 and -135 into xenon-133 and -135, respectively, precludes such analysis after a short time. Close-in, rapid collection should result in higher concentration of radionuclides, facilitating analysis, because they would have less time to dilute in the atmosphere. Hafemeister states that airborne sensors or ground sensors closer to a test can enhance the concentration of radionuclides by a factor of more than a million.[120] Close-in collection should also result in more confident determination of which nation conducted a test by greatly reducing the number of countries from which the radionuclides could have originated.

There could be obstacles to airborne or seaborne collection systems operating on or over international waters. For example, according to press reports, North Korea fired several surface-to-air missiles around the time of the 2009 nuclear test that "appeared to be aimed at keeping U.S. and Japanese surveillance planes away from the nuclear test site."[121]

Improve the Capability of Monitoring Systems

Increase the Sensitivity of Detection Equipment

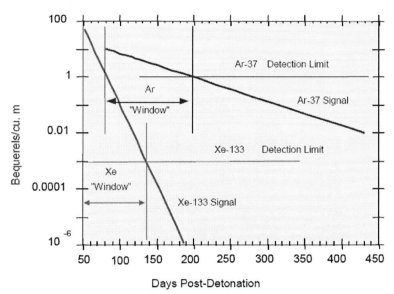

Source: Charles Carrigan, "Using OSI [On-Site Inspection] Field Studies and Tests to Define Noble Gas Sampling and Analysis Requirements," Paper presented at International Noble Gas Experiment-2009 Conference, Daejeon, Korea, November 9-14, 2009, Lawrence Livermore National Laboratory, LLNL-PRES-41961.
Notes: 1 Becquerel = 1 radioactive disintegration per second. Calculations are derived from a model based on data obtained from the Non-Proliferation Experiment (NPE), an underground blast conducted in 1993 at the Nevada Test Site that used nonnuclear explosives to simulate a 1-kiloton nuclear explosion. It used helium-3 gas to simulate argon-37 and sulfur hexafluoride gas to simulate xenon-133.

Figure 5. Detection "Window" for Argon-37 and Xenon-133; Lowering the Detection Limit Keeps "Window" Open Longer.

While the capability to detect radioactive noble gases is very good, it could be improved. So doing would increase the probability of detection, both remote and onsite, by enabling a detector to pick up a signal from a radioisotope at a lower concentration or for a longer time. Figure 5 illustrates the point for onsite detection. It shows a detection limit or threshold for argon-37 and xenon-133 (horizontal lines). It shows the signal from these two isotopes diminishing over time (diagonal lines), with the xenon signal diminishing faster than the argon signal because the former has a shorter half-life, 5.3 days vs. 34.8 days. The "window," or the period in which an isotope can be detected (vertical lines), opens when the gas reaches the surface, with xenon and argon reaching the surface about 50 and 80 days, respectively, after a detonation as a result of barometric pumping, and closes when the amount of either gas falls below the detection threshold.[122] Thus if the detection threshold can be lowered, the window closes later. While the graph shows the signal as starting out at its peak, in practice the signal would begin at zero and at some point would rise rapidly. As a result, a more sensitive detector might also "open" the window slightly earlier.

Study Numbers, Types, and Basing for Aircraft that Collect Nuclear Debris

The Air Force Technical Applications Center (AFTAC) operates two WC-135 "Constant Phoenix" aircraft, which are designed to collect particulates and gases from a nuclear explosion. The WC-135 is a component of the U.S. Atomic Energy Detection System.[123] AFTAC states,

> The Air Force maintains one primary and one backup WC-135 to support airborne nuclear collections. The aircraft are operated by the 55th Wing, 45th Reconnaissance Squadron at Offutt Air Force Base, Neb. Both the primary and backup aircraft are equipped with an AFTAC collection suite that provides the capability to collect the gaseous and particulate debris that might be released from a nuclear explosion. The Air Force is conducting an Analysis of Alternatives to determine solutions that can support changing mission requirements and will provide long term, viable alternatives to the current capability as it reaches end of life (the WC-135 airframes are almost 50 years old).[124]

The Air Force elaborated on the preceding statement: "Currently, the WC-135 must be evaluated for re-skinning the wings in around 2022, and AFMC [Air Force Materiel Command] asserts TF33 engine sustainment through 2040. Otherwise, there is not an explicit end-of-life date." The analysis of alternatives "will examine the WC-135, plus other manned and unmanned aircraft, and assess the number of each aircraft appropriate for the mission."[125]

One of the two WC-135s is the primary aircraft; the other is a backup. The Air Force stated, "Either aircraft can fly the mission. Also both aircraft can be flown simultaneously. However, one of the aircraft is usually in Primary Depot Maintenance (PDM) and therefore would be unavailable. If both aircraft are out of PDM then they both can support mission."[126] Thus the USAEDS airborne collection asset at most times is a single aircraft nearly 50 years old based thousands of miles from North Korea and also from Iran.

Given the prospect that several nations, over a vast geographic area, might conduct nuclear tests, it would be of value to collect samples as soon as possible to narrow the region where the test occurred, to minimize the loss of samples with time, and to have a chance of obtaining samples of xenon isotopes with forensic value. Accordingly, it may be desirable to have more than two aircraft for this purpose, and to have some forward-based. Forward basing might be less costly for large, long-range Reaper- or Global Hawk-type drones than for WC-135s and similar aircraft.[127] For example, since these drones are remotely operated, personnel controlling the mission and operating the sensors (as distinct from the ground crew) would not have to be forward-based.

Also at issue is whether to extend the service life of WC-135s or procure new aircraft. Finally, it may be worth considering whether to add airborne sensors to the IMS, which would have to be done in accordance with Article IV, paragraphs 11 and 23, of the CTBT.

Congress is aware of the importance of collecting samples promptly. In the Nuclear Forensics and Attribution Act, it found,

> Many of the radioisotopes produced in the detonation of a nuclear device have short half-lives, so the timely acquisition of samples is of the utmost importance. Over the past several decades, the ability of the United States to gather atmospheric samples—often the preferred method of sample acquisition—has diminished. This ability must be restored and modern technologies that could complement or replace existing techniques should be pursued.

Improve Onsite Inspection Capability

Since the previous administration did not seek entry into force of the CTBT but did favor improving means of monitoring nuclear testing, it requested only those funds for the CTBTO Preparatory Commission that directly supported the IMS. It requested these funds in the State Department's International Affairs Function 150 budget in the Nonproliferation, Antiterrorism, Demining, and Related Programs account. The FY2007 budget justification, for example, stated that the requested funds, $19.8 million, would "pay the U.S. share for the ongoing development and implementation of the International Monitoring System (IMS), which supplements U.S. capabilities to detect nuclear explosions. Since the United States does not seek ratification and entry-into-force of the CTBT, none of the funds will support Preparatory Commission activities that are not related to the IMS."[128] While the PrepCom budget shows no nation-by-nation link between funds received and funds spent, this quotation illustrates the attitude toward expenditures that would be of value only if the CTBT were to enter into force, such as OSIs. Consistent with this policy, the administration directed U.S. R&D funding away from OSI issues and toward IMS technologies.

With the Obama Administration favoring the CTBT, and with OSIs a key part of the verification regime, more might be done to make them more effective. One approach would be to develop more sensitive detectors. A second would be to integrate geophysical methods for detecting anomalies hundreds of feet underground with gas sampling techniques to help inspectors locate a suspected test more precisely. A third would be to conduct field experiments on how noble gases reach the surface. The only OSI-type gas sampling experiment was performed in conjunction with the 1993 NPE (see "Increase the Sensitivity of Detection Equipment"). Conducting similar experiments (perhaps releasing gases in mine shafts to reduce costs) under various geologic, containment, hydrologic, and barometric conditions would help develop and calibrate computer models of gas leakage from underground tests, making results of the type found in 1993 applicable to a wider range of conditions under which OSIs might be conducted.

Conduct Further R&D on Satellite Detection

Given the immense value of data provided by satellites, Congress might explore whether additional R&D might be warranted on satellite-borne means of detecting signatures that a clandestine nuclear program or test, or preparations for a nuclear test, might produce. While the IMS does not include satellites, the Provisional Technical Secretariat, which operates the IMS, might want to conduct such R&D as well, both because it can utilize commercial satellite imagery and because the IMS might, at some point, have access to its own satellite data. The CTBT provides (Article IV, paragraphs 11 and 23) for the possibility of adding monitoring technologies such as satellites to the IMS if agreed pursuant to Article VII (Amendments).

Evaluate Classified Projects

The United States is presumably conducting classified R&D in areas related to the subject matter of this report. The relevant congressional committees may wish to determine what efforts, if any, are being made along these lines and whether the level of effort in each such area is appropriate. For example, many evasion scenarios set forth by CTBT opponents were created decades ago, some in the 1950s. They have been studied and debated ever since, and study of such scenarios remains a daily concern of the Intelligence Community. The ability to defeat evasive scenarios would increase confidence in detection capability, while an inability to defeat them would help guide detection R&D. Either way, efforts to develop and to defeat these scenarios would challenge scientists working on detection, just as with any other offense-defense competition. However, few new evasion scenarios or technologies appear in the public record out of concern that public discussion of them could aid would-be evaders.

Look for New Signatures to Help Determine if a Test Is Nuclear

Examine Costs and Benefits of Long-Range Detection of Argon-37

As noted earlier, it may be feasible and useful to detect argon-37 at a distance. However, moving from "may be feasible" to an operational system would require characterizing background levels of this isotope; determining the value that might be gained by detecting this isotope in addition to detecting xenon-133; studying the worldwide distribution of calcium, especially at likely test sites; developing automated detection equipment that could be used at remote locations, such as at IMS radionuclide stations; and determining whether the cost of this effort is worth the benefit.

Study Signatures of a Chemical Explosion

As the case of the 2009 North Korean test shows, it would be useful to determine if an explosion was nuclear or chemical in order to reveal if a nation had conducted a nuclear test or was bluffing. Effluents of a chemical explosion would probably not permit making that determination because they would be hydrocarbons and there is a huge atmospheric background of such materials from vehicles, industry, forest fires, mining explosions, etc. However, there might be other signatures, such as in the preparation, seismic waves, or post-event activity. For example, detailed study of seismic waves might reveal slight differences between those generated by nuclear or chemical explosions. This was a goal of the 1993 NPE, though the apparent inability to prove conclusively that the 2009 North Korean event was or was not nuclear indicates that more work along these lines may be warranted. At the same time, it would be important to guard against the prospect that a nation could create signatures of a chemical explosion as cover for a nuclear test. The ability to monitor signatures of nonnuclear explosions is especially important in situations like the 2009 event prior to CTBT entry into force. After entry into force, should it occur, onsite inspections would be available to help resolve such situations.

End Notes

[1] "Text of the North Korean Announcement of Nuclear Test," *Reuters,* May 25, 2009, http://www.nytimes.com/2009/05/25/world/asia/25nuke-text.html. For information on North Korea's nuclear weapons program, see CRS Report RL34256, *North Korea's Nuclear Weapons: Technical Issues*, by Mary Beth Nikitin.

[2] In a "gun assembly" weapon, one piece of uranium-235 is fired into another such piece to create a critical mass. The Hiroshima bomb was of this design. U.S. scientists had such confidence in this design that they did not test it prior to use. Gun-assembly weapons can only use highly enriched uranium, not plutonium.

[3] For a history of nuclear test bans, see Appendix A in CRS Report RL34394, *Comprehensive Nuclear-Test-Ban Treaty: Issues and Arguments*, by Jonathan Medalia.

[4] One kiloton is equivalent to the explosive force of 1,000 tons of TNT. For comparison, the explosive yield of the Hiroshima bomb was 15 kilotons.

[5] For the status of signatures and ratifications, and text of the treaty, see the website of the Comprehensive Nuclear-Test-Ban Treaty Organization Preparatory Commission, http://www.ctbto.org. For current developments on the CTBT, see CRS Report RL33548, *Comprehensive Nuclear-Test-Ban Treaty: Background and Current Developments*, by Jonathan Medalia.

[6] U.S. White House. Office of the Press Secretary. "Remarks by President Barack Obama," Hradcany Square, Prague, Czech Republic, April 5, 2009, http://www.whitehouse.gov/the_press_office/Remarks-By-President-Barack-Obama-InPrague-As-Delivered/.

[7] U.S. Office of the Director of National Intelligence. Public Affairs Office. "Statement by the Office of the Director of National Intelligence on the North Korean Nuclear Test," news release 19-06, October 16, 2006.

[8] Information provided by Office of the Director of National Intelligence, personal communication, July 17, 2009.

[9] Thom Shanker and David Sanger, "North Korean Fuel Identified as Plutonium," *New York Times,* October 17, 2006.

[10] Comprehensive Nuclear-Test-Ban Treaty Organization Preparatory Commission, "The CTBT Verification Regime Put to the Test – The Event in the DPRK on 9 October 2006," http://www.ctbto.org/press-centre/highlights/2007/thectbt-verification-regime-put-to-the-test-the-event-in-the-dprk-on-9-october-2006/page-2/. An atmospheric transport model, as discussed later, shows how winds move gases or particles through the atmosphere. Xenon is a noble gas, i.e., one that is chemically inert. Nuclear explosions create radioactive isotopes of some noble gases. The IMS has some stations that can detect radioactive isotopes of xenon, such as xenon-133.

[11] Swedish Defence Research Agency (FOI), "FOI found radioactive xenon following explosion in North Korea," press release, December 19, 2006, http://www.foa.se/FOI/Templates/NewsPage____5412.aspx.

[12] U.S. Office of the Director of National Intelligence. Public Affairs Office. "Statement by the Office of the Director of National Intelligence on North Korea's Declared Nuclear Test on May 25, 2009," ODNI News Release No. 23-09, June 15, 2009, http://www.dni.gov/press_releases/20090615_release.pdf.

[13] Comprehensive Nuclear-Test-Ban Treaty Preparatory Commission, "Homing in on the Event," May 29, 2009, http://www.ctbto.org/press-centre/highlights/2009/homing-in-on-the-event/.

[14] For seismograms of these two events and of an earthquake from the same region, see Won-Young Kim, Paul Richards, and Lynn Sykes, "Discrimination of Earthquakes and Explosions Near Nuclear Test Sites Using Regional High-Frequency Data," poster SEISMO-27J presented at the International Scientific Studies Conference, June 2009, http://www.ctbto.org/fileadmin/user_upload/ISS_2009/Poster/SEISMO-27J%20%28US%29%20-%20Won_Young_Kim%20_Paul_Richards%20and%20Lynn_Sykes.pdf.

[15] Comprehensive Nuclear-Test-Ban Treaty Organization Preparatory Commission, "Experts Sure about the Nature of the DPRK Event," (referring to the May 2009 North Korean test), June 12, 2009, http://www.ctbto.org/press-centre/highlights/2009/experts-sure-about-nature-of-the-dprk-event/.

[16] Geoffrey Forden, "DPRK: Drilling for Nuke Verification," *Arms Control Wonk*, July 20, 2009, http://www.armscontrolwonk.com/2392/dprk-nuke-verification-will-require-drilling. The amount of chemical explosive needed to implement this scenario may be less than it would appear. For example, one study observes a range of calculations in which it takes a nuclear explosive with a yield of 1 to 2 kilotons to produce the seismic signature of 1 kiloton of chemical explosive. That study calculates that 1.25 kilotons of nuclear explosives produces the seismic signature of 1 kiloton of chemical explosive. James Kamm and Randy Bos, "Comparison of Chemical and Nuclear Explosions: Numerical Simulations of the Non-Proliferation Experiment," Los Alamos National Laboratory report LA-12942-MS, UC-700 and UC-703, June 1995, pp. 89-92, http://www.osti.gov/ bridge/servlets/purl/72900-YlaqIV/webviewable/72900.pdf. Another study finds, "The basic results from the U.S. Department of Energy's (DOE's) Non-Proliferation Experiment (NPE) for seismic signal generation are that the source function for a chemical explosion is equivalent to that of a nuclear explosion of about twice the yield...." Marvin Denny et al., "Seismic Results from DOE's Non-Proliferation Experiment: A Comparison of Chemical and Nuclear Explosions," Lawrence Livermore National Laboratory, UCRL-JC-119214 preprint, January 1995, p. 1, http://www.osti.gov/energycitations/servlets/purl/93630-EAQRwr/webviewable/93630.pdf. (The NPE was an underground nonnuclear explosion of about 1 kiloton yield conducted in 1993 to simulate a nuclear explosion.)

[17] In 1985, the Defense Nuclear Agency conducted a test, "Minor Scale," using 4,800 tons of high explosive. U.S. Department of Defense. Defense Threat Reduction Agency. *Defense's Nuclear Agency, 1947-1997*, Washington, 2002, pp. 269-270.

[18] See "Nonproliferation, Arms Control, and International Security," Lawrence Livermore National Laboratory, c. 1995, p. 8, https://www.llnl.gov/etr/pdfs/01_95.02.pdf; and "Non-Proliferation Experiment (NPE)," Globalsecurity.org, http://www.globalsecurity.org/wmd/ops/npe.htm.

[19] Comprehensive Nuclear-Test-Ban Treaty Organization Preparatory Commission, "Experts Sure about the Nature of the DPRK Event."

[20] A large chemical explosion designed to mimic a nuclear explosion but that is not detonated all at once could generate signals that can be differentiated from a nuclear explosion. Similarly, mining explosions are often ripple-fired and, as a result, generate a different seismic signal than would a nuclear explosion.

[21] The CTBTO and Technical Secretariat would come into existence only upon entry into force of the CTBT. As an interim measure, the states that had signed the CTBT in 1996 adopted a resolution establishing the CTBTO Preparatory Commission as a means "to ensure the rapid and effective establishment of the future Comprehensive Nuclear-TestBan Treaty Organization." "Resolution Establishing the Preparatory Commission for the Comprehensive Nuclear-TestBan Treaty Organization," adopted November 19, 1996, U.N. document CTBT/MSS/RES/1. Upon entry into force of the CTBT, the CTBTO Preparatory Commission would become the CTBTO and the Provisional Technical Secretariat would become the Technical Secretariat.

[22] Pursuant to Article II of the treaty, the Conference of the States Parties is composed of all states that are parties to the treaty. The Executive Council has 51 member states and is the executive organ of the CTBTO.

[23] U.S. Congress. Senate. Committee on Foreign Relations. *The INF Treaty*. S.Hrg. 100-522, 100th Congress, 2nd Session, 1988, part 1, p. 289.

[24] Nuclear Threat Initiative, "China's Nuclear Tests: Dates, Yields, Types, Methods, and Comments," http://www.nti.org/db/china/testlist.htm.

[25] While the IMS is to be completed by the time the CTBT enters into force, it could be completed sooner. CTBTO PrepCom believes it can project 90% completion, but the remainder depends on political, financial, and environmental factors. The support from Member States and countries hosting stations is necessary for completing the IMS. Information provided by Comprehensive Nuclear-Test-Ban Treaty Preparatory Commission, March 3, 2010.

[26] For an up-to-date list of these facilities, see http://www.ctbto.org/map/#ims.

[27] For details on the IMS, see http://www.ctbto.org/verification-regime/.

[28] The instrument that records seismic signals is a "seismograph" or "seismometer"; the visual record of these signals is a "seismogram." For an old but useful description of the science of seismic detection, see U.S. Congress, Office of Technology Assessment, *Seismic Verification of Nuclear Testing Treaties*, OTA-ISC-361, 139 pages, 1988, http://www.fas.org/ota/reports/8838.pdf.

[29] For example, IMS hydrophones near the coast of Chile detected signals from an underwater detonation of 20 kilograms of TNT, a tiny fraction of the yield of a nuclear weapon, off the coast of Japan, 16,300 km away. International Scientific Studies Conference (summary brochure), Vienna, Austria, June 10-12, 2009, p. 3, http://www.ctbto.org/fileadmin/user_upload/pdf/ISSAFC2_Web.pdf.

[30] Il-Young Che et al., "Infrasound Observation of the Apparent North Korean Nuclear Test of 25 May 2009," *Geophysical Research Letters*, vol. 36, L22802, doi: 10.1029/2009GL041017, 2009, 5 p.

[31] Ibid.

[32] Vitaly Fedchenko, "North Korea's Nuclear Test Explosion, 2009," Stockholm International Peace Research Institute (SIPRI) fact sheet, December 2009, pp. 3-4, http://books.sipri.org/files/FS/SIPRIFS0912.pdf.

[33] The difference in apparent magnitude (or yield) of the infrasound and seismic signals results from the great difference in density and compressibility between air and rock. Because the Earth is so stiff, even the relatively high pressure caused by an underground nuclear explosion moves the surface only a little, while air is so compressible that the small upward motion of the Earth's surface caused by the explosion generates only a small atmospheric pressure wave. Information provided by Raymond Jeanloz, Professor of Earth and Planetary Sciences, University of California, Berkeley, e-mail, January 5, 2010.

[34] Katie Walter, "Sleuthing Seismic Signals," *Science & Technology Review*, March 2009, pp. 4-12.

[35] Gabriele Rennie, "Monitoring Earth's Subsurface from Space," *Science & Technology Review*, April 2005, p. 5.

[36] Paul R.J. Saey, "Ultra-Low-Level Measurements of Argon, Krypton and Radioxenon for Treaty Verification Purposes," *ESARDA Bulletin*, no. 36 (July 2007), pp. 42-56.

[37] David Hafemeister, "Progress in CTBT Monitoring Since Its 1999 Senate Defeat," Science and Global Security, vol. 15 (2007), pp. 159-160.

[38] For 236 scientific posters from 2009 detailing various aspects of the IMS and technologies for monitoring nuclear explosions, see International Scientific Studies, "Scientific Contributions," http://www.ctbto.org/specials/the-international-scientific-studies-project-iss/scientific-contribtutions/.

[39] See James Ely et al., "Estimation of Ground-Level Radioisotope Distributions for Underground Nuclear Test Leakage," poster, International Scientific Study, http://www.ctbto.org/fileadmin/user_upload/ISS_2009/Poster/OSI17B%20%28US%29%20-%20James_Ely%20etal.pdf.

[40] If a state party to the treaty refused to permit an OSI, Article V ("Measures to redress a situation and to ensure compliance, including sanctions") would presumably come into play. It provides for actions to "redress a situation," including collective measures and bringing the matter to the attention of the United Nations.

[41] U.S. Air Force. "Air Force Technical Applications Center," http://www.afisr.af.mil/library/factsheets/factsheet.asp?id=10309.

[42] Argonne National Laboratory, "Krypton," Human Health Fact Sheet, August 2005, 2 p., http://www.ead.anl.gov/pub/doc/krypton.pdf.

[43] The interaction is that when a neutron strikes the nucleus of a calcium-40 atom, the nucleus immediately emits an alpha particle (two neutrons and two protons), producing argon-37.

[44] These neutrons are generated by cosmic rays, naturally-occurring uranium, and other sources.

[45] R. Purtschert, R. Riedmann, and H.H. Loosli, "Evaluation of Argon-37 as a means for identifying clandestine subsurface nuclear tests," Proceedings of the 4th Mini Conference on Noble Gases in the Hydrosphere and in Natural Gas Reservoirs, Potsdam, Germany, February 28-March 2, 2007, p. 1, http://bib.gfz-potsdam.de/pub/minoga/ minogajurtschert-r.pdf.

[46] Personal communication, February 5, 2010. These are Professor Purtschert's personal views and not necessarily those of any institution.

[47] N.N. Greenwood and A. Earnshaw, *Chemistry of the Elements,* Oxford, England, Butterworth Heinemann, Publisher, 1998, p. 109.

[48] U.S. National Aeronautics and Space Administration. "World Book at NASA," http://www.nasa.gov/worldbook/ earth_worldbook.html.

[49] Personal communication, January 29, 2010.

[50] Personal communication, February 2, 2010.

[51] Information provided by Comprehensive Nuclear-Test-Ban Treaty Preparatory Commission, personal communication, July 30, 2009. For a description of how the radioxenon equipment works, see Kalinowski et al., "The Complexity of CTBT Verification. Taking Noble Gas Monitoring as an Example," *Complexity,* vol. 14, no. 1, published online July 14, 2008, pp. 92-93.

[52] Comprehensive Nuclear-Test-Ban Treaty Organization Preparatory Commission, "Experts Sure about Nature of the DPRK Event."

[53] Half-life data are from Lawrence Berkeley Laboratory, "Exploring the Table of Isotopes: Isotopes of Xenon (Z=54)," http://ie.lbl.gov/education/parent/Xe_iso.htm. Xenon-131m is of limited value for detecting nuclear explosions because they generate very little of it, and because, given its longer half-life, it is often in the background, at least regionally, generated by nuclear reactors or medical isotope production reactors. Lars-

Erik De Geer, "Radioxenon signatures from underground nuclear explosions," poster for the International Scientific Studies Project, Vienna, Austria, June 10-12, 2009, http://www.ctbto.org/fileadmin/user_upload/ISS_2009/Poster/RN-22D%20%28Sweden%29%20-%20Lars-Erik_DeGeer.pdf. The "m" in xenon-131m and xenon-133m refers to a metastable isomer, which has the same nucleus as xenon-131 or xenon-133, respectively, but in a higher-energy state. In contrast, xenon-133 refers to that isotope in its lower-energy, or ground, state.

[54] For further discussion of gamma-ray spectra, see CRS Report R40154, *Detection of Nuclear Weapons and Materials: Science, Technologies, Observations*, by Jonathan Medalia, Chapter 1 and Appendix.

[55] The same approach is used to detect xenon-135, which emits a beta particle and a 250-keV gamma ray simultaneously. Information provided by Joseph Sanders, Sandia National Laboratories, personal communications, September 16 and October 20, 2009.

[56] Comprehensive Nuclear-Test-Ban Treaty Preparatory Commission, "Major Step Forward in Detecting Nuclear Explosions: CTBTO-WMO [World Meteorological Organization] Cooperation Enhances Nuclear Test-Ban Verification," press release, September 1, 2008, http://www.ctbto.org/press-centre/press-releases/2008/major-stepforward-in-detectingnuclear-explosions/.

[57] Atomic Energy of Canada Limited, "Chalk River Laboratories," http://www.aecl.ca/Science/CRL.htm.

[58] P.R.J. Saey et al., "A long distance measurement of radioxenon in Yellowknife, Canada, in late October 2006," *Geophysical Research Letters*, vol. 34 (October 2007), http://www.agu.org/pubs/crossref/2007/2007GL030611.shtml.

[59] The detectors can detect one radioactive disintegration per second in 5,000 cubic meters of air. Robert Pearce et al., "The Announced Nuclear Test in the DPRK on 25 May 2009," *CTBTO Spectrum*, September 2009, p. 27, http://www.ctbto.org/fileadmin/user_upload/pdf/Spectrum/09_2009/Spectrum13_dprk2_p26-29.pdf.

[60] Ibid., p. 28. For further information on ATM, see Comprehensive Nuclear-Test-Ban Treaty Organization Preparatory Commission, "Atmospheric Transport Modelling and Data Fusion," http://www.ctbto.org/verification-regime/the-international-data-centre/atmospheric-transport-modellingand-data-fusion/page-1-atmospheric-transportmodelling-and-data-fusion/; Comprehensive Nuclear-Test-Ban Treaty Organization Preparatory Commission, "Major Step Forward in Detecting Nuclear Explosions," press release, 01 September 2008, http://www.ctbto.org/press-centre/press-releases/ 2008/major-step-forward-in-detectingnuclear-explosions/; and Tibor Toth, "Building Up the Regime for Verifying the CTBT," *Arms Control Today*, September 2009, p. 10. For several scientific posters on atmospheric transport modeling, see "Atmospheric Transport Modeling/Posters," in the International Scientific Studies website, http://www.ctbto.org/specials/the-international-scientific-studies-project-iss/scientific-contribtutions/ atmospheric-transport-modelingposters.

[61] Personal communication, Comprehensive Nuclear-Test-Ban Treaty Organization Preparatory Commission, December 8, 2009.

[62] See, for example, De Geer, "Radioxenon signatures from underground nuclear explosions," and Kalinowski et al., "The Complexity of CTBT Verification. Taking Noble Gas Monitoring as an Example," p. 94.

[63] Ibid., and Hui Zhang, "Off-Site Air Sampling Analysis and North Korean Nuclear Test," (deals with the 2006 test), 2007, p. 7, paper presented at the 2007 meeting of the Institute of Nuclear Materials Management, http://belfercenter.ksg.harvard.edu/files/NKSampling_INMM07_Hui.pdf.

[64] Personal communications, October 20 and 28, 2009.

[65] De Geer, "Radioxenon signatures from underground nuclear explosions."

[66] Jungmin Kang, Frank von Hippel, and Hui Zhang, "The North Korean Test and the Limits of Nuclear Forensics," letter to the editor, *Arms Control Today*, January/February 2007, p. 42.

[67] "Responses to Jonathan Medalia (Congressional Research Service), Questions related to the Comprehensive Nuclear Test Ban Treaty," information provided by DOE and NNSA laboratories, August 2009, p. 2.

[68] Fission products are atoms, usually radioactive, of elements lighter than uranium or plutonium that are produced when uranium or plutonium atoms fission, or split.

[69] U.S. Department of Defense and Department of Energy. *The Effects of Nuclear Weapons,* third edition, compiled and edited by Samuel Glasstone and Philip Dolan, Washington, U.S. Govt. Print. Off., 1977, p. 37.

[70] Richard Rhodes, *Dark Sun: The Making of the Hydrogen Bomb* (New York, Simon & Schuster, 1995), p. 371. See also Charles Ziegler, "Waiting for Joe-1: Decisions Leading to the Detection of Russia's First Atomic Bomb Test," *Social Studies of Science,* May 1988, pp. 197-229. Radioactive isotopes of lead would be created by neutron bombardment ("activation") of materials in the ground, not by fission of uranium or plutonium in a weapon.

[71] Joint Working Group of the American Physical Society and the American Association for the Advancement of Science, *Nuclear Forensics: Role, State of the Art, and Program Needs*, 2008, p. 3, http://iis-db.stanford.edu/pubs/22126/APS_AAAS_2008.pdf.

[72] A.J. Fahey et al., "Postdetonation Nuclear Debris for Attribution," *Proceedings of the National Academy of Sciences*, vol. 107, no. 47 (November 23, 2010), pp. 20207-20212; for abstract, http://www.pnas.org/content/107/47/20207.

[73] Vitaly Khalturin et al., "A Review of Nuclear Testing by the Soviet Union at Novaya Zemlya, 1955-1990," *Science and Global Security*, vol. 13 (2005), p. 21.

[74] Information provided by Joseph Sanders, Sandia National Laboratories, personal communication, September 11, 2009.

[75] See C.R. Carrigan et al., "Trace Gas Emissions on Geological Faults as Indicators of Underground Nuclear Testing," *Nature*, vol. 382, August 8, 1996, pp. 528-531; and Lars-Erik De Geer, "Sniffing out Clandestine Tests," *Nature*, vol. 382, August 8, 1996, pp. 491-492.

[76] John Holdren (chair) et al., *Technical Issues Related to Ratification of the Comprehensive Test Ban Treaty*, Committee on Technical Issues Related to Ratification of the Comprehensive Test Ban Treaty, National Academy of Sciences, National Academy Press, Washington, 2002, p. 45. The source cited is V.N. Mikhailov et al., *Northern Test Site: Chronology and Phenomenology of Nuclear Tests at the Novaya Zemlya Test Site*, July 1992.

[77] Personal communication, November 21, 2007.

[78] Lawrence Livermore National Laboratory and U.S. Department of Defense. Defense Nuclear Agency, *Caging the Dragon: The Containment of Underground Nuclear Explosions*, DOE/NV-388 and DNA TR 95-74, 1995, by James Carrothers, p. 1, http://www.scribd.com/doc/6602337/Caging-the-Dragon-The-Containment-of-Underground-NuclearExplosions. (On the cover: "Distribution of this document is unlimited.")

[79] U.S. Department of Defense and Department of Energy. *The Effects of Nuclear Weapons*, third edition, p. 261.

[80] U.S. Congress. Office of Technology Assessment. *The Containment of Underground Nuclear Explosions*. OTA-ISC-414, October 1989, pp. 31-55, available at http://www.nv.doe.gov/library/publications/historical/OTA-ISC-414.pdf.

[81] Carrothers, *Caging the Dragon*, 726 p.

[82] U.S. Department of Energy. Nevada Operations Office. *Radiological Effluents Released from U.S. Continental Tests, 1961 through 1992*, DOE/NV-317 Rev. 1, UC-702, August 1996, p. 2, http://www.nv.doe.gov/library/publications/historical/DOENV_317.pdf.

[83] Ibid. "Plowshare" tests explored peaceful uses of nuclear explosions, such as digging canals or harbors, in the 1960s and 1970s. Tests intended to create large craters for such purposes of course could not be contained.

[84] Office of Technology Assessment. *The Containment of Underground Nuclear Explosions*, p. 32. The Atomic Energy Commission was a predecessor agency of the Department of Energy.

[85] U.S. Department of Energy. Nevada Operations Office, *United States Nuclear Tests, July 1945 through September 1992*, DOE/NV—209-REV 15, December 2000, pp. 30-89, http://www.nv.doe.gov/library/publications/historical/ DOENV_209_REV15.pdf.

[86] U.S. Department of Energy, *Radiological Effluents Released from U.S. Continental Tests, 1961 through 1992*, pp. 210, 211, 222, 223, 231.

[87] U.S. Department of Energy, *Radiological Effluents Released from U.S. Continental Tests, 1961 Through 1992*.

[88] Office of Technology Assessment, *The Containment of Underground Nuclear Explosions*, pp. 4-5; original text bold.

[89] Ibid., p. 34.

[90] Mika Nikkinen, Matthias Zahringer, and Robert Werzi, "The Radionuclide Processing System of the CTBTO," poster presented at International Scientific Studies 2009, http://www.ctbto.org/fileadmin/user_upload/ISS_2009/Poster/RN-30%20%28PTS%29%20-%20Mika_Nikkinen%20etal.pdf.

[91] "Responses to Jonathan Medalia," August 2009, p. 1.

[92] See, for example, Jim Wolf, "North Korea, Iran Joined on Missile Work: U.S. General," *Reuters*, June 11, 2009, http://www.reuters.com/article/newsOne/idUSTRE55A4E720090611. See also CRS Report RL30613, *North Korea: Back on the Terrorism List?* by Mark E. Manyin.

[93] U.S. Department of Energy, *United States Nuclear Tests, July 1945 through September 1992*, pp. xvi, 18-89.

[94] Siegfried Hecker, "A Return Trip to North Korea's Yongbyon Nuclear Complex," November 20, 2010, http://iis-db.stanford.edu/pubs/23035/Yongbyonreport.pdf.

[95] David Albright and Paul Brannan, "Satellite Image Shows Building Containing Centrifuges in North Korea," Institute for Science and International Security, November 21, 2010, http://isis-online.org/isis-reports/detail/satelliteimage-shows-building-containing-centrifuges-in-north-korea/. See also David Albright and Paul Brannan, "Taking Stock: North Korea's Uranium Enrichment Program," Institute for Science and International Security, October 8, 2010, http://www.isis-online.org/uploads/isis-reports/documents/ISIS_DPRK_UEP.pdf.

[96] Hecker, "A Return Trip to North Korea's Yongbyon Nuclear Complex."

[97] Jay Solomon and Adam Entous, "North Korea Nuclear Fears Grow," *Wall Street Journal,* November 22, 2010, p. 8.

[98] "Chances of Another N.Korean Test 'Low,'" *Chosun Ilbo* (Republic of Korea), October 25, 2010.

[99] "Is N.Korea Preparing for Another Nuke Test?," *Chosun Ilbo* (Republic of Korea), October 21, 2010.

[100] "N.Korea Seeks to Develop Smaller Nuclear Warheads: Minister," *Agence France-Presse,* November 2, 2010.

[101] "Gov't Yet to Confirm Whether NK Is Preparing Another Nuke Test," *KBS World News,* November 17, 2010.

[102] "Satellite Images Confirm New Activities at N.Korea Nuke Test Site," *Kyodo News* (Japan), November 17, 2010.

[103] "More Reports Confirm Activities at N.K. Nuke Site," *Korea Herald,* November 19, 2010.

[104] "N.Korea's Twin Nuclear Threats," *Chosun Ilbo* (Republic of Korea), November 20, 2010. Cheong Wa Dae, the Blue House, is the executive office and official residence of the President of South Korea.

[105] "S.Korea Has Yet to Confirm NK's Possible Nuke Test," *KBS World News,* November 20, 2010.

[106] Personal communication, Annika Thunborg, Comprehensive Nuclear-Test-Ban Treaty Organization Preparatory Commission, December 8, 2009.

[107] See Senator Jon Kyl, "Why We Need to Test Nuclear Weapons," *Wall Street Journal,* October 21, 2009, p. 23.

[108] For discussions of decoupling and other evasion scenarios, see David Hafemeister, "CTBT Evasion Scenarios: Possible or Probable?," *CTBTO Spectrum,* issue 13, September 2009, pp. 22-25, http://www.ctbto.org/fileadmin/user_upload/pdf/Spectrum/09_2009/Spectrum13_hafemeisterj22-25.pdf, and Robert Barker, "CTBT Monitoring Limitations & Verification Implications: Cheating Scenarios," presentation to the National Academies' CTBT Review Committee, September 9, 2009. The latter document is available through the committee's website, http://www8.nationalacademies.org/cp/projectview.aspx?key=49131; follow the link to the Public Access Records Office at the bottom of the page, and use that link to file a request.

[109] John Holdren (chair) et al., *Technical Issues Related to Ratification of the Comprehensive Test Ban Treaty,* Committee on Technical Issues Related to Ratification of the Comprehensive Test Ban Treaty, National Academy of Sciences, National Academy Press, Washington, 2002, pp. 46-48. See also Harold Karan Jacobson and Eric Stein, *Diplomats, Scientists, and Politicians: The United States and the Nuclear Test Ban Negotiations,* University of Michigan Press, Ann Arbor, 1966, pp. 153-154.

[110] United Nations. General Assembly. "Letter dated 29 June 2006 from the Permanent Representative of Sweden to the United Nations addressed to the Secretary-General," Annex, "Weapons of Terror: Freeing the World of Nuclear, Biological, and Chemical Arms," document A/60/934, July 10, 2006, p. 13, http://www.wmdcommission.org/files/ english.pdf; and Martin Matishak, "Nuclear Test Ban Could Become Reality Without North Korea, Experts Say," *Global Security Newswire,* June 4, 2009, http://www.globalsecuritynewswire.org/gsn/nw_20090602_5876.php. Jessica Tuchman Mathews said, "If only North Korea and Iran remain [as states that must ratify the CTBT for it to enter into force], the more than 160 nations that have joined the treaty will not allow them to block it. An amendment will be drawn that allows provisional entry into force without them." Jessica Tuchman Mathews, "This Time, Ban the Test," *International Herald Tribune,* October 21, 2009, http://carnegieendowment.org/publications/index.cfm?fa=view&id=24021.

[111] As an example of a strategic plan, see U.S. Department of Energy. National Nuclear Security Administration. "Nuclear Explosion Monitoring Research and Engineering Program: Strategic Plan," https://na22.nnsa.doe.gov/ndd/ strategicplan.

[112] Personal communication, June 23, 2009. Jeanloz continues, "Interestingly, the question of containment of gases in the Earth's crust is also important for energy and environmental issues such as carbon sequestration. While the time scale is much longer for sequestration (centuries to millenia) than for nuclear explosion monitoring (hours to days), the issue of gas containment in the crust is pretty much the same, and study of long-term sequestration would benefit from a better understanding of short-term containment, such as for CTBT monitoring." Jonathan Katz, Professor of Physics at Washington University in St. Louis, states, "the issues of noble gas seepage and carbon dioxide (CO_2) sequestration are not quite the same. Unlike noble gases, CO_2

will react with some rocks and ground water, and will liquefy under pressure at room temperature. Both effects make a difference for diffusion." Personal communication, August 4, 2009.

[113] Email from Raymond Jeanloz, Professor of Geophysics, University of California, Berkeley, April 20, 2009.

[114] Information provided by Thorne Lay, Professor of Earth and Planetary Sciences, University of California, Santa Cruz, personal correspondence, April 20, 2009. The 1997 report is Thorne Lay et al., *Research Required to Support Comprehensive Nuclear Test Ban Treaty Monitoring,* National Research Council, National Academies Press, 1997.

[115] H.R. 730 passed the Senate with an amendment by unanimous consent on December 23, 2009. On January 21, 2010, the House agreed to the Senate amendment, 397-10. The President signed the bill into law February 16. 2010.

[116] Personal communications, July 30, 2009, and December 8, 2009.

[117] Personal communication, September 15, 2009.

[118] In 2007 and 2008, the European Union provided a total of €3.986 million, part of which was to be used for noble gas monitoring. See "Council Joint Action 2007/468/CFSP of 28 June 2007," *Official Journal of the European Union,* July 6, 2007, pp. L 176/31-L 176/38; and "Council Joint Action 2008/588/CFSP of 15 July 2008," *Official Journal of the European Union,* July 17, 2008, pp. L 189/28-L 189/35.

[119] Personal communication, NNSA staff, November 20, 2009.

[120] David Hafemeister, "Input to the NAS CTBT Study," presentation to the CTBT Review Committee of the National Academy of Sciences, September 9, 2009, p. 24.

[121] Jean Lee, "Defying World Powers, N. Korea Conducts N Test," *Associated Press,* May 25, 2009, http://www.breitbart.com/article.php?id=D98DCSF00&show_article=1.

[122] Charles Carrigan, "Using OSI Field Studies and Tests to Define Noble Gas Sampling and Analysis Requirements," presentation at INGE [International Noble Gas Experiment] 2009, Daejeon, Korea, November 9-14, 2009, Lawrence Livermore National Laboratory document LLNL-PRES-41961, p. 11. This prediction assumes good test containment and the barometric and geologic conditions present for a specific (nonnuclear) test conducted at the Nevada Test Site. This test, the Non-Proliferation Experiment (NPE), was conducted on September 22, 1993, and used some 1,400 tons of chemical explosive, along with small quantities of gases intended to simulate certain radioactive gases. Other conditions could produce different results. For further information on NPE, see U.S. Department of Energy. *Symposium on the Non-Proliferation Experiment: Results and Implications for Test Ban Treaties,* CONF-9404100, April 19-21, 1994, https://na22.nnsa.doe.gov/cgi-bin/prod/nemre/index.cgi?Page=Symposium+1994.

[123] U.S. Air Force. "WC-135 Constant Phoenix," fact sheet, http://www.af.mil/information/factsheets/factsheet.asp?id=192.

[124] Information provided by Air Force Technical Applications Center through Air Force Legislative Liaison Office, email, October 26, 2009.

[125] Information provided by Air Force Legislative Liaison Office, email, October 29, 2009.

[126] Information provided by U.S. Air Force Legislative Liaison Office, November 24, 2009.

[127] The MQ-9 Reaper is a large remotely-piloted aircraft designed for ground attack or intelligence missions. Several characteristics may make it suitable for collecting radionuclide samples. Its range is 3,682 miles, its payload is 3,750 pounds, its ceiling is up to 50,000 feet, it has long endurance, and it can be loaded into a container for deployment by aircraft, e.g., C-130 Hercules, worldwide. U.S. Air Force. "MQ-9 Reaper," fact sheet, http://www.af.mil/information/ factsheets/factsheet.asp?id=6405. The RQ-4 Global Hawk might also be used to collect radionuclide samples. Its mission is long-range high-altitude intelligence, surveillance, and reconnaissance. It is larger than the Reaper, has a range of 10,939 miles, a payload of 2,000 or 3,000 pounds, depending on the model, and a ceiling of 60,000 feet. U.S. Air Force. "RQ-4 Global Hawk," fact sheet, http://www.af.mil/information/factsheets/factsheet.asp?id=13225. By way of contrast, the Predator has a range of 454 miles, a payload of 450 pounds, and a ceiling of 25,000 feet. U.S. Air Force. "MQ-1 Predator," fact sheet, http://www.af.mil/information/factsheets/factsheet.asp?fsID=122.

[128] U.S. Department of State. *Summary and Highlights: International Affairs Function 150, Fiscal Year 2007 Budget Request,* p. 40, at http://www.state.gov/documents/organization/60297.pdf.

Chapter 5

NORTH KOREA'S SECOND NUCLEAR TEST: IMPLICATIONS OF U.N. SECURITY COUNCIL RESOLUTION 1874[*]

*Mary Beth Nikitin, Mark E. Manyin,
Emma Chanlett-Avery and Dick K. Nanto*

SUMMARY

The United Nations Security Council unanimously passed Res. 1874 on June 12, 2009, in response to North Korea's second nuclear test. The resolution puts in place a series of sanctions on North Korea's arms sales, luxury goods, and financial transactions related to its weapons programs, and calls upon states to inspect North Korean vessels suspected of carrying such shipments. The resolution does allow for shipments of food and nonmilitary goods. As was the case with an earlier U.N. resolution, 1718, that was passed in October 2006 after North Korea's first nuclear test, Resolution 1874 seeks to curb financial benefits that go to North Korea's regime and its weapons program. This report summarizes and analyzes Resolution 1874. In summary, the economic effect of Resolution 1874 is not likely to be great unless China cooperates extensively and goes beyond the requirements of the resolution and/or the specific financial sanctions cause a ripple effect that causes financial institutions to avoid being "tainted" by handling any DPRK transaction.

On the surface, sanctions aimed solely at the Democratic People's Republic of Korea (DPRK, the official name of North Korea) and its prohibited activities are not likely to have a large monetary effect. Governments will have to interpret the financial sanctions ban of the resolution liberally in order to apply sanctions to the bank accounts of North Korean trading corporations. A key to its success will be the extent to which China, North Korea's most important economic partner, implements the resolution. A ban on luxury goods will only be effective if China begins to deny North Korea lucrative trade credits.

---

[*] This is an edited, reformatted and augmented version of a Congressional Research Service publication, CRS Report for Congress R40684, from www.crs.gov, dated April 15, 2010.

Provisions for inspection of banned cargo on aircraft and sea vessels rely on the acquiescence of the shipping state. In the case of North Korean vessels, it is highly unlikely that they would submit to searches. Resolution 1874 is vague about how its air cargo provisions are to be implemented, in contrast to the specific procedures set forth regarding inspecting sea-borne cargo. While procedures are specified for sea interdictions, the authority given is ambiguous and optional. Further, DPRK trade in small arms and ammunition is relatively insignificant, and therefore the ban on those exports is unlikely to have a great impact.

INTRODUCTION[1]

Since the breakdown of the Six-Party Talks over verification issues in December 2008, North Korea has carried out a series of increasingly provocative acts that have challenged the Obama Administration and the world community. In January and February, North Korea presented the newly inaugurated Obama Administration with a tough set of negotiating positions. North Korea reportedly did not respond to subsequent overtures by the United States to restart talks. On April 5, 2009, North Korea launched a long-range ballistic missile, the Taepo Dong 2, over Japan, but failed to achieve a complete test of the system or place a satellite into orbit. This test led to United Nations Security Council (UNSC) condemnation. In response, North Korea said it would abandon the Six-Party Talks, restart its nuclear facilities and conduct a nuclear test. It asked international and U.S. inspectors to leave the country.

On May 25, 2009, North Korea conducted an underground nuclear explosion.[2] In response, the UNSC on June 12 unanimously passed Res. 1874,[3] which puts in place a series of sanctions on North Korea's arms sales, luxury goods, and financial transactions related to its weapons programs and calls upon states to inspect North Korean vessels suspected of carrying such shipments. The resolution does allow for shipments of food and nonmilitary goods. As was the case with an earlier resolution, 1718, that was passed in October 2006 after North Korea's first nuclear test, Res. 1874 seeks to curb financial benefits that go to North Korea's regime and its weapons program. This report summarizes and analyzes Resolution 1874. In summary, the economic effect of Resolution 1874 is not likely to be great unless China cooperates extensively and goes beyond the requirements of the resolution and/or the specific financial sanctions cause a ripple effect that causes financial institutions to avoid being "tainted" by handling any DPRK transaction.

In June 2009, the Obama Administration formed an interagency team to coordinate sanctions efforts against North Korea with other nations. The team is led by Philip S. Goldberg, a former ambassador to Bolivia, and consists of representatives from the State Department, the White House, the National Security Agency, the Treasury Department, and others.[4] (See "Implementation of Sanctions" below.) Many observers cited the designation of a high-level coordinator as a way the United States could produce more success in implementing Res. 1874 than was had in implementing its predecessor. In February 2010, Ambassador Goldberg also took over as Assistant Secretary of the State Department's Bureau of Intelligence and Research (INR). He will continue in his role as Coordinator for Implementation of UNSC Resolution 1874 on North Korea.

Main Provisions of Resolution 1874

Resolution 1874 condemns the May 25 nuclear test, demands that North Korea not conduct additional nuclear tests or ballistic missile tests, says North Korea should suspend its ballistic missile program and re-establish the missile launch moratorium, calls on the DPRK to abandon all nuclear weapons and existing nuclear programs in a "complete, verifiable and irreversible manner" and calls on North Korea to return to the Non-Proliferation Treaty (NPT) and the Six-Party Talks.

The resolution includes a ban on all arms transfers from the DPRK and all arms except exports of small arms or light weapons to the DPRK. As with past UNSC resolutions, this ban includes weapons of mass destruction (WMD) or missile-related technology. The resolution also provides for new economic and financial sanctions on the DPRK. It calls on states not to provide grants, assistance, loans, or public financial support for trade if such assistance could contribute to North Korea's proliferation efforts. It also calls on states to deny financial services, including freezing assets, where such assets could contribute to prohibited DPRK programs. The resolution is not an embargo, however, and explicit exclusions are made for humanitarian and denuclearization aid. These are broad and far-reaching sanctions, if effective, but several problems arise in implementation (discussed below).

Interdiction Procedures

Due to concerns over North Korea's past track record on proliferation of nuclear and missile technology, the Security Council deliberations focused on ways to interdict North Korean shipments of banned items. Past Security Council resolutions (1718 (2006) and 1695 (2006)) have tackled this issue, but the new resolution includes specific guidelines for inspecting and interdicting ships that transport banned materials. Resolution 1874 calls on all states to "inspect, in accordance with their national legal authorities and consistent with international law, all cargo to and from the DPRK, in their territory, including seaports and airports," if that state has information that the cargo is prohibited by UNSC Resolutions. Res. 1874 does not, however, provide the authority to do so without the flag state's consent.[5] Reportedly due to objections by Russia and China, the resolution does not authorize the use of force if the inspection is refused.[6] In that case, the requesting state is asked to report the matter to the Security Council.

If a suspect ship is on the high seas, U.N. member states are "called upon" to request the right to board and inspect. If refused, the resolution obligates the flag state to direct their vessel to port for inspection. The resolution "authorizes" seizure of banned items. The resolution prohibits "bunkering services" such as refueling or servicing of a ship with suspected cargo. This is significant because North Korea reportedly ships most goods under its own flag and typically uses small vessels that would need refueling.

Designations

The sanctions committee under U.N. Security Council Resolution 1718 first designated three North Korean companies at the end of April 2009. Resolution 1874 required designations to be reviewed within 30 days, and the Security Council sanctions committee on July 16, 2009, designated for sanctions three North Korean trading companies, an Iran-based company, and North Korea's General Bureau of Atomic Energy. It also designated five North

Korean officials, including the director of another North Korean trading company.[7] (For a full discussion see "Implementation of Sanctions" below.) No additional designations have been made since July 2009.

Reporting Requirements and Panel of Experts
Resolution 1874 also established reporting mechanisms on the implementation of the resolution. Within 45 days of the resolution's adoption, all U.N. member states were to report to the Security Council on "concrete measures" they have taken to implement the arms embargo and financial measures. The Sanctions Committee, originally established by UNSC Res. 1718, submitted a proposed agenda for its work covering "compliance, investigations, outreach, dialogue, assistance and cooperation." The newly established Panel of Experts is to contribute expertise to the Committee's work, particularly in evaluating cases of noncompliance.[8]

The resolution also asks the U.N. Secretary-General to establish a Panel of Experts, with a maximum of seven experts to analyze reports and make recommendations regarding implementation of Res. 1874 and 1718 for an initial one-year period ending with a report to the Security Council in spring 2010. The Secretary General appointed a panel with members from the United States, China, France, Japan, Russia, South Korea, and the United Kingdom.[9] Victor Comras is the panel's U.S. expert. According to the resolution, the panel is to "gather, examine and analyze information from States, relevant U.N. bodies, and other interested parties regarding implementation" and make recommendations to the Council, Committee, or member states on improved implementation. It is also tasked with producing an interim and final report summarizing its findings and recommendations. Despite this mandate, it is still unclear the extent to which the panel will make judgments about U.N. member states' compliance with the resolution. However, the panel is playing a role in investigating seized shipments and noncompliance cases.

The panel provided an interim report to the Security Council in November 2009, as required by the resolution. According to press reports, the experts panel noted that the sanctions have had an impact on North Korea's trading activity. However, the reports also said the panel assessed that North Korea was actively circumventing the sanctions through masking of transactions by use of intermediaries, false manifests, and false description of cargo.[10] It also reportedly said that North Korea's use of trading companies continued.

Cases of Noncompliance
Several cases of alleged noncompliance with UNSC Resolution 1874 sanctions surfaced in press reports in 2009. Each shipment involved multiple countries and other evasion techniques. Only one publicized interdiction to date involved an air shipment. In July 2009, Italian authorities seized yachts, banned luxury items under UNSC Resolution 1874, bound for North Korea. In August 2009, the *ANL Australia*'s cargo of conventional weapons was seized in the UAE.[11] In September 2009, a shipment of protective clothing was intercepted in South Korea on its way to North Korea.[12] An Ilyushin Il-76 cargo plane was seized at an airport in Thailand in December 2009. The cargo included conventional weapons allegedly exported from North Korea. In November 2009, South Africa interdicted a shipment of tank components from North Korea en route to the Republic of Congo.[13] (Detailed discussion of these cases is below.)

IMPLEMENTATION OF SANCTIONS[14]

The Obama Administration faces several key decisions regarding the U.S. role in enforcing Resolution 1874 and applying new U.S. sanctions against North Korea. The Administration faces a decision on how assertive to be in confronting North Korean ship traffic to attempt searches. It also faces a decision on the U.S. role in enforcing the ban on WMD-related North Korean financial transactions. U.S. officials have said that the Obama Administration is emphasizing the Resolution's call on states to deny financial services to North Korea, especially access to foreign banks by North Korean trading companies.[15] Administration officials also have said that they are considering reinstating North Korea on the U.S. list of state sponsors of terrorism; the Bush Administration removed North Korea from the list in October 2008.[16] Finally, the Administration may have to calculate the degree of pressure to apply to China if Beijing does little to enforce the Security Council sanctions, as was the case following Resolution 1718.

The Hyundai Economic Research Institute of South Korea has estimated that if U.N. members enforce the sanctions in Resolution 1874 against North Korea, North Korea could lose between $1.5 billion and $3.7 billion. Other estimates place the loss close to $4 billion.[17] However, Resolution 1874 does not make enforcement of sanctions mandatory but instead "calls on" U.N. members to take enforcement steps. If sanctions are to have this kind of impact, several key countries will have act forcefully and will have to interpret the sanctions language of the resolution liberally.

There appear to be four key areas of sanctions enforcement:

1) The Ban on Financial Transactions Related to North Korea's Trade in Weapons of Mass Destruction (WMD) and Weapons of Mass Destruction Technology

North Korea's state trading companies are key vehicles for transferring WMD and WMD technology to other countries and for transmitting the foreign exchange earnings back to Pyongyang. The trading companies conduct these transactions through accounts maintained in banks in numerous countries around the world. The trading companies are particularly active in China and undoubtedly have accounts throughout the Chinese banking system.[18] In order to shut down these financial transactions, governments and banks in a number of countries will have to freeze these bank accounts. However, they face the dilemma that the trading companies conduct other transactions through the same accounts. These include the financing of legitimate commerce but also laundering money acquired through North Korea's smuggling of counterfeit products, including counterfeit U.S. dollars and U.S. products. Neither of these activities are banned by Resolution 1874. Governments will have to interpret the financial sanctions ban of the resolution liberally in order to apply sanctions to the bank accounts of the trading corporations. Obama Administration officials have indicated that they are urging other governments to apply such a liberal interpretation to the activities of the trading companies.[19] In early July 2009, Ambassador Philip Goldberg and Under Secretary of the Treasury Stuart Levey visited China and Malaysia. Goldberg was appointed as a special envoy to coordinate sanctions against North Korea. They emphasized to Chinese and Malaysian officials the need to restrict activities of North Korean trading companies. They reportedly raised with Malaysian officials the use of a Malaysian bank by North Korea to facilitate the sale of North Korean arms to Burma.[20] Ambassador Goldberg and his delegation also visited South Korea, Japan, Thailand, and Singapore. U.S. officials have said that the Obama Administration is emphasizing the Resolution's call on states to deny financial services to North Korea, especially access to foreign banks by North Korean trading companies.[21] Ambassador Goldberg and an interagency team also visited Egypt and the United Arab Emirates in October 2009, to urge compliance with 1874 provisions.

The U.N. Security Council's sanctions committee designated three North Korean companies at the end of April 2009. Japan and the United States had recommended 10 and 14 trading companies to be sanctioned at points in the sanctions committee's deliberation, but China and Russia reportedly objected. The number finally was scaled back to three, two trading companies and one North Korean bank.[22] In line with Resolution 1874, the Security Council sanctions committee on July 16, 2009, designated for sanctions three North Korean trading companies, an Iran-based company, and North Korea's General Bureau of Atomic Energy. It also designated five North Korean officials, including the director of another North Korean trading company.[23] The U.S. Treasury Department previously had imposed U.S. sanctions on one of these North Korean trading companies, the Namchongang Trading Corporation, and the Iran-based Hong Kong Electronics. Treasury Department officials disclosed in late June 2009 that the Department was targeting 17 North Korean trading companies and banks for U.S. and international sanctions.[24]

In its interim report, the UNSCR Panel of Experts reportedly discussed North Korea's continued use of trading companies. For example, one news report said the experts had found that "The Korea Mining Development Trading Corp, sanctioned for involvement in ballistic missile sales, continued to operate through subsidiaries. The Kwangson Banking Corp and Amroggang Development Bank had been determined to be acting for the listed Tanchon Commercial Bank and Korea Hyoskin Trading Corp."[25]

2) Search of Sea-Borne Traffic

The specific provisions set out in Resolution 1874 appear to give the United States and allies the means to gain access to North Korean ships and thus shut down WMD-related ship traffic.[26] This will be dependent on a number of countries cooperating with the United States, particularly in applying the resolution's provision for searching North Korean ships in their ports and denying provisions of fuel and supplies to North Korean ships that refuse to be searched. China is particularly important, since North Korean ships frequently visit Chinese ports. Singapore, Indonesia, and Malaysia would be important with respect to North Korean ships that seek to pass through the Singapore and Malacca Straits that connect the Pacific and Indian Ocean, the route to the Middle East and Burma. Middle East-bound ships also stop at ports in India and Pakistan. India has searched North Korean ships in the past. Pakistan's cooperation may be more uncertain, since it has had close relations with North Korea in past years, including purchases of North Korean missiles and missile technology.[27]

The first test case of sea-borne traffic was the North Korean ship, the Kang Nam. The Kang Nam was shadowed by the U.S. Navy as it headed south from North Korea, hugging the coast of China as it approached the South China Sea. South Korean officials believed that the Kang Nam was bound for Burma with a shipment of arms. However, before reaching the international waters of the South China Sea, the Kang Nam turned back and returned to North Korea on July 7, 2009.[28] While attending a regional meeting in Thailand in late July,

Secretary of State Hillary Clinton as well as Japanese officials stated that Burmese Foreign Minister Nyan Win had pledged that Burma would abide by U.N. sanctions on North Korea.[29]

An important application of sanctions against sea-borne traffic came in the form of several intercepted shipments of North Koreans bound for Iran in the second half of 2009. Three vessels were intercepted, which contained North Korean weapons that Western intelligence and Israeli intelligence officials and non-government experts believe were bound for Hezbollah and Hamas, terrorist groups on the official U.S. list of international terrorist organizations.[30] The largest of these shipments was aboard a ship that was searched in Dubai before departing for Iran in July 2009. All three ships reportedly contained North Korean components for 122 mm Grad rockets and rocket launchers. The shipment intercepted in Dubai contained 2,030 detonators for the Grad rockets and related electric circuits and solid fuel propellant for rockets. The Iranian Revolutionary Guards is known to have supplied significant quantities of these rockets and rocket launchers to Hezbollah and Hamas, which have frequently fired them into Israel.[31]

In addition, the South African government seized a shipment of large tank components bound for the Republic of Congo in November 2009. Press reports have said that the shipment originated in North Korea and passed through the Chinese port of Dallan.

3) Inspecting North Korea's Air Cargo

Resolution 1874 is vague in how its air cargo provisions are to be implemented, in contrast to the specific procedures set forth regarding inspecting sea-borne cargo. However, many experts believe that North Korea uses air traffic much more than sea traffic in order to transfer and exchange WMDs, WMD technology, and WMD scientists and technicians.[32] The key to inspections of North Korea's air cargo is the air traffic between North Korea and Iran. North Korea and Iran have extensive collaboration in the development of ballistic missiles.[33] The U.S.- based Institute for Foreign Policy Analysis estimated in 2009 that North Korea earns about $1.5 billion annually from sales of missiles to other countries.[34] It appears that much of this comes from missile sales and collaboration with Iran.[35] Iran and North Korea reportedly use the Pyongyang-Tehran air route for the transfer of missiles and weapons of mass destruction technology and for mutual visits of nuclear and missile officials, scientists, and technicians. North Korea and Iran reportedly emphasized air travel and traffic after 2002 in response to the Bush Administration's announcement of a Proliferation Security Initiative. Aircraft use Chinese air space and reportedly refuel at Chinese airports.[36] A weakness of Resolution 1874 is that it does not specify procedures for the inspection of North Korea-related air cargo similar to the procedures outlined for sea-borne cargo.

China would have the prime responsibility for searches of aircraft on the Pyongyang-Tehran air route. The Obama Administration indicated that Ambassador Goldberg raised the air traffic issue with Chinese officials during his visit to China in early July 2009, but they did not indicate how Chinese officials responded.[37] Chinese officials have not spoken publicly about the air traffic issue, but they have urged caution regarding searches of North Korean ships.

The seizure of an Ilyushin-T76 transport aircraft filled with North Korean arms in Bangkok, Thailand, in December 2009 was another successful application of sanctions but also pointed up the apparent lack of Chinese cooperation in intercepting North Korea-Iran air traffic. The Ilyushin had flown from Pyongyang to Bangkok through hundreds of miles of

Chinese air space with no Chinese effort to direct the aircraft to land and be searched.[38] The Ilyushin reportedly had been leased a few days before the flight, on December 2, 2009, by Union Top Management, a firm based in Chinese Hong Kong. The sea-borne cargo of North Korean arms seized in Dubai in July 2009 had visited several Chinese ports and was transported from Dalian, China, to Shanghai aboard a Chinese ship, again without a Chinese effort to conduct a search.[39]

The flight plan of the Ilyushin reportedly showed that its ultimate destination was Iran.[40] The weapons reportedly included two 1958 multiple 240 mm rocket launchers, rocket launching tubes, 24,240 mm rockets, shoulder-launched missiles, and components of surface-to-air missiles.[41] Israeli and Lebanese newspapers quoted Western intelligence sources as concluding that most of these weapons likely were bound for Hezbollah.[42] Charles Vick, a noted expert on arms and the arms trade, observed that the rocket-related weapons in the shipment are used often by Hezbollah and Hamas against Israel.

It is unknown how much income North Korea lost from Iran by the interception of the Ilyushin and the three earlier seizures at sea. The value no doubt is in the tens of millions of dollars, perhaps more.

4) The Ban on Financial Support for Trade with North Korea Except for Humanitarian Goods

Resolution 1874 reaffirmed Resolution 1718 of October 2006, including the ban on the export of luxury goods to North Korea. Luxury consumer goods are a key benefit to North Korea's elite, the core support group of the Kim Jong-il regime. In the past, the major sources of luxury goods have been Europe and China. Chinese traders report a high demand for Chinese consumer goods by the North Korean elite.[43] An analysis of Chinese trade statistics for 2008 indicates that Chinese exports of luxury consumer goods to North Korea was between $100 million and $160 million, about 5%-8% of China's total 2008 exports of $2 billion to North Korea.[44] Moreover, most of China's exports are reportedly financed by Chinese trade credits to North Korea, which have generous long-term repayment provisions.[45] In short, there is evidence that a sizeable portion of Chinese goods come into North Korea largely cost-free to the North Korean government. Thus, this sanction will not be enforced unless China's begins to deny North Korea these lucrative trade credits.

IMPLICATIONS OF RESOLUTION 1874

Trade, Aid, and Finance[46]

The DPRK is really two economies.[47] The first is that of the military, the Korean Workers Party, and the governing elite. This economy has considerable industrial capacity and first priority for resources. This part of the economy appears to be growing as the military reportedly has taken over some trading companies that previously were private. In many products, particularly food, the first economy tends to be parasitic. It lives off the production from the second economy, the rest of the country. This second economy consists mostly of agriculture, services, light manufacturing, and the range of economic activity typical of a less developed nation. As a whole, the DPRK economy is one of the world's most isolated and moribund. It is in dire straits with a considerable share of its population on the edge of starvation and in need of outside food aid. Without humanitarian aid and trade with China, many of its people would starve. For 2009, the Food and Agriculture Organization and World Food Program estimated that the DPRK faced a cereal deficit of about 836,000 tons—enough to leave 8.7 million people in need of food assistance.[48] The industrial side of the economy also faces problems with antiquated equipment, lack of raw materials, and unreliable electrical supply.

The challenge in implementing the new U.N. economic and financial sanctions lies in separating funds and transactions that are related to the military from the normal economic and financial transactions of the country. Even though the economy as a whole is in shambles, the military and ruling elite are able to command sufficient resources to pursue their nuclear and ballistic missile programs. For example, officials from the Korean Peoples Army (KPA) reportedly have been authorized to acquire any material, resource or item from other commercial projects for use in North Koreas' nuclear programs.[49] A broad interpretation of the sanctions would apply to any transaction that could be interpreted to assist the military.

The irony of Pyongyang's nuclear and missile program is that its 2009 nuclear test and series of missile launches likely cost the government enough to cover much of its need for fertilizer and basic food imports for the year.[50] What seems clear is that if providing an essential level of food to the country's population were a priority goal for the regime, it would have the economic resources to do so.[51] North Korea finds itself in a stereotypical "guns and butter" dilemma. By diverting scarce resources to pay for "guns" it is robbing the greater economy of "butter" (or in North Korea's case, rice) and, in the process, creating a humanitarian disaster.

The additional sanctions in U.N. Resolution 1874 target outside resources flowing into the DPRK that are associated with its prohibited activities. Outside resources include development assistance, loans, finance, and certain exports and imports. Since most official development assistance is to meet basic human needs, countries and international organizations may continue to provide humanitarian aid to North Korea should they desire to do so.[52]

Aid

In the 1990s, Pyongyang's policies (along with bad weather) pushed as many as 2 million of its citizens into death by starvation. In more recent years, other countries have stepped in to provide humanitarian aid even though the ruling regime arguably caused the humanitarian crisis in the first place. This time it appears that Pyongyang's gamble may not work. The Western world seems to be suffering from a combination of "aid fatigue," the effects of the global financial crisis, declining budgetary resources, plus a reluctance to "buy the same horse twice" (i.e., to provide food and fuel aid in exchange for denuclearization steps that are later reversed). Even though Resolution 1874 does not preclude humanitarian aid, this confluence of events, history, and negative responses to the DPRK's attempt to become a nuclear power could cut into inflows of essential food and fuel for the large segment of the population living on the edge of starvation.

Data on total aid to North Korea for 2008 has not been reported yet, but for 2007, the DPRK received $97.6 million in official development assistance (mostly humanitarian aid) from major aid donors that report to the Organisation for Economic Cooperation and

Development (excludes South Korea, China, and Russia). Of this, $32.5 million came from the United States; $16.6 million from the European Community; $26.7 million bilaterally from Germany, France, Australia, Norway, Sweden, and Switzerland; and $10.4 million from the United Nations and other multilateral agencies. U.S. assistance has now stopped. The European Community has limited its funds to humanitarian aid and food security assistance and has progressively shifted from relief and emergency response to providing support to and/or rehabilitation of agriculture in two North Korean provinces.[53] The United Nations World Food Programme has scaled back its humanitarian food assistance for the DPRK after several months of funding shortfalls. In March 2009 (before the nuclear test), it reported that operations were at 15% of planned levels. Approximately 2 million out of the 6.2 million people targeted by their operation were receiving rations (incomplete) of fortified foods.[54]

South Korea provided $54.1 million in humanitarian aid to North Korea in 2008, down from $395.7 million in 2007. Virtually all ($50.2 million) of the aid in 2008 was through non-governmental organizations. How much of this NGO assistance may continue is problematic.[55]

Given the declines in humanitarian aid to the DPRK, Pyongyang may be counting on increased production from its agricultural sector to feed its people. Prospects for this, however, are not favorable. According to estimates by the Bank of Korea, in 2008, the North Korean economy grew at 3.7% following two years of negative growth of -1.1% in 2006 and -2.3% in 2007. The economy as a whole is regaining some of the ground lost during the past two years. Agricultural output grew by an estimated 8.2% in 2008 attributable mainly to better weather, but this did not offset the disastrous declines in farm production that amounted to -9.4% in 2007 and -2.6% in 2006.[56] In short, the agricultural sector in the DPRK has recovered somewhat, but the adequacy of basic nutrition still is questionable for millions of people.

Financial Support

U.N. Resolution 1874 called upon all member states not to provide public financial support for trade with the DPRK (including the granting of export credits, guarantees or insurance to their nationals or entities involved in such trade) where such financial support could contribute to the DPRK's nuclear-related or ballistic missile-related or other WMD-related programs or activities. In 2008, China exported $2.0 billion in goods to the DPRK (see Table 2). With respect to the U.N. sanctions, only a small proportion of this total would seem to be associated with prohibited activities. Other links between exports of "dual use" items such as food, fuel, machinery, and electronics would be difficult to trace. Nevertheless, the $100 million to $160 million in Chinese exports of "luxury" goods[57] to North Korea may be essential to help maintain elite loyalty to the regime and to the military policies that have led to the nuclear and missile programs.

The amount of China's financial support for trade with the DPRK is not reported. In most of the world, except for cash transactions, most international trade is financed through trade credits issued by banks or other financial institutions. A news report from along the Sino-DPRK border indicates that much of the trade is financed by credits from Beijing.[58] Since North Korea's nuclear and missile programs have such a high priority in Pyongyang, it does not seem likely that the military would finance specific inputs into such programs with Chinese trade credits. After U.N. Resolution 1874, this seems even more unlikely. Imports not specific to the nuclear or missile programs ("dual use items") probably enter as general imports and are subsumed into standard non-prohibited categories of purchases that would go primarily for civilian uses. Without cooperation from Chinese officials, attempting to ferret out Chinese trade finance supporting exports of prohibited items only would be nearly futile. As for concessionary finance by Beijing, most of the $1.3 billion deficit in the DPRK's trade with China in 2008 must have been financed by long-term credits or loans (presumably from Beijing), though other sources of financing presumably would include rising Chinese foreign direct investment in North Korea, DPRK export earnings, illicit activities, or from foreign exchange generated from activities such as the Kaesong Industrial Complex. Note also that in 2008, North Korea's deficit in trade with Russia was $83 million.[59]

Since the DPRK is not a member of the World Bank or Asian Development Bank, it is not eligible to borrow for trade finance from these international financial institutions. National Export-Import banks also do not fund trade in prohibited items. Over the period 2005-2007, the 21 industrialized nations that form the Development Assistance Committee of the Organisation for Economic Cooperation and Development reported no bank credits for trade for the DPRK. Gross non-bank trade credits, however, amounted to $6 million in 2005, $110 million in 2006, and $17 million in 2007.[60] These data also do not include credits from China or Russia.

As for loans, the extent of borrowing from western commercial banks by the DPRK is relatively small. In December 2008, consolidated claims on the DPRK by banks that report to the Bank for International Settlements totaled $2.0 billion, down from a peak of $4.2 billion in June 2008. All reporting banks with claims on North Korean entities were from Europe, with France accounting for nearly half of the total.[61] These figures, however, do not include Russia or China. How much of this lending activity is purely commercial and how much went to North Korea's prohibited activities is unknown. Also, funds are fungible. A loan to a commercial activity in one sector may free up resources that then can be used for military purposes. The potential impact of the U.N. sanctions on this activity, therefore, is also unknown, but its upper limit would be around $2 billion in lending from Western nations.

On the surface, therefore, financial sanctions aimed solely at the DPRK's prohibited activities are not likely to have a large monetary effect. The total amounts of such activity are not large, and what can be attributed to nuclear or missile activity would be even smaller. Still, as can be deduced from the 2005 Banco Delta Asia sanctions (see text box below), if financial institutions are put in a position in which they have to choose between dealing with the United States or dealing with the DPRK, they often will close the North Korean accounts, even if those accounts are for legitimate purposes. The BDA sanctions also showed that even amounts as relatively small as $25 million are important to Pyongyang. A BDA-type strategy, therefore, might be to let financial institutions know that any prohibited financial activity related to the U.N. sanctions could bring their whole institution under scrutiny and possible sanctions similar to those imposed on the BDA. The financial institution may then terminate all transactions with the DPRK because it feels unable to separate out the legitimate and prohibited transactions.

> **The Banco Delta Asia Sanctions**
>
> On September 15, 2005, the U.S. Treasury imposed USA PATRIOT Act Section 311 designations against Banco Delta Asia (BDA) in Macau. In the action, Treasury stated that the bank was a "primary money laundering concern" because, among other findings, sources indicated that senior officials in Banco Delta Asia were working with DPRK officials to accept large deposits of cash, including counterfeit U.S. currency, and agreeing to place that currency into circulation. On September 20, 2005, the Financial Crimes Enforcement Network of Treasury imposed special measures against Banco Delta Asia that prohibited U.S. institutions or agencies from opening or maintaining correspondent accounts on behalf of BDA and required covered financial institutions to exercise due diligence to ensure that no correspondent account was being used indirectly to provide services to BDA. Some $25 million in North Korean assets were frozen.
>
> The U.S. action against BDA generated an avalanche of responses both in financial and political circles. It caused such a run on accounts at the bank that the government of Macau had to take over BDA's operations and place a temporary halt on withdrawals. According to press reports, the Macau government shut down all North Korea-related accounts including those belonging to nine DPRK banks and 23 DPRK trading companies. These reportedly included accounts from the core organs of the North Korean Regime.
>
> The financial effects of the BDA action were larger than expected. The crackdown also spread around the region. In Macau, the North Korean trading firm used by Pyongyang as a *de facto* consulate rolled up its operations as the Macau government placed BDA into receivership. Not only did the action deprive major DPRK companies of an international financial base and cut into the secret personal accounts of the Pyongyang leadership, but it appears to have obstructed some legitimate North Korean trade.
>
> On February 13, 2007, a new Six-Party Talks agreement on North Korea's nuclear program and energy needs was concluded. In announcing this agreement, Assistant Secretary of State Christopher Hill pledged to settle with North Korea the issue of U.S. financial sanctions against BDA and the freezing of North Korean accounts of $25 million. After several failed attempts to transfer the $25 million, the DPRK recovered its funds in June 2007 when the New York Federal Reserve Bank agreed to transfer them through its facilities to a bank in Russia.[62]

On June 18, 2009, the Financial Crimes Enforcement Network (FinCEN) of the U.S. Treasury Department issued an advisory for all U.S. financial institutions to take risk mitigation measures against the possibility that the DPRK would use deceptive financial practices to hide illicit conduct. Specifically, FinCEN noted that with respect to correspondent accounts held for North Korean financial institutions, as well as their foreign branches and subsidiaries, there is now an increased likelihood that such vehicles may be used to hide illicit conduct and related financial proceeds in an attempt to circumvent existing sanctions, particularly those of U.N. Resolution 1874. FinCEN advised financial institutions to apply enhanced scrutiny to any such correspondent accounts and to avoid providing financial services for North Korea's procurement of luxury goods. In order to assist in applying enhanced scrutiny, FinCEN supplied a list of North Korean banks. It also encouraged financial institutions worldwide to take similar precautions.[63]

Trade in Arms

The U.N. sanctions also ban exports of North Korean arms, including small arms and light weapons. Stopping exports of large armaments will depend on the effectiveness of interdictions and threats of interdictions of shipments by cooperating countries discussed elsewhere in this memorandum. DPRK trade in small arms and ammunition is relatively insignificant. Recently reported purchases of such items from the DPRK included imports of $45.5 thousand by Brazil in 2007, of $3.1 million by the United Arab Emirates in 2006, and $364.4 thousand by Ethiopia and $121.4 thousand by Mexico in 2005.[64] The small arms export ban, therefore, is not likely to have a large effect on the economy of the DPRK, but it could affect the ability of certain military-owned factories to buy needed raw materials and technology.

Import and Export Trade

Between one-half and three-quarters of the DPRK's imports and exports are with China. More than one-half of North Korea's exports and one-third of its imports have been with South Korea, primarily through activities in the Kaesong Industrial Complex located in North Korea just north of the DMZ. The United States and Japan have virtually no trade with North Korea. The vast majority of China's imports from the DPRK is in non-prohibited items such as ores, coal, iron/steel, apparel, fish, and minerals. The top six imports in Table 1 account for about 85% of China's total imports from North Korea. The ores, coal, and fish/seafood originate primarily from Chinese investments in enterprises in the DPRK.

Table 1. China's Major Imports from the DPRK ($million)

Commodity	Description	2003	2004	2005	2006	2007	2008
	Total	395.5	582.2	496.5	467.7	581.5	754.0
26	Ores, Slag, Ash	15.0	58.9	92.3	118.4	164.0	212.7
27	Mineral Fuel, Oil	17.2	53.0	112.2	102.3	170.0	207.6
72	Iron and Steel	46.8	75.0	72.2	35.2	45.2	78.4
62	Woven Apparel	52.2	49.1	58.3	63.3	60.4	77.3
03	Fish and Seafood	207.0	261.2	92.4	43.3	29.9	40.0
25	Salt; Sulfur; Earths and Stone	0.7	1.1	1.3	4.2	7.5	19.3

Source: Congressional Research Service with Data from Global Trade Atlas. Notes: Commodity numbers are 2-digit Harmonized Tariff System Codes.

As shown in Table 2, China's major exports to the DPRK include mineral fuels (petroleum), machinery/boilers, electrical machinery, knit apparel, plastic, vehicles, man-made filaments, and cereals. With the exception of knit apparel, these exports are essential to the functioning of the North Korean economy. It is noteworthy that China exports less in cereals to North Korea than it imports in fish and seafood, contradicting the general impression that trade in food is primarily one-way from China to the DPRK.

China recognizes the leverage it wields through its exports of petroleum to the DPRK. According to a news report from Japan, following the DPRK's second nuclear test, China imposed its own "sanctions" on the DPRK by reducing crude oil shipments through its pipeline with North Korea. Previously, following the DPRK's missile test on April 5, 2009, China had tightened inspections of weapons-related exports to North Korea.[65] China also cancelled a joint venture with North Korea to produce vanadium (used to toughen steel alloys used in missile casings) and has intercepted a shipment of 70 kg of vanadium hidden in a truckload of fruit crossing the border into North Korea.[66]

Table 2. China's Major Exports to the DPRK ($million)

Commodity	Description	2003	2004	2005	2006	2007	2008
	Total	628.0	794.5	1,084.7	1,231.9	1,392.4	2,033.2
27	Mineral Fuel, Oil	180.7	204.4	285.7	347.5	402.0	586.0
84	Machinery; Reactors, Boilers	27.0	39.6	77.1	83.0	103.8	145.5
85	Electrical Machinery, Etc.	39.6	45.8	56.6	97.6	69.3	100.6
61	Knit Apparel	3.6	4.8	6.2	10.1	23.8	87.0
39	Plastic	24.6	32.0	52.2	52.0	54.6	80.0
87	Vehicles, Not Railway	8.4	18.3	28.3	28.0	53.7	67.3
54	Manmade Filaments	14.6	18.0	28.9	38.6	52.3	55.0
10	Cereals	50.0	15.3	50.3	16.9	36.5	34.9

Source: Congressional Research Service with Data from Global Trade Atlas.
Notes: Commodity numbers are 2-digit Harmonized Tariff System Codes.

Since the sanctions under Resolution 1874 are narrowly focused on items related to the North Korean nuclear and missile programs, pressure from China would entail using broader trade tools.

The U.N. sanctions also include exports of luxury goods. Figure 1 shows China's exports of luxury goods to the DPRK by month from July 2005 to November 2009 using international trade categories corresponding closely to the lists of banned goods. As indicated in the figure, there seems to be little change in Chinese exports of luxury goods following either of the two U.N. resolutions. Figure 1 also shows that in December of each year, Pyongyang seems to go on a buying spree in China. There was a surge in imports of luxury items in that month, particularly in 2006 ($15.1 million) and in 2008 ($50.4 million). In 2008, the imports included $16.6 million in articles of leather, $6.3 million in articles of fur, $5.7 million in crustaceans and shell fish, $4.6 million in exercise and pool equipment, and $4.5 million in motor vehicles. In December 2009, there was a smaller spike in purchases of luxury goods followed by a drop in January 2010 and a slight recovery in February. Whether this decline in 2010 is due to a lack of foreign exchange or the U.N. sanctions is not determinable at this time.

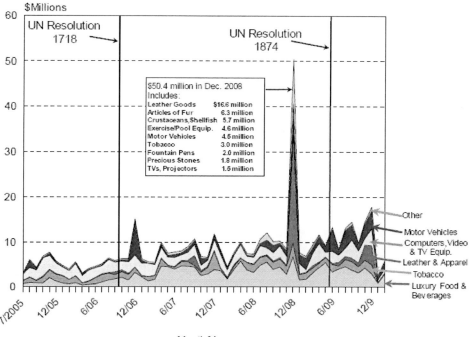

Source: Underlying data accessed through Global Trade Atlas.

Notes: Computers include only those less than 10 kg (laptops). From August to November 2009, China reported trade with the DPRK as trade with "Other Asia, not elsewhere specified." These "Other Asia" data are used in this chart for the August to November period. The list of luxury items are from the U.S. Department of Commerce and from Marcus Noland, "The (Non) Impact of UN Sanctions on North Korea," Peterson Institute for International Economics, Working Paper Series, December 2008, pp. 14-16, The lists of banned products are not specific and are not accompanied by HTS (Harmonized Tariff System) codes. The actual HTS codes used are listed in Appendix to this report.

Figure 1. China's Exports of Luxury Goods under U.N. Sanctions to the DPRK.

In summary, the economic effect of Resolution 1874 is not likely to be great unless

- China cooperates extensively and goes beyond the requirements of the resolution and/or
- the specific financial sanctions create a ripple effect that causes financial institutions to avoid being "tainted" by handling any DPRK transaction.

North Korea's Proliferation, Nuclear and Missile Programs[67]

At a press conference on June 16, President Obama stated that "North Korea also has a track record of proliferation that makes it unacceptable for them to be accepted as a nuclear power. They have not shown in the past any restraint in terms of exporting weapons to not only state actors but also non-state actors."[68] North Korea is known to have sold ballistic missiles and associated materials to "several Middle Eastern countries, including Iran, and, in our assessment, assisted Syria with the construction of a nuclear reactor," according to DNI Admiral Dennis Blair's testimony to Congress.[69] North Korea appears not to simply export missile technology, but to collaborate with Iran and perhaps others in missile development.[70] Resolution 1874 may bolster the ability of the international community to prevent North Korea from proliferating its WMD and missile technologies to other countries and to halt supply of North Korea's programs only to the extent that countries are willing to sanction relevant entities, share sensitive information and stop suspicious shipments.

Some analysts point out that the measures authorized under the resolution will not prevent the proliferation of nuclear material or sensitive information such as test data or weapons design due to their portability. However, other analysts and the Obama Administration contend that if all countries implement what is called for in the resolution, at the minimum North Korea would be discouraged from attempting to ship or procure sensitive goods. Others point out that, generally, increased monitoring and sharing of information about North Koreans' activities abroad may improve U.S. intelligence related to WMD programs.

As evidenced in the reports to the UNSC Sanctions Committee for Res. 1718, many countries have existing laws or participate in multilateral export control regimes that prohibit trade in WMD and missile-related technology. The Proliferation Security Initiative (PSI) has facilitated international cooperation on WMD interdiction issues.[71] However, the extent to which countries are now willing to sanction their own companies involved in such transactions by placing them on the UNSC sanctions list (as discussed above) will be a key determinant.

Pyongyang has had an active procurement network for its nuclear program for decades.[72] Pyongyang may need to procure items from abroad for further advances. Therefore, increased international vigilance, stopping of shipments and financial pressures combined may have a limiting effect on North Korea's own programs as well as on its proliferation to others. This may largely depend on China's willingness to curb traffic, as discussed in the "Implementation of Sanctions" section above.

North Korea's Policies and Internal Situation[73]

As with all analysis that involves the secretive regime in Pyongyang, the impact of the resolution on North Korea's domestic situation is nearly impossible to gauge with any degree of precision. However, North Korea's actions surrounding the nuclear test have provided observers with some clues about the internal dynamics of Kim's government. In the past, North Korea's provocations tended to be viewed by the majority of analysts as ploys to strengthen its negotiating position at the Six-Party Talks. Pyongyang's more recent behavior, however, has generally shifted the predominant view among Korea-watchers: it now seems that North Korea is determined to be a nuclear state, even at the price of angering its closest allies.

Financial sanctions were designed to target the country's elite and military enterprises. Most analysts suggest that the regime has proven quite resourceful at remaining firmly in power despite a bevy of sanctions in past years. Even at the expense of large swathes of the general population, the inner circle of elites has been kept happy with limited resources. However, some argue that if sanctions are carried out effectively, they may have an impact on internal power struggles as elites vie for resources. Some suggest that the sanctions levied against Banco Delta Asia in 2005 appeared to be effective at targeting the regime, and that the pain inflicted by those sanctions led to North Korea's return to the nuclear negotiations. Others point out, however, that this return was preceded by North Korea's first nuclear test, indicating that effective sanctions may simply strengthen the hardliners' resolve.

Further complicating assessments of how the resolution may affect North Korea's internal policies is the assumption that officials in Pyongyang are contemplating a transfer of power. Kim Jong-il's reported stroke in August 2008 elevated attention among international observers to the question of succession in the North Korean regime. Pyongyang's behavior while Kim was ill was characterized as provocative and aggressive, suggesting that hardline elements held sway in decisions such as the missile launch, nuclear test, and withdrawal from the Six-Party Talks. Kim has apparently recovered and re-asserted his authority over the regime. Now back in power, Kim himself is thought to be overseeing the anticipated succession. The strengthening of the National Defense Commission and suspected constitutional adjustments, together with stepped-up propaganda in praise of his third son Kim Jong Eun, suggest that Pyongyang is attempting to manage a transition to a new leader.

Because decision-making within the regime remains opaque, it is not clear how elites in Pyongyang may be considering Beijing's reaction in their calculations. In the past, it seems that North Korean elites were able to depend on China ultimately to ensure their survival. If North Korea has actually alienated some influential players in Beijing with this round of provocations, enhanced Chinese enforcement of the sanctions regime could inflict more pain than earlier attempts. However, some analysts believe that China, recognizing that different parties within North Korea are competing for influence, may feel even more restrained from pressuring North Korea for fear of alienating a future power base.

ASSESSMENTS OF UNSC RESOLUTION 1718 (2006)[74]

UNSC Resolution 1874 tightens, expands, and adds to many of the existing restrictions that were included in UNSC Resolution 1718, which the Security Council unanimously passed on October 14, 2006, five days after North Korea's first nuclear test.[75] As with Resolution 1874, Resolution 1718 was passed in the hope that it would curb financial inflows that went to North Korea's regime and its weapons programs, while imposing minimal humanitarian hardships on the broader North Korean population.

Less than three weeks after the UNSC passed Resolution 1718, North Korea announced it would return to the Six-Party Talks that it had been boycotting for nearly a year. The announcement came after secret meetings with U.S. and Chinese officials. While it is possible that Kim Jong-il's government planned to quickly return to the talks after its nuclear test, it is also possible that the speedy passage and unanimous support of 1718 spurred the regime's decision.

However, most analysts consider Resolution 1718 ineffective in economically penalizing North Korea. The coverage of the provisions was relatively limited, provisions enforcing transparency on sanctioning countries were relatively weak, military enforcement options were not included in the resolution, and there was no defined list of the prohibited products. Instead, creating the lists was left to individual countries, who then reported them to the U.N. Sanctions Committee. This administrative feature of the sanctions regime allowed countries to avoid or soften implementation of the resolution. China and South Korea appeared to soften implementation with North Korea's decision to return to the Six-Party Talks. Neither country, for instance, published detailed lists of the luxury goods they planned to sanction. Together, the two accounted for 61% and 75% of DPRK trade in 2006 and 2007, respectively.

There is strong evidence that China did not rigorously implement the resolution's provisions.[76] According to an analysis by the Peterson Institute's Marcus Noland, for instance, it appears that exports from China increased after 2006.[77] In 2007, North Korea-China trade in general increased by 13%, followed by a 41% increase in 2008. In those years, Chinese exports to North Korea rose by 13% and 46%, respectively.[78] While this rise in overall trade is not necessarily indicative of an increase in luxury goods shipments, it appears to indicate that the sanctions either had no or little deterrent effect on Chinese enterprises' normal commerce with their North Korean counterparts.[79] Even more damaging, informed sources have told CRS that most of the North Korean trading companies and banks sanctioned by the Security Council continued to operate in China at the end of 2009.

As for South Korea, in the aftermath of North Korea's test, it halted humanitarian assistance. Food aid shipments from Seoul dropped from 400,000 in 2005 to 100,000 in 2006.[80] However, overall trade between the Koreas jumped by 33% in the calendar year after Resolution 1718 was adopted.[81] Much of this increased trade was due to the expansion of the Kaesong Industrial Complex (KIC), a facility in North Korea in which South Korean manufacturers employ North Korean workers. The North Korean government derives tens of millions of dollars from the complex, from rental fees and the portion of the workers' wages it collects.[82]

APPENDIX. CHINA'S EXPORTS OF LUXURY GOODS TO THE DPRK

HTS Number	Description	2006	2007	2008
	Luxury Items Listed by the United States			
24	Tobacco	14,117,739	12,950,218	16,952,464
2203-2208	Alcoholic Beverages	5,137,988	5,084,449	6,652,041
33	Perfumery, Cosmetic Products	1,322,454	1,672,327	1,688,481
42	Leather Art; Saddlery, Etc.	772,645	1,441,805	19,155,523
5007	Woven Fabrics Of Silk Or Silk Waste	0	10,422	0
621410	Shawls, Scarves Etc Of Silk Or Silk Waste Not Knit	1,645	2,750	0
4303	Articles Of Apparel Etc. Of Furskin	823,388	2,454,154	485,978

HTS Number	Description	2006	2007	2008
4304	Artificial Fur And Articles Thereof	590,483	209,337	6,427,779
8703	Motor Cars & Vehicles For Transporting Persons	9,087,018	7,179,104	10,981,707
870710	Bodies F Mtr Car/Vehicles For Transporting Persons	38,627	0	18,296
871110	Motocycles (Incl Mopeds), Pist. Eng. Cyl, Not, Exc 50Cc	7,625	49,633	19,863
871120	Motorcycles (Including Mopeds),Cycl,Exc50Cc,Nt250C	152,403	205,782	187,336
871190	Motorcycles (Including Mopeds), Nesoi, Side Cars	23,031	385,307	220,720
890310	Inflatable Yachts, Vessels, For Plesure, Sports	400	1,300	100
890399	Yachts Etc For Pleas, Sport, Nesoi; Row Bts, Canoes	21,620	4,200	21,845
57	Textile Floor Coverings	81,286	123,635	170,494
71	Precious Stones	49,118	23,837	3,916,863
8528	Tv Recvrs, Incl Video Monitors & Projectors	19,734,504	17,852,328	18,054,879
8521	Video Recrdng/Reproduc Appar Wheth/Nt Video Tuner	6,455,725	6,144,654	6,167,653
8522	Parts And Accessories For Items 8519 To 8521	694	20,990	40,080
847130	Portable Digtl Automatic Data Process Mach Not > 10 Kg	909,043	1,359,392	1,915,003
91	Clocks and Watches	309,593	536,805	959,410
97	Art and Antiques	2,188	1,180	1,770
92	Musical Instruments	884,475	1,025,490	1,861,885
6911	Ceramic Tableware Etc. Of Porcelain Or China	616,051	518,996	219,608
6912	Ceramic Tablewre, Kitchnwre Etc, Earthenware Etc	1,940	0	0
9506	Artls & Equip F Genrl Physcl Exerc Etc; Pools; Pts	175,268	275,992	5,063,675
701321	Drinking Glasses Other Than Glass-Ceramics, Of Lead Crystal	0	0	0
701331	Table/Kitchenware (Exc Drinking Glasses) O/T Glass-Ceramics, Of Lead Crystal	0	0	0
701333	Other Drinking Glasses, O/T Of Glass-Ceramics, Of Lead Crystal	0	4,020	636

Appendix. (Continued)

HTS Number	Description	2006	2007	2008
701341	Table/Kitchenware,Excl Drinking Glasses, O/T Glass-Ceramics, Of Lead Crystal	0	195	756
701391	Glassware, Nes Of Lead Crystal, Other Than That Of 70.10 Or 70.18	0	61,487	23,208
960839	Fountain Pens, Stylograph Pens And Other Pens, O/T Indian Ink Drawing Pens	11,005	29,792	2,016,092
Total U.S.		61,327,956	59,629,581	103,224,145	61,327,956
Additional Luxury Goods listed by the European Union, Australia, Canada, and Japan				
9006	Photographic Cameras;Photographic Flash-Light App O/T Discharge Lamps Of 85.39	6,795	33,656	17,992
9007	Cinematographic Cameras & Projectors, W/N Incorp Sound Record Or Reprdc App	34,164	0	2,162
8471less	Computers no portables	12,253,274	14,130,377	16,226,703
847130				
160250	Prepared Or Preserved Bovine Meat Etc. Nesoi	3494	89216	59504
1604	Prep Or Pres Fish; Caviar & Caviar Substitutes	784,372	937,967	2,286,515
1605	Crustaceans, Molluscs Etc. Prepared Or Preserved	8,940,342	34,820,072	41,175,401
Total Additional Luxury Goods		22,022,441	50,011,288	59,768,277
Total U.S. Plus Additional Luxury Goods		83,350,397	109,640,869	162,992,422

Source: Congressional Research Service. List of luxury items from Marcus Noland, "The (Non) Impact of UN Sanctions on North Korea," Peterson Institute for International Economics, Working Paper Series, December 2008, pp. 14-16, and U.S. Department of Commerce. Data from Global Trade Atlas.

Note: The lists of banned products are not specific and are not accompanied by HTS (Harmonized Tariff System) codes. The above totals differ somewhat from those by Marcus Noland for 2006 and 2007. Nesoi=not elsewhere specified or indicated.

End Notes

[1] Larry Niksch, a longtime Specialist in Asian Affairs who retired from CRS in early 2010, was a co-author of this report.

[2] http://www.dni.gov/press_releases/20090615_release.pdf.

[3] For full text, see http://www.un.org/Docs/sc/unsc_resolutions09.htm.

[4] Michael D. Shear, "U.S. Interagency Team to Focus On Sanctions Against N. Korea ," *The Washington Post*, June 27, 2009, p. A7.
[5] "Flag state" refers to the country that exercises regulatory control over a commercial ship that has registered under its flag. Some states may allow foreign vessels to register under their flag, known as "flag of convenience."
[6] Blaine Harden, "North Korea Says It Will Start Enriching Uranium," *Washington Post*, June 14, 2009. The resolution is under Chapter 7, Article 41 of the U.N. Charter, and does not authorize use of force during interdiction attempts. The full text of Article 41 follows: "The Security Council may decide what measures not involving the use of armed force are to be employed to give effect to its decisions, and it may call upon the Members of the United Nations to apply such measures. These may include complete or partial interruption of economic relations and of rail, sea, air, postal, telegraphic, radio, and other means of communication, and the severance of diplomatic relations."
[7] "U.N. Expands Sanctions Imposed on North Korea," *Wall Street Journal Asia*, July 17, 2009, p. 13.
[8] Other U.N. Security Council Sanctions Committees have appointed a panel of experts to help the committee monitor implementation of sanctions, i.e., related to arms embargoes on the Sudan, Sierre Leone, Somalia, Liberia, etc. U.N. Security Council Resolution 1540 also established a panel of experts, but that panel focuses on reporting and encouraging states to develop national infrastructure to prevent illicit trade in WMD, as opposed to sanctions violations.
[9] http://www.un.org/sc/committees/1718/pdf/S2009416%20E.pdf. Please note that the Chinese expert on this original list was later replaced with another expert.
[10] "Sanctioned N. Korean firms operating via dummies: U.N. report," *Japan Economic Newswire*, November 19, 2009.
[11] "Cargo of North Korea materiel is seized en route to Iran," *Wall Street Journal*, August 31, 2009.
[12] There is some dispute as to whether protective clothing is prohibited under the resolution. This type of clothing could be used to protect against chemical attacks. "S. Korea searched suspicious N.K. containers: sources," *Yonhap News*, October 6, 2009
[13] "South Africa reports NKorea sanctions violation," *Associated Press*, February 26, 2010.
[14] This section was originally prepared by Larry Niksch.
[15] U.S. Department of State, Bureau of Public Affairs, Background Briefing on North Korea, July 15, 2009.
[16] "U.S. Mulls Relisting N. Korea As State Sponsor of Terrorism," *Asia Pulse*, June 8, 2009. See CRS Report RL30613, *North Korea: Terrorism List Removal*, by Larry A. Niksch.
[17] "North Korea to Face Huge Losses from U.N. Sanctions: Report," *Asia Pulse*, June 11, 2009. Yun Deok-min, "China's Nuclear Headache," *JoongAng Daily Online*, June 16, 2009.
[18] John S. Park, *North Korea, Inc., Gaining Insights into North Korean Regime Stability from Recent Commercial Activities*, U.S. Institute of Peace, USIP Working Paper, Washington, DC, April 22, 2009.
[19] U.S. Department of State, Bureau of Public Affairs, "Background Briefing on North Korea," July 15, 2009.
[20] "U.S. Seeks Malaysia's Help to Block N. Korea's Access to Banks," *Kyodo News*, July 6, 2009.
[21] U.S. Department of State, Bureau of Public Affairs, "Background Briefing on North Korea," July 15, 2009.
[22] "3 Entities Subject to Asset Freeze Over N. Korea Nuke, Missile Program," *Kyodo News*, April 24, 2009.
[23] "U.N. Expands Sanctions Imposed on North Korea," *Wall Street Journal Asia*, July 17, 2009, p. 13.
[24] Jay Solomon, "U.S. goes after North Korea's Finances," *Wall Street Journal Asia*, July 1, 2009, p. 8.
[25] "N.Korea maneuvers to evade UN sanctions," *Reuters*, November 18, 2009.
[26] David E. Sanger, "U.S. to confront, not board, North Korean ships," *New York Times* (internet), June 17, 2009.
[27] Paul Kerr, "Iran, North Korea Deepen Missile Cooperation," *Arms Control Today*, January/February 2007, http://www.armscontrol.org/act/2007_01-02/IranNK
[28] Choe Sang-hun, "South Korea Says Freighter from North Turns Back," *New York Times*, July 7, 2009, p. 5.
[29] State Department, "Remarks at the ASEAN Regional Forum," Hillary Rodham Clinton, July 23, 2009; "Japan Officials Say Burma FM Pledges Nation to Oblige by UN Sanctions on DPRK," *Agence France Presse*, July 23, 2009.
[30] Joby Warrick, "Arms smuggling heightens Iran fears," *Washington Port*, December 3, 2009, p. A14. "Iran bought masses of N Korean arms," *Chosun Ilbo Online*, December 4, 2009.
[31] Ibid.
[32] Paul Eckert, "Anti-proliferation Group Only Symbolic Without China," *Reuters News*, May 27, 2009.
[33] There also are numerous reports that the two countries may be cooperating in the nuclear field. Two CRS Reports lay out extensive information on North Korean-Iranian collaboration: CRS Report RL33590, *North Korea's Nuclear Weapons Development and Diplomacy*, by Larry A. Niksch and CRS Report RL30613, *North Korea: Terrorism List Removal*, by Larry A. Niksch.

[34] Jon Herskovitz, "How North Korea Earns Money from Arms Sales," *Reuters News*, July 4, 2009.
[35] "What's Behind the New U.N. sanctions on N.Korea?" *Reuters News*, June 12, 2009.
[36] "N.Korea's Arms Export Routes Getting Harder To Track," *Chosun Ilbo Online*, June 29, 2009. Yi Chol-hui, "North's Air Cargo: Missiles," *Chungang Ilbo* (internet), June 16, 2003. "N.K. Exported Weapons Via Overland Routes in China, Russia," *Korea Herald Online*, July 2, 2009. William Triplett, "Gaps at the G-8 Gates," *Washington Times*, July 13, 2006, p. A16. Paul Eckert, "Anti-proliferation Group Only Symbolic without China," *Reuters News*, May 27, 2009.
[37] U.S. Department of State, Bureau of Public Affairs, "Background Briefing on North Korea," July 15, 2009.
[38] Nicholas Kralev, "Illegal N. Korean arms fly in Chinese airspace," *Washington Times*, December 17, 2009, p. A1.
[39] "City firm linked to N Korean arms shipment," *The Standard Online* (Hong Kong), December 23, 2009. "Iran bought masses of N Korean arms," *Chosun Ilbo Online*, December 4, 2009.
[40] Daniel Michaels and Margaret Coker, "Seized arms Iran-bound, report says," *Wall Street Journal Asia*, December 21, 2009.
[41] "Details of mysterious weapons—authorities stunned to find RPG rocket launchers," *Krungthep Thurakit* (Bangkok, internet), December 16, 2009. "Rocket launchers, but no nuclear components," *The Nation Online* (Bangkok), December 16, 2009.
[42] "Korean arms cache caught en route to Mideast," *Daily Star Online* (Beirut), December 15, 2009.
[43] Robert J. Saiget, "China, DPRK Trade Said Booming Despite Rocket Tensions," *Agence France Presse*, April 6, 2009.
[44] For details on Chinese exports of luxury goods, see the Appendix to this report.
[45] Ibid.
[46] This section was prepared by Dick Nanto.
[47] For details, see CRS Report RL32493, *North Korea: Economic Leverage and Policy Analysis*, by Dick K. Nanto and Emma Chanlett-Avery
[48] World Food Programme, "8.7 Million North Koreans Need Food Assistance," December 10, 2008.
[49] John S. Park, *North Korea, Inc., Gaining Insights into North Korean Regime Stability from Recent Commercial Activities*, U.S. Institute of Peace, USIP Working Paper, Washington, DC, April 22, 2009.
[50] "N. Korea 'Squandered $700 Million to Create Tensions'," *The Chosun Ilbo*, July 6, 2009, Online Digital Chosun.
[51] Balbina Hwang, "Shattering Myths and Assumptions: The Implications of North Korea's Strategic Culture for U.S. Policy," *International Journal of Korean Unification Studies*, vol. 18, no. 1 (2009), p. 42.
[52] For more on assistance to North Korea, including details of U.S. aid, see CRS Report R40095, *Foreign Assistance to North Korea*, by Mark E. Manyin and Mary Beth Nikitin.
[53] European Commission, *North Korea - Food Security Programme 2007 (LRRD Component)*, EuropeAid/126276/C/ACT/KP, Brussels, Belgium, 2008, p. 3.
[54] United Nations World Food Programme, *WFP Does What Little It Can for North Koreans*, March 5, 2009.
[55] CRS Report RL32493, *North Korea: Economic Leverage and Policy Analysis*, by Dick K. Nanto and Emma Chanlett-Avery, p. 34.
[56] Bank of Korea, Income Statistics Team, *Gross Domestic Product of North Korea in 2008*, Seoul, Korea, June 26, 2009, http://eng.bok.or.kr/contents/total/eng/boardView.action.
[57] For details on Chinese exports of luxury goods, see the Appendix to this report.
[58] Robert J. Saiget, "China, DPRK Trade Said Booming Despite Rocket Tensions," *Agence France-Presse, Hong Kong AFP*, April 6, 2009.
[59] Ibid., p. 42.
[60] Organisation for Economic Cooperation and Development, *Development Statistics*, DAC Private Flows to the DPRK, Non-bank gross export credits, http://stats.oecd.org.
[61] Bank for International Settlements, *Consolidated banking statistics, Table 9D: Consolidated foreign claims of reporting banks - ultimate risk basis*, accessed June 17, 2009.
[62] CRS Report RL33324, *North Korean Counterfeiting of U.S. Currency*, by Dick K. Nanto.
[63] Financial Crimes Enforcement Network, U.S. Department of the Treasury, *North Korea Government Agencies' and Front Companies' Involvement in Illicit Financial Activities*, Advisory FIN 2009-A002, Washington, DC, June 18, 2009, http://www.fincen.gov/statutes_regs/guidance/html/fin-2009-a002.html.
[64] United Nations COMTRADE database.

[65] "China Imposes Own 'Sanctions' on DPRK by Reducing Crude Oil Shipment, Stepping Up Customs Inspection on Exports to the DPRK," *Asahi Shimbun (in Japanese)*, June 13, 2009, Translation in U.S. Forces Korea J2, Korea, Open Source Digest, Volume II, Issue 114, June 16, 2009 .

[66] "China foils smuggling of missile-use material to North Korea," *Chosun Ilbo*, July 25, 2009, Internet edition.

[67] This section was prepared by Mary Beth Nikitin.

[68] http://www.whitehouse.gov/video/President-Obama-and-President-Lee-of-the-Republic-of-Korea-Talk-to-the-Press/

[69] http://intelligence.senate.gov/090212/blair.pdf

[70] "North Korea's Nuclear and Missile Programs," *International Crisis Group*, June 18, 2009.

[71] China does not participate in PSI. South Korea announced its participation shortly after the May 2009 North Korean nuclear test. See also CRS Report RL34327, *Proliferation Security Initiative (PSI)*, by Mary Beth Nikitin.

[72] "Nuclear Black Markets: Pakistan, A.Q. Khan and the Rise of Proliferation Networks," *IISS Strategic Dossier*, 2007.

[73] This section was prepared by Emma Chanlett-Avery.

[74] This section was prepared by Mark Manyin.

[75] Resolution 1718 called on North Korea to abandon its nuclear and missile programs and imposed sanctions on several types of activities. The resolution banned trade with North Korea in materials related to ballistic missiles or weapons of mass destruction, and barred exports of luxury goods to the DPRK. It also banned trading with North Korea in large weapons systems. It also froze funds and other financial assets owned by people connected with North Korea's unconventional weapons program and banned travel by such people.

[76] Trade in heavy weapons systems such as missiles generally are not recorded, complicating any assessment of 1718's arms embargo.

[77] Marcus Noland, "The (Non) Impact of U.N. Sanctions on North Korea," Peterson Institute for International Economics, Working Paper 08-12, 2008.

[78] Global Trade Atlas using Chinese data.

[79] For more on this point, see Noland, "The (Non) Impact of U.N. Sanctions on North Korea," p. 5, 9-10.

[80] South Korean Export-Import Bank's "DPRK Support Fund," provided via South Korean Ministry of Unification.

[81] South Korean Ministry of Unification.

[82] See CRS Report RL34093, *The Kaesong North-South Korean Industrial Complex*, by Dick K. Nanto and Mark E. Manyin.

INDEX

A

access, 2, 13, 16, 56, 63, 64, 104, 117, 118
accounting, 17, 50, 123
agencies, 14, 47, 54, 55, 71, 77, 98, 122, 124
agriculture, 18, 120, 122
Air Force, 82, 87, 99, 102, 107, 111
airports, 66, 115, 119
Appropriations Act, 67
Argentina, 25
argon, 82, 83, 101, 102, 104, 107
armed forces, 58
arms control, 29, 77, 79
arms sales, viii, 6, 15, 113, 114
ASEAN, 133
Asia, 4, 9, 13, 14, 15, 19, 37, 40, 41, 42, 44, 70, 73, 123, 124, 127, 129, 133, 134
atmosphere, 30, 75, 82, 83, 87, 89, 91, 101, 105
atmospheric pressure, 81, 90, 107
Austria, 106, 108
authorities, 66, 82, 115, 116, 134
authority, 7, 11, 33, 67, 68, 74, 114, 115, 129

B

ballistic missiles, 15, 16, 37, 57, 65, 95, 119, 128, 135
ban, viii, 75, 77, 113, 114, 115, 117, 120, 125
banks, 15, 117, 118, 122, 123, 124, 125, 130, 134
base, 53, 96, 115, 118, 124, 129
Beijing, 4, 5, 8, 9, 10, 12, 23, 28, 29, 30, 33, 36, 37, 38, 41, 69, 72, 73, 117, 122, 123, 129
Belgium, 22, 134
benefits, viii, 5, 9, 93, 113, 114
bilateral relationship, 32
Boris Yeltsin, 32
Brazil, 25, 125

breakdown, 35, 47, 114
Britain, 71
Burma, 6, 118, 133
burn, 49, 69

C

calcium, 82, 83, 104, 107
carbon dioxide, 89, 110
cash, 17, 37, 122, 124
challenges, 4, 13, 24, 36, 69
chemical, 60, 62, 78, 79, 81, 104, 106, 111, 133
Chile, 106
China, viii, ix, 1, 2, 3, 4, 5, 8, 9, 10, 12, 13, 15, 19, 23, 27, 28, 29, 30, 32, 35, 38, 40, 41, 43, 44, 45, 48, 53, 56, 62, 66, 69, 71, 75, 77, 80, 93, 100, 106, 113, 114, 115, 116, 117, 118, 119, 120, 121, 122, 123, 125, 126, 127, 128, 129, 130, 131, 133, 134, 135
CIA, 51, 54, 69, 70, 71
citizens, 10, 12, 13, 14, 34, 36, 121
climate change, 4
Clinton Administration, vii, 1, 4, 8, 15, 17
CNN, 18, 68
coercive tools, vii, 22, 23, 38
Cold War, vii, 1, 3, 27, 29, 32
collaboration, 6, 18, 89, 119, 133
commercial, 6, 10, 50, 79, 87, 104, 121, 123, 133
communication, 105, 107, 108, 109, 110, 111, 133
Communist Party, 12
community, 5, 8, 9, 12, 16, 21, 24, 26, 32, 39, 99, 114, 128
compliance, 6, 8, 23, 38, 77, 78, 79, 97, 107, 116, 118
Comprehensive Nuclear-Test-Ban Treaty (CTBT), viii, 75, 76
Comprehensive Test Ban Treaty, 109, 110
computer, 76, 81, 84, 91, 103

conflict, 3, 28, 37, 47
confrontation, 65
Congo, 116, 119
Congress, viii, 1, 2, 13, 14, 16, 33, 34, 40, 41, 43, 45, 46, 48, 49, 54, 55, 57, 61, 62, 65, 66, 67, 68, 69, 70, 71, 72, 74, 75, 76, 79, 96, 97, 98, 99, 103, 104, 106, 109, 113, 128
consent, viii, 24, 28, 39, 64, 66, 75, 77, 111, 115
Consolidated Appropriations Act, 67
construction, viii, 7, 8, 45, 46, 47, 51, 52, 62, 65, 70, 94, 128
cooling, 49, 50, 51, 58, 59, 60, 62
cooperation, 4, 6, 12, 17, 24, 30, 40, 47, 53, 66, 93, 94, 116, 118, 119, 123, 128
cost, 14, 26, 28, 33, 40, 67, 104, 120, 121
covering, 55, 116
crust, 83, 99, 110
currency, 1, 4, 7, 10, 15, 37, 124
Czech Republic, 105

D

danger, 11, 26, 31, 34
decay, 83, 84, 85, 87, 90, 101
deficit, 121, 123
Delta, 15, 37, 123, 124, 129
democracy, 14, 22, 24, 25, 36, 39
Democratic People's Republic of Korea, vii, 1, 3, 19, 67, 70, 73, 77, 113
denuclearization, vii, 1, 2, 3, 5, 6, 16, 45, 48, 53, 55, 56, 63, 67, 68, 115, 121
Department of Commerce, 127, 132
Department of Defense, 16, 17, 21, 22, 67, 106, 108, 109
Department of Energy, 64, 67, 74, 89, 91, 106, 108, 109, 110, 111
destruction, 34, 36, 115, 119, 135
detectable, 86, 89, 90, 92, 97
detection, 75, 76, 78, 79, 82, 83, 84, 85, 88, 90, 92, 93, 97, 98, 100, 102, 104, 106
detonation, 80, 90, 91, 100, 102, 103, 106
diplomacy, 2, 3, 4, 17, 33, 57
diplomatic efforts, 33
diplomatic relations, vii, 1, 3, 8, 17, 32, 133
dismantlement, 48, 56, 58, 62, 65, 66, 67, 68
distribution, 10, 22, 86, 104
divergence, 12, 24, 39
diversity, 23, 38
DNA, 109
DPRK transaction, ix, 113, 114, 127

E

East Asia, 4, 9, 40, 42, 44, 73
economic activity, 120
economic assistance, 8
economic cooperation, 12
economic crisis, 66
economic development, 8, 10
economic landscape, 4
economic reform, 8
economic relations, 17, 37, 133
economic resources, 121
effluents, 75, 76, 83, 91, 92, 93
Egypt, 15, 77, 118
eight-year freeze, viii, 45, 47
election, 9, 37
embargo, 33, 115, 116, 135
emergency, 8, 17, 122
energy, viii, 9, 16, 18, 46, 59, 64, 65, 67, 78, 80, 83, 84, 85, 92, 108, 110, 124
enforcement, 41, 117, 129, 130
England, 107
enriched uranium, viii, 34, 35, 41, 45, 46, 47, 48, 52, 53, 54, 55, 62, 65, 69, 70, 94, 95, 105
environment, 16, 30, 80
equipment, 18, 51, 53, 54, 55, 60, 61, 63, 64, 65, 66, 67, 69, 76, 78, 81, 82, 83, 84, 85, 88, 92, 93, 96, 98, 100, 104, 107, 121, 126
European Commission, 134
European Community, 122
European Union (EU), 41, 47, 48, 69, 94, 100, 111, 132
execution, 13
Executive Order, 36, 41
explosives, 47, 71, 78, 79, 87, 96, 101, 106
export control, 128
exports, 9, 114, 115, 120, 121, 122, 123, 125, 126, 130, 134, 135

F

fabrication, 49, 58, 59, 60, 62, 69, 94
fear, 5, 6, 8, 10, 28, 29, 30, 31, 95, 129, 133,
financial, viii, 5, 25, 36, 65, 66, 100, 106, 113, 114, 115, 116, 117, 121, 122, 123, 124, 127, 128, 129, 135
Financial Crimes Enforcement Network, 124, 134
financial institutions, ix, 113, 114, 122, 123, 124, 127
financial resources, 100
financial support, 115, 122
fission, 71, 87, 108

food, viii, 2, 4, 8, 9, 10, 12, 13, 14, 16, 26, 113, 114, 120, 121, 122, 126
force, viii, 27, 31, 35, 66, 75, 76, 77, 79, 82, 87, 88, 93, 97, 98, 100, 103, 105, 106, 110, 115, 133
foreign assistance, 97
foreign banks, 117, 118
foreign direct investment, 123
foreign exchange, 117, 123, 127
foreign policy, vii, 1, 3, 4, 23, 24, 32, 34, 38, 39
forest fire, 104
France, 71, 73, 110, 116, 122, 123, 133, 134
freedom, 14, 22
funding, 8, 14, 19, 33, 36, 48, 58, 66, 67, 68, 99, 103, 122
funds, 13, 16, 37, 66, 67, 74, 103, 121, 122, 123, 124, 135
fusion, 108

G

gallium, 49
gamma rays, 83, 84, 85
GAO, 14, 19
gas centrifuge, viii, 7, 45, 46, 52, 94
geology, 89, 90, 91, 92
germanium, 85
Germany, 107, 122
governments, 3, 5, 6, 14, 15, 56, 57, 80, 117
greed, 9, 17, 51, 58, 61, 64, 111
Gross Domestic Product, 134

H

half-life, 78, 82, 83, 84, 87, 101, 102, 107
Hamas, 119, 120
health, 10, 17, 18
Hezbollah, 119, 120
history, 23, 25, 38, 53, 65, 105, 121
Hong Kong, 118, 120, 134
hostility, 7, 23, 26, 30, 38
human rights, 2, 4, 12, 13, 14, 24, 32, 36, 39, 68
humanitarian aid, 2, 36, 121, 122
hydrogen bomb, 96
hypothesis, 85, 86
Hyundai, 7, 42, 117

I

imports, 55, 121, 123, 125, 126
India, 77, 118
indoctrination, 12

Indonesia, 77, 118
inspections, 8, 47, 50, 63, 76, 77, 79, 81, 82, 97, 98, 105, 119, 126
inspectors, viii, 5, 8, 16, 45, 46, 47, 51, 53, 56, 62, 64, 70, 74, 97, 103, 114
institutions, ix, 17, 29, 34, 113, 114, 122, 123, 124, 127
intelligence, viii, 8, 10, 28, 34, 41, 45, 47, 49, 53, 55, 71, 74, 76, 77, 80, 96, 111, 119, 120, 128, 135
International Atomic Energy Agency, 32, 47, 53, 64, 70
international diplomacy, 4
international financial institutions, 123
international inspectors, viii, 45, 46, 56, 64
international law, 66, 80, 115
international relations, 22
international standards, 18
international trade, 122, 126
intervention, 11, 26, 28
iodine, 84, 89, 90, 101
Iran, 4, 5, 6, 15, 40, 43, 44, 57, 65, 74, 76, 77, 93, 94, 95, 102, 109, 110, 115, 118, 119, 120, 128, 133, 134
Iraq, 33
iron, 70, 125
ISC, 106, 109
isotope, 49, 69, 78, 82, 83, 84, 85, 86, 87, 102, 104, 107, 108
Israel, 40, 77, 94, 119, 120

J

Japan, viii, 1, 2, 3, 4, 8, 15, 34, 35, 41, 45, 47, 48, 62, 64, 69, 72, 75, 93, 100, 106, 110, 114, 116, 118, 125, 126, 132, 133
joint ventures, 17
journalists, 7
judiciary, 12
jurisdiction, 99

K

Kazakhstan, 89, 90
krypton, 82, 83, 107

L

lead, 17, 25, 33, 36, 37, 55, 58, 64, 76, 87, 89, 97, 98, 99, 108
leadership, 1, 4, 5, 7, 9, 10, 11, 21, 26, 124
leakage, 56, 103

leaks, 60
legislation, 14, 68
Liberia, 133
light, viii, 7, 8, 25, 33, 37, 45, 46, 47, 52, 53, 56, 57, 66, 115, 120, 125
loans, 115, 121, 123

M

machinery, 122, 125
Malaysia, 117, 118, 133
market economy, 32, 36
matter, 90, 98, 100, 104, 107, 115
Mexico, 68, 125
Middle East, 6, 65, 66, 94, 118, 128
military, 3, 4, 6, 7, 8, 11, 15, 21, 24, 26, 27, 28, 29, 30, 32, 33, 40, 58, 65, 72, 120, 121, 122, 123, 125, 128, 130
military exercises, 6, 7, 11
military junta, 33
mission, 8, 14, 21, 54, 102, 103, 111
money laundering, 15, 124
Mongolia, 13, 19, 86
moon, 42, 43, 44
moratorium, 15, 34, 37, 115
Moscow, 23, 29, 30, 31, 32, 38

N

NAS, 111
National Aeronautics and Space Administration, 107
National Defense Authorization Act, 74
National Research Council, 99, 111
national security, 6, 13, 21, 26, 30, 31
National Security Agency (NSA),111, 114
negotiating, 5, 6, 56, 79, 114, 128
NGOs, 17
noble gases, 57, 78, 81, 82, 83, 90, 91, 92, 93, 99, 102, 103, 105, 110
North Korea's nuclear weapons program, vii, 1, 3, 8, 26, 46, 64, 93, 105
North Korean refugees, 14
North Korean vessels, viii, 113, 114
Northeast Asia, 19
Norway, 122
NPT, 6, 8, 32, 33, 47, 52, 67, 115
nuclear explosions, viii, 75, 76, 77, 78, 81, 82, 83, 84, 87, 92, 98, 103, 107, 108, 109
nuclear nonproliferation, vii, 16, 23, 32, 38, 47
nuclear program, 3, 4, 7, 9, 16, 22, 23, 24, 25, 26, 27, 29, 31, 32, 33, 35, 36, 37, 38, 40, 41, 46, 47, 48, 58, 61, 62, 63, 65, 94, 98, 104, 115, 121, 124, 128

nuclear talks, 58
nuclear weapons, iv, vii, 1, 2, 3, 5, 6, 8, 9, 16, 25, 26, 28, 29, 31, 32, 35, 36, 41, 45, 46, 47, 48, 49, 53, 54, 55, 56, 57, 58, 62, 64, 65, 67, 71, 76, 87, 93, 95, 96, 105, 115
nuclei, 83, 84
nucleus, 107, 108

O

Obama, viii, 1, 2, 4, 5, 6, 7, 9, 14, 16, 17, 64, 72, 73, 75, 77, 103, 105, 114, 117, 119, 127, 128, 135
officials, viii, 2, 3, 5, 6, 7, 8, 12, 14, 15, 34, 45, 46, 47, 48, 49, 50, 52, 57, 58, 61, 63, 64, 65, 77, 94, 116, 117, 118, 119, 121, 123, 124, 129
oil, viii, 8, 9, 16, 33, 37, 45, 47, 48, 126
open-source information, vii, 45
operations, 2, 16, 22, 36, 51, 61, 62, 63, 94, 95, 122, 124

P

Pacific, 3, 9, 27, 41, 70, 73, 83, 87, 118
Pakistan, 15, 41, 53, 71, 77, 118, 135
Pentagon, 33, 57
permit, 59, 64, 76, 82, 98, 104, 107
personal communication, 105, 107, 108, 109
personal views, 107
petroleum, 125, 126
Philippines, 19
plants, 48, 53, 56, 73, 82
plutonium, vii, 8, 31, 34, 35, 36, 41, 45, 46, 47, 48, 49, 50, 51, 52, 53, 55, 56, 58, 60, 61, 62, 63, 64, 65, 67, 69, 71, 72, 76, 77, 80, 87, 93, 94, 95, 105, 108
plutonium production program, viii, 45, 50, 55
policy, vii, 1, 2, 3, 4, 5, 9, 11, 15, 21, 22, 23, 24, 30, 31, 32, 33, 34, 37, 38, 39, 41, 58, 103
politics, 3, 26, 29, 32
population, 2, 13, 14, 121, 129
positive relationship, 27, 38
positron, 84
post-Cold War period, vii, 1, 3
potassium, 83
presidency, 1, 30, 36, 41
president, viii, 2, 3, 4, 6, 7, 8, 12, 13, 16, 23, 28, 31, 32, 33, 34, 35, 36, 37, 38, 41, 46, 48, 53, 62, 63, 67, 68, 73, 75, 77, 105, 110, 111, 127, 135
President Clinton, viii, 33, 35, 38, 75
President Obama, viii, 6, 75, 77, 127
presidential campaign, 5
prisoners, 13, 16

prisoners of war, 16
PRK, 3, 15, 19, 70, 77, 123, 134
project, 8, 17, 24, 33, 34, 35, 36, 37, 39, 51, 52, 106, 107, 108
proliferation, vii, 1, 5, 6, 24, 25, 34, 45, 61, 62, 63, 64, 65, 66, 95, 115, 127, 128, 133, 134
Pyongyang, vii, 1, 2, 3, 4, 5, 6, 7, 8, 9, 10, 12, 14, 15, 16, 17, 18, 19, 20, 22, 23, 24, 25, 26, 27, 28, 29, 30, 31, 32, 33, 34, 35, 36, 37, 38, 39, 40, 42, 44, 46, 50, 53, 56, 57, 58, 59, 60, 63, 64, 65, 68, 95, 117, 119, 121, 122, 123, 124, 126, 128, 129

R

radiation, 49, 51, 83, 84, 91
radio, 14, 62, 87, 133
radioactive disintegration, 101, 108
radioactive isotopes, 78, 82, 83, 87, 105
radioisotope, 102
ratification, viii, 75, 77, 98, 103
reconciliation, 37
recovery, 17, 32, 127
Red Army, 40
reform, 1, 7, 8, 10, 19, 29, 42
refugee flows, 10
refugees, 13, 14
resolution, viii, 2, 4, 5, 15, 17, 22, 36, 37, 38, 66, 68, 106, 113, 114, 115, 116, 117, 118, 127, 128, 129, 130, 133, 135
resources, 12, 15, 16, 25, 67, 68, 100, 120, 121, 123, 129
response, viii, 3, 5, 7, 26, 28, 37, 46, 47, 54, 58, 62, 71, 80, 98, 100, 113, 114, 119, 122
rhetoric, 8, 34, 58
rights, iv, 2, 4, 12, 13, 14, 24, 32, 36, 39, 68
risk, 4, 5, 11, 13, 25, 26, 28, 65, 70, 124, 134,
rods, 36, 41, 46, 47, 49, 50, 51, 59, 60, 72
romanticism, 40, 44
Russia, viii, 1, 6, 8, 19, 32, 35, 42, 45, 48, 53, 66, 69, 70, 71, 75, 93, 100, 108, 115, 116, 118, 122, 123, 124, 134

S

Saipan, 19
sanctions, vii, viii, 1, 3, 5, 6, 7, 8, 9, 10, 15, 24, 36, 41, 46, 47, 61, 64, 68, 72, 98, 107, 113, 114, 115, 116, 117, 118, 119, 121, 122, 123, 124, 125, 126, 127, 128, 129, 130, 133, 134, 135
science, 17, 18, 22, 75, 76, 81, 99, 106
Secretary of Defense, 6, 15
Secretary of the Treasury, 117

security, 3, 6, 9, 13, 18, 21, 22, 23, 24, 26, 27, 30, 31, 33, 38, 39, 43, 71, 122
Senate, viii, 36, 54, 57, 69, 71, 72, 73, 74, 75, 77, 106, 107, 111
Senate Foreign Relations Committee, 69
services, 10, 66, 76, 115, 117, 118, 120, 124
signals, 76, 78, 81, 86, 96, 97, 98, 106, 107
signs, 1, 77, 81, 95
Singapore, 61, 118
Six-Party Talks, viii, 1, 2, 3, 5, 6, 7, 8, 9, 15, 16, 17, 35, 36, 37, 41, 45, 46, 48, 50, 51, 53, 54, 55, 56, 58, 60, 65, 66, 67, 69, 71, 73, 94, 114, 115, 124, 128, 129, 130
smuggling, 117, 133, 135
solution, vii, 22, 23, 24, 25, 38, 39
Somalia, 133
South Africa, 25, 116, 119, 133
South Korea, viii, 1, 2, 3, 4, 5, 6, 7, 8, 9, 10, 12, 13, 14, 15, 16, 19, 25, 26, 28, 29, 31, 32, 33, 35, 36, 37, 40, 41, 42, 43, 44, 45, 47, 48, 50, 51, 56, 59, 60, 64, 69, 75, 78, 93, 95, 96, 100, 110, 116, 117, 118, 122, 125, 130, 133, 135
Southeast Asia, 13
sovereignty, 24, 25, 27, 29, 36, 39
Soviet Union, 27, 28, 29, 30, 32, 47, 52, 65, 68, 87, 89, 109
State of the Union address, 34
State Sponsor of Terrorism (SST), viii, 46, 62, 73
succession, 1, 7, 10, 11, 12, 129
Sun, 19, 39, 42, 55, 108
surveillance, 51, 55, 64, 101, 111
survival, 4, 5, 12, 129
Sweden, 110, 122
Switzerland, 39, 43, 82, 122
Syria, 6, 15, 61, 62, 65, 74, 128

T

Taiwan, 25
target, vii, 1, 3, 121, 128
tension, 2, 8, 26, 29, 34, 56
territory, 7, 58, 66, 97, 115
terrorism, 9, 19, 37, 58, 63, 117
terrorist groups, 119
terrorists, 80
Thailand, 19, 116, 118, 119
threats, 7, 24, 26, 30, 38, 58, 125
torture, 13
trade, 9, 12, 30, 32, 33, 40, 44, 93, 113, 114, 115, 120, 121, 122, 123, 124, 125, 126, 127, 128, 130, 133, 135
Trading with the Enemy Act, viii, 37, 46, 48, 62, 73
trafficking, 13, 15

Index

transactions, viii, 113, 114, 116, 117, 121, 122, 123, 128
transmission, 14, 19, 84
transparency, 48, 53, 130
transport, 77, 83, 84, 90, 99, 105, 108, 115, 119
Treasury, 15, 36, 114, 117, 118, 124, 134
treaties, 29, 80

U

U.N. Security Council, v, 5, 9, 15, 18, 46, 66, 113, 115, 118, 133
U.S. assistance, 66, 122
U.S. Department of Commerce, 127, 132
U.S. Department of the Treasury, 134
U.S. foreign policy, vii, 1, 3, 4
U.S. policy, 1, 2, 4, 9, 15, 22, 37, 41
U.S. sanctions, vii, viii, 1, 3, 5, 6, 46, 68, 117, 118
U.S. Treasury, 15, 36, 118, 124
UNHCR, 13
United Kingdom (UK), 93, 116
United Nations (UN), viii, 5, 8, 9, 12, 13, 16, 28, 28, 37, 41, 42, 46, 53, 58, 66, 68, 72, 80, 97, 107, 110, 113, 114, 122, 127, 132, 133, 134,
United Nations High Commissioner for Refugees, 13
uranium, vii, 7, 8, 34, 35, 36, 41, 45, 46, 47, 48, 49, 51, 52, 53, 54, 55, 56, 59, 61, 62, 63, 64, 65, 68, 69, 70, 71, 76, 80, 87, 93, 94, 95, 105, 107, 108
uranium enrichment plant, viii, 7, 45, 46, 47, 52, 56, 68
uranium enrichment program, vii, 8, 41, 45, 47, 51, 53, 54, 55, 61, 62, 65
USA PATRIOT Act, 124

V

vehicles, 95, 96, 104, 117, 124, 125, 126
vessels, viii, 66, 113, 114, 115, 119, 133
Vietnam, 28, 29, 30

vulnerability, 23, 24, 25, 26, 27, 28, 29, 30, 31, 32, 33, 35, 36, 37, 38, 39

W

war, 4, 8, 12, 16, 26, 27, 28, 29, 33, 40, 57, 58, 66
warhead estimates, vii, 45
Washington, 4, 5, 7, 9, 18, 20, 23, 24, 27, 28, 29, 30, 31, 32, 33, 34, 36, 37, 38, 39, 40, 42, 43, 44, 71, 72, 73, 74, 106, 108, 109, 110, 133, 134
waste, 49, 60
water, viii, 7, 8, 33, 37, 45, 46, 47, 52, 53, 81, 89, 91, 111
weapons of mass destruction (WMD), 34, 36, 66, 67, 115, 117, 118, 119, 122, 128, 133, 135,
White House, 20, 44, 72, 73, 105, 114
withdrawal, 8, 16, 31, 32, 54, 67, 129
workforce, 65
World Bank, 123
World War I, 28
worldwide, 70, 84, 104, 111, 125

X

xenon, 78, 81, 82, 83, 84, 85, 86, 87, 92, 96, 100, 101, 102, 103, 104, 105, 108

Y

Yemen, 15
yield, viii, 23, 24, 38, 39, 45, 56, 57, 71, 75, 77, 78, 79, 80, 81, 83, 87, 90, 92, 94, 96, 98, 105, 106, 107
Yongbyon site, viii, 8, 45, 64

Z

zirconium, 87